In the Wake of Medea

# In the Wake of Medea

## Neoclassical Theater
## and the Arts of Destruction

Juliette Cherbuliez

FORDHAM UNIVERSITY PRESS

*New York 2020*

Fordham University Press gratefully acknowledges
financial assistance and support provided for the
publication of this book by the University of Minnesota.

Copyright © 2020 Fordham University Press

All rights reserved. No part of this publication may be
reproduced, stored in a retrieval system, or transmitted in
any form or by any means—electronic, mechanical,
photocopy, recording, or any other—except for brief
quotations in printed reviews, without the prior
permission of the publisher.

Fordham University Press has no responsibility for the
persistence or accuracy of URLs for external or third-party
Internet websites referred to in this publication and does
not guarantee that any content on such websites is, or will
remain, accurate or appropriate.

Fordham University Press also publishes its books in a
variety of electronic formats. Some content that appears in
print may not be available in electronic books.
Visit us online at www.fordhampress.com.

Library of Congress Cataloging-in-Publication Data

Names: Cherbuliez, Juliette, 1970– author.
Title: In the wake of Medea : neoclassical theater and the
arts of destruction / Juliette Cherbuliez.
Description: New York : Fordham University Press, 2020. |
Includes bibliographical references and index. | Summary:
"Through the figure of Medea, shows how important
violence was for seventeenth-century French tragedy and
contextualizes that violence in a longer literary and
philosophical history from Ovid to Pasolini"—Provided
by publisher.
Identifiers: LCCN 2020000605 | ISBN 9780823287826
(hardback) | ISBN 9780823287819 (paperback) |
ISBN 9780823287833 (epub)
Subjects: LCSH: Medea, consort of Aegeus, King of
Athens (Mythological character)—In literature. | French
literature—History and criticism. | Violence in literature.
Classification: LCC PQ423 .C47 2020 |
DDC 842/.509351—dc23
LC record available at https://lccn.loc.gov/2020000605

Printed in the United States of America
22 21 20    5 4 3 2 1
First edition

*for Claire Goldstein, in gratitude for a friendship which, bringing joy to intellectual inquiry and rigor to lipstick choice, leaves its bright traces on every page*

CONTENTS

*A Note on Translations and Names*     ix

    Introduction: Coming after Violence in Literature     1
    Medea, a Manifesto     37
1. Surface Selves: *Médée*, 1634     53
2. The Medean Presence: Violence Unmade and Remade     94
3. Staying Power: Performing the Present Moment of Tragedy     120
4. Flying toward Futurity: Spectacularity and Suspension     143
5. Medea Overlived: The Future of Catastrophe     174
    Epilogue: The Cosmopolitics of Literature     199

*Acknowledgments*     207
*Notes*     209
*Bibliography*     227
*Index*     239

## A NOTE ON TRANSLATIONS AND NAMES

I have chosen translations based not just on their rendition but also on their accessibility, indicating any of my own modifications. Wherever possible, I have attempted to preserve ambiguities instead of eliding them. These translations can feel awkward to a contemporary reader, but they also make available the uncertainty or multiplicity of meanings that might have also been in the original.

Mythological names present their own problems, especially in a book generally about premodern French theater that also draws broadly on ancient and contemporary sources. Thus, names in italics (*Médée*, *Hercule mourant*) always refer to the titles of works, given in their original spelling. Names in French (Médée, Hercule) indicate characters in French works, whereas names in English (Medea, Hercules, Glauca, Creusa) refer to the figure more broadly, with all its mythological, cultural, and theoretical freight. My hope is that these multiple names, and the inevitable slippage among them, do not cause confusion but instead compel a productive consideration of both the specificity of a figure and its far-ranging connections beyond any one artistic context.

In the Wake of Medea

# Introduction:
# Coming after Violence in Literature

You are beginning a book about Medea, so it is likely that you expect blood. This is understandable: Once spilled and seen, blood is usually indelible, whether on cloth or in memory. Consider the Abbey Theatre performance of Fiona Shaw in *Medea*, directed by Deborah Warner, which came to the Brooklyn Academy of Music (BAM) in 2002. She stood in a pool of water, her forearms and front slick, and her white tunic streaked scarlet. Her power, helplessness, grief, and rage radiated from her body, which had just become that of a murderer. Under Carrie Cracknell's direction, Helen McCrory (National Theater, London, 2014) also wore white: a gauzy sheath that became visibly heavy when tainted pink. At the Almeida in 2015, artistic director Rupert Goold promised to up the ante; in the poster for this version of Euripides' *Medea* adapted by Rachel Cusk, Kate Fleetwood has her hands in a blender, icon of modern domesticity, fondling chunks of flesh and sinew. There are echoes here of the same actress playing Lady Macbeth under the same director, her forearms red and her gaze steady. The poster was misleading, however: Cusk's adaptation of the infanticidal denouement upset audiences deeply, perhaps because these children suffer horribly—but not directly at their mother's hands, and strangely without

Figure 1. Fiona Shaw in *Medea*. Abbey Theatre, Brooklyn Academy of Music, 2000. Photograph copyright Stephanie Berger.

Introduction: Coming after Violence in Literature    3

Figure 2. Publicity Poster of Rachel Cusk's adaptation of *Medea* with Kate Fleetwood. Almeida Theater. 2015. Image by Paul Thompson.

blood: They reportedly overdose. It was perhaps the suggestion of a bloodless death that was untenable to this public, whether it assigned some agency to the children themselves or only removed Medea's hand from the action. We expect gore from a mother who murders her children, and we expect to be shocked at the viscera, as seen in the production with Shaw at BAM in 2002. Cradling one of the children in her arms while running behind the set's transparent partition upstage, we watched her exit. Then blood spattered against the partition. The audience flinched collectively.

We expect blood because we know *Medea* as the story of a woman who kills her children. Mythology's quintessential foreigner, Medea is the princess from the kingdom of Colchis, the limits of the Greeks' known world. She falls in love with Jason when he arrives with his Argonauts to steal the Golden Fleece, guarantor of Colchis's sovereignty and key to Jason's retrieval of his father's throne at Iolchos. She betrays her kingdom and, while fleeing with the Argonauts, massacres her brother. Once back in Iolchos, she contrives the death of Jason's uncle. This is all backstory to most versions of the play, including and especially that of Euripides. In those, after Jason agrees to marry into the Corinthian house, Medea kills the king and his daughter, and burns down Corinth. She kills her own children before flying away in a dragon-drawn chariot.

Never mind all the other bodies, or the three cities whose sovereignty is violated, today we interpret *Medea* as a domestic revenge drama, sometimes something closer to a soap opera. Contemporary productions tend to stage Euripides' tragedy so that the audience cannot simply reject her. Hence the tendency to offer nods to the contemporary moment: There were children's toys on Warner's stage; Goold's chorus was a mommy-baby group of privileged women; and the children in Cracknell's *Medea* camped out cuddling in sleeping bags in front of the TV. By including these nods to the contemporary moment, directors and actors seem to want to say there's something universal about the Medea story, And this universality should drive our affective response. Medea cannot be only crazy or totally other; she must be at the edge of what we identify with. Contemporary productions hone that edge enough to give an audience a sentimental attachment to the protagonist so that we can't quite hate and reject her; we instead feel pity or sublime horror at the possibility of it all. While seeing the blood gives us what feels like metonymic confirmation of Medea's infanticide, its shocking visibility also functions in the same way that certain understandings of catharsis seem to operate: It becomes not just a visible manifestation of our horror but also a material symbol of its evacuation.

I never have much to say about these productions, even and especially when they affect me deeply. In mobilizing our sympathy, our identification even, and then in attaching the violence primarily to children's blood, they elide a foundational part of the Medean story that we desperately need to confront: that part which is precisely about the impossibility of accepting, understanding, or otherwise assimilating such violence, and so the part of that character which is constitutively foreign, absolutely unlike the world that regards her, yet nevertheless integral to the fabric of how we constitute the social and rehearse its limits. The bloodiness of these productions obfuscates the part of Medea that works with fire: torching, burning, lighting up.

So you will find more fire than blood here. Fire is first of all the medium for Medea's magic arts. Her spells dominate her father's fire-breathing bulls, which Jason must tame as one condition for approaching the Golden Fleece. It is through fire that Medea's arts also cause the poisoned gifts given to Jason's bride to kill her: "The golden garland set upon her head

Introduction: Coming after Violence in Literature 5

Figure 3. "Médée rajeunit Eson. *La Métamorphose d'Ovide figurée* (Lyon: Jean de Tournes, 1557). Attributed to Bernard Salomon. Courtesy Douglas H. Gordon Collection of French Books, Albert and Shirley Small Special Collections Library, University of Virginia.

was sending forth a wonder, a stream of all-consuming fire."[1] This same fire can be said, literally and symbolically, to bring down Corinth, as it kills also its king. Medea's blazing power is multivalent, however, since fire figures—especially in premodern Medean texts—as the dominant metaphor for all kinds of passion, whether amorous or murderous. It is also associated specifically with Medea's power to aid and even create life. Bernard Salomon's mid-sixteenth-century *Metamorphose Figurée*, a cycle of 178 woodcuts and verse interpretations, depicts this power in its illustration of the rejuvenation of Jason's father Aeson. In the image for this episode, derived from the account in book 7 of Ovid's *Metamorphoses*, torches surrounding her table and the fire under her cauldron signal the life-giving power of her art. Salomon's illustrations offered a template for seventeenth- and eighteenth-century illustrations of the same incidents. In these, the scene remains largely the same, featuring the old man's body alongside the torch-lit table and cauldron fire, while the power of fire seems to spread through billowing smoke that mingles with the heavens. Like Medea's

Figure 4. "Rejeunisement d'Eson," by Jean Mathieu, in Nicholas Renouard, *Les Métamorphoses d'Ovide, traduites en prose Françoise* (Paris, 1619). Source: Bibliothèque nationale de France, Département de la Réserve des livres rares.

Figure 5. "Rajeunissement d'Eson," by Bernard Picart et al., in Antoine Banier, *Les Métmorphoses d'Ovide en latin, traduites en françois* (Amsterdam: Wetstein & Smith, 1732). Source: Bibliothèque nationale de France.

own escape fueled by the power of the dragon-drawn chariot, fire is indexed to the power of her knowledge, whether invigorating or deadly.

Fire is elemental, fundamental, primitive, and vibrant. Blood and fire have something paradoxical in common: Both are signs of vitality and death, of civilization and ruin. Both are then signs of destruction. As such, however, the divergences in their properties are significant. When still warm, blood glistens, is viscous, and promises to stain and stay. Fire can look like liquid and shines in its own way, but it can't be touched. Rather it envelops and consumes, even though it seems ephemeral and self-consuming. You can see its remains, its trace, but only after its absence. Blood is violence's evidence, whereas fire is its agent. Symbolically, blood traces relations of kin, family, honor; blood is the social. Fire, like blood, is life when it is contained. Uncontrolled, it appears to be beyond the law; it is *bios*, or *Gaia*: whatever word one wants for the power and destruction of life beyond humans. Yet when fire is anthropogenic, when it is caused and controlled by humans, fire too figures the essence of the political, since it is fundamentally the confronting and wielding of power.[2] The aftermath of blood, as I have already suggested, is a scar or a stain: a memento. The aftermath of fire is destruction of the social and the environment, but it also brings an awareness that the "balance of nature," any lasting state of equilibrium, is illusory.[3] Fire is never fully extinguished: It will always return.

*In the Wake of Medea* reads aspects of seventeenth-century French dramatic poetry as a meditation on this fiery kind of violence: one that is often called primitive when it is highly sophisticated, one that appears to be both destructive and constitutive of the social. It offers these readings in a double context: First, I advance a reevaluation of the politics of Medean violence, and, second, I propose an alternative, nonlinear history for neoclassical theater that acknowledges the persistent and recurring nature of Medean violence. The cornerstone of this project is Pierre Corneille's 1634 *Médée*, whose nonlinear history, I show, spirals out to include both Ovid and Pier Paolo Pasolini as well as dramaturges Jean Racine and Jean Rotrou. Medean violence occurs in plays featuring the character of Medea (*Médée, La Conquête de la Toison d'or*), as well as those where the character does not appear (*Hercule mourant, Athalie*). Violence appears in these plays' dominant forms of description; it is incarnated in characters; it intervenes in the temporality of tragic action. It is integral to the structure of the plays I treat, and to the demands they make on their audiences, whether in print or on stage. Medean violence does not serve to purge ills, though we might wish it to do so. It does, however, disrupt: by forcing a pause, delay, or an acceleration in events—concentrating moments of terror, bringing the past to bear directly on the present, or forcing a reconsideration of how histories are negotiated. Even when incidents of violence serve as moments of solidarity or as invitations to a cohesive social structure—wartimes survived, battle scars as memories, heroes immortalized—they also appear as confirmations that peace has an aftermath and so never feels final. Tragedy's role might not be to evacuate violence but to help us see the impossibility of its leaving us: This is all of literature's art of destruction. Both in tragedy and beyond, Medean violence tracks this art.

## The Medean Presence in Premodern Tragedy

Medean violence can be seen to permeate and mobilize tragedy in particular because the premodern tragic form is fundamentally political: It addresses the fiery side of power. However, *In the Wake* offers neither a generic intervention into the nature of violence in tragedy nor a characterological study of Medea. Tragedy here is less a genre than a dynamic form of political poetics, whose crystallization we might locate in the tragic genre, but which also leaks out into and among other premodern dramatic forms—tragicomedy and *pièces à machines* (machine plays that create special effects through innovative technology), as well as poetry, film, image, and philosophical inquiry.[4] Tragedy then becomes a mode of rehearsal, a practice of considering the politics of violence.

This is also not a study of the character of Medea, who does not even appear in all the representations I examine.[5] Rather Medea is an avatar of a practice of violence with specific characteristics. Here I recall Jean-Pierre Vernant and Pierre Vidal-Naquet's classic assertion that the human being and human actions in the tragic universe should be understood not "as realities to be pinned down and defined in their essential qualities . . . but as problems that defy resolution, riddles with double meanings that are never fully decoded."[6] This is particularly fitting for the premodern Medea, whose multivalence, exceptionality, and powerful yet minor status suggests that we need to look beyond notions of ubiquity, dominance, or institutional value to theorize the politics of violence in neoclassical theater.

Neoclassical French tragedy has been traditionally limited to one role within the history of tragedy. Not known for its displays of either blood or fire, it remains exemplary of a tradition that evolved from a violent Renaissance theater conveniently figured by the first tragedy printed in French: Jean de La Péruse's *Médée* (printed in 1555). From these Senecan tragedies of the sixteenth and early seventeenth centuries evolved, so the story used to go, the neoclassical ideal of "a portrait of civic life which was invented for the regulation of the passions," or in other words, of a "tragedy without love."[7] This particular story depends in part on a sense of periodization for which the path connecting the work of Renaissance tragic poet Robert Garnier to the "baroque" works of such early seventeenth-century dramaturges as Alexandre Hardy and Pierre Du Ryer continues through the tragicomedies and tragedies of Pierre Corneille to arrive at Jean Racine, in an evolutionary line that is as smooth and uninterrupted as the image that we have of Louis XIV's alliance of government and culture is totalizing and effective. That this narrative has obtained stubbornly since the nineteenth century is testament to the very long politics of periodization. From the late eighteenth century on, playwrights and philosophers looking for a politics of the theater proper to their own politics strove to characterize neoclassical rigidity and sterility as elements of a genre that functioned as apology for what they considered to be the old-régime culture of absolutism. This narrative was reinforced by nineteenth-century Romantics who also wished to stage a second Revolution—in the realm of aesthetics, by striving to reinvent sentimentality.[8] In the avant-garde movements of twentieth-century theater, Racinian poetics emerged as Aristotle's henchman, the revanchist standard-bearer of elitism.[9]

To maintain this narrative, the backbone of many a European theater history course even today, French tragedy had to be made to go from an undisciplined, baroque genre where anything was admissible on stage, including battles, death, unseemly behavior, and the like, to a highly regulated and codified genre where passion was expressed, and contained, through the carefully metered poetic word. In many of these histories, Pierre Corneille, his work, and the controversies it elicited function as a kind of fulcrum in this evolution. And *Médée*, his first tragedy—billed originally as a *tragi-comédie*—marks the tipping point. In a landmark 1980 essay, Marc Fumaroli offered Corneille's first tragedy *Médée* as a figure of the dawn and dusk of neoclassical theater. Corneille wrote *Médée* just before the watershed of *Le Cid*, which premiered in December 1636, and the public debates it initiated about suitable theater, which changed French political theater. Fumaroli also sees Médée working powerfully at the end of the century's tragic tradition, figuring the simultaneous apogee and death of French neoclassical tragedy in Racine's 1677 *Phèdre*.[10] The eponymous queen whose illicit love of her stepson is the motor behind her fitful self-destruction, announces her imminent death thus: "J'ai pris, j'ai fait couler dans mes brûlantes veines/ Un poison que Médée apporta dans Athènes"

(I've taken, I've put into my burning veins / A poison that Medea brought to Athens). The queen's identification of this burning drug with its maker also places Médée at the epicenter of French tragedy's last great moment. In this scene of self-destruction, Médée ushers both Phèdre and all of neoclassical French tragedy to their common death.

In Fumaroli's reading Médée, in Corneille and then in Racine, inaugurates and closes neoclassical tragedy. For others, *Médée* similarly offers a defining limit to the genre as one that refused violence, whether as rejected vestige of baroque violence or as the mark of a new warrant for state power.[11] Whether seen as a remnant of a past when violence was acceptable, or—seemingly conversely—a precursor to modernity, analyses of *Médée* put it to work toward a traditional narrative of a unified progression and toward an increasingly perfected genre that respected and reinforced ideal cultural values, including and especially the elimination of violence.

Recent scholarship has done much to unsettle this narrative, in part through an increased historicization of the relationship between aesthetics and violence in the early part of the seventeenth century, especially with regard to the aftermath of the Wars of Religion, and so to an increasingly complex understanding of periodization.[12] Certainly, some of this story nevertheless should continue to guide our understanding of the sociopolitical valences of neoclassical tragedy. Beginning with Louis XIII and his minister the Cardinal de Richelieu, the social practice and aesthetic form of theater were increasingly subject to state-directed codification and constraint, with norms of "honnêteté" guiding both audience behavior and dramatic subject, and aesthetic ideals of "purity" having roots in political fears of foreign, especially Italian, state influence.

Amid such discourses of decorum and purity, theater's violence never really went away. In *Le Cid* the shocking slap that Chimène's outraged father offers Rodrigue's father in the play's first scenes is overshadowed first by the fatal duel in which Rodrigue saves his aged father's honor, which is in turn effaced by the battlefield triumph of Rodrigue against the Moors, a son's heroic act also supplanting a father's humiliation. In Corneille's next tragedy *Horace* (premiered 1640), anxious anticipation of the battle between the Horaces and the Curiaces structures the tension of the play until it occurs, after which it is then the subject of not one but three onstage reports. Horace's triumph is confirmed, however, by the murder of his sister, whom he chases offstage with his sword drawn. The drama of *Rodogune* (premiered in the 1644–45 season) revolves around fear, disgust, and hatred of the scheming, murderous Cléopâtre, who attempts to kill her sons with sword and with poison, which she finally swallows herself. In Racine's oeuvre, neoclassical tragedy lives in the aftermath of violence and the fear of its resurgence. The memory of the Trojan War massacres shapes the political compass driving *Andromaque* (premiered 1667), while its anticipation warrants the fear and expectation of sacrifice in *Iphigénie* (premiered 1674). The temporality of violence, whether as future threat or historical motivation, seems to fold mourning or dread into the present. Certainly, violence gives tragedy its rhythm, but the tragic is formed between those moments when its characters' world is "mis à feu et à sang," as the French saying goes, made into a bloodbath, put to fire and sword—or literally, put to fire and blood.

When neoclassical tragedy eschewed actions representative of violence, it transformed these actions into fears, motivations, histories, descriptions, and offstage events. But this was no relegation, nor was such constraint purely an attempt at the erasure of violence. Rather, as we shall see, explorations of ostentatious violence on stage and its relationship to spectators were very much part of neoclassical debates about the social function of theater. The answers to these debates did not always include the banishment of such violence. Violence could be both pleasant and instructive.

## Plaire et dètruire: *Debates about Violence on the Neoclassical Stage*

The Horacian adage of *utile dulci*, "please and instruct," which guided so many debates in the premodern period about the possibilities and danger of art, poetry, and theater, was rendered in French "plaire et instruire." In debates that occurred during the seventeenth century, it might also been rendered as "plaire et détruire," to please and destroy. That is, violence was often at the heart of the moral and political messages of these plays, and debates acknowledged this. These debates, from those involving dramatist/critics La Mesnardière and d'Aubignac through theologians Nicole and Bossuet, are often seen as part of a more general antitheatricality in Europe. Yet even antitheatrical clerical voices did not absolutely condemn theatrical practice, and some even established certain social virtues for the stage.[13] For example, critic, dramatist, and physician Hippolyte-Jules Pilet de La Mesnardière asserted as early as 1639 that good theater should be "similar to good legislators, giving to virtue and vice alike the reward that each is due."[14] The question about what was *vraisemblable* (which is often translated as "plausible" but which I prefer to translate as "realistic" because of its normative moralizing connotations) in theater became linked intimately to that of *bienséance* (decorum), wherein both imposed a value of what characters should model as behavior befitting ideal subjects. D'Aubignac's famous measure of *vraisemblance* against what a public expected and tolerated exemplifies this standard. Corneille would, throughout his career, advocate for a theatrical *vraisemblance* that also admitted the *vrai* of the historical record.[15]

There was also a practical side to all of the moral discussions, one which admitted the material and lived, social conditions of theater making, the work of actors, the livelihood of writers, and especially the pleasures of spectators. This, and really any, view onto any moral or political reading of European poetry—and especially its incarnated version, theater—has long operated under cover of the Horatian assertion that it should benefit or please readers, and ideally do both simultaneously. In the seventeenth century, both a more worldly defender of theater such as Charles de Saint-Évremond and his opponent the Jesuit René Rapin based their arguments on the Horatian paradigm, albeit with divergent ends in mind.[16] Horace derived his normative principle, via Aristotle, from a long tradition of philosophical debates about the politics of poetry, so it is fascinating that we tend to consider the Horatian ideal outside of any sociopolitical or temporal context, as if the wisdom of the sages were handed down to practitioners as sacred edicts and followed accordingly. Horace's major preoccupation in the *Ars poetica* is audience approbation, and his classic phrase appears in an argument about guaranteeing authorial success. At stake for Horace was how to achieve success among one's peers as well as appreciation from posterity. Poetry is not useful in a vacuum; even for Horace its claims to morality were mobilized toward pragmatic and political ends.[17]

As early as Ovid, therefore, the instrumentality of *utile dulci* was integrated into poetry. Ovid's exilic work is also a meditation on the dangers and displeasures—to the author in particular—of writing for a public.[18] The politics of poetry, as many scholars have shown, are thus local and historicized, even as their rhetorical claims make bids for eternity and universality. Thus seventeenth-century debates challenging dramaturges and poets on the merits of their work tend to be exposed as post hoc justification, if anything. It is arguable that this justification is a part of the work of mediating the contingent, local, and strategic "good" of literature, a moral category that emerges out of the need for a defense, not out of the desire for creation. What this also means is that discussions about the morality of poetry, theater, and leisure writing in general are always mediating their other effects beyond morality.

Accordingly, theorists and practitioners at the time rarely addressed the question of violence as an unmediated or simple moral issue. They addressed the issue in a way that to our eyes seems almost oblique: in the context of debates about the moral and political categories of *bienséance* and *vraisemblance*. Physical violence was not always seen as beyond the bounds of decorum, and its role depended on the moral quandary it created. One of the few mentions of onstage aggression is in d'Aubignac's 1657 *Pratique du théâtre*, one of the principal sources for understanding seventeenth-century theater and acting practices. At the beginning of book 2, d'Aubignac investigates the thorny problem of whether history should be altered by poet-dramaturges. He offers the example of Horace's sister Camille. History tells us she was killed by her brother, but the stage is not there to give history lessons:

> C'est une pensée bien ridicule d'aller au théâtre pour apprendre l'histoire. La scène ne donne point les choses comme elles ont été, mais comme elles devaient être, et le poète y doit rétablir dans le sujet tout ce qui ne s'accommodera pas aux règles de son art, comme fait un peintre quand il travaille sur un modèle défectueux. C'est pourquoi la mort de Camille par la main d'Horace son frère, n'a pas été approuvée au théâtre, bien que ce soit une aventure véritable, et j'avais été d'avis, pour sauver en quelque sorte l'histoire, et tout ensemble la bienséance de la scène, que cette fille désespérée voyant son frère l'épée à la main, se fût précipitée dessus: ainsi elle fût morte de la main d'Horace, et lui eût été digne de compassion, comme un malheureux innocent, l'histoire et le théâtre auraient été d'accord.[19]

It's certainly a ridiculous idea to go to the theater in order to learn history. The stage does not offer things as they were, but as they should be. And the poet should reform everything that does not adhere to the rules of his art, as does a painter with a defective model. This is why Camille's death at the hands of her brother Horace was not approved for the theater, even though it is a true story. I was of the opinion that, in order to save the story as well as the decorum of the scene, at the sight of her brother with his sword drawn, this desperate girl might have thrust herself upon it. Thus she would have been dead by Horace's hand, while he would remain worthy of compassion, as an unhappy innocent, [and] history and theater would have been in agreement.

D'Aubignac's solution to the problem of *vraisemblance* is *not* to eliminate the death of Camille by the hand of her brother, but to preserve compassion for him by eliminating his act of murder.[20] Camille running herself through with her brother's sword—we may think of Phèdre's own attempt to grab Hippolyte's arm—seems a perverse solution. Although it was perhaps one that would not be admitted many decades later, it suggests that the question of violence on stage was not always considered in terms only of what acts should be represented, but also with regard to the moral codes that such violence upheld, the relationships that it defined, and the power it held in both its absence and its presence.

Early modern moralists differed greatly in their motivations, and even the long-standing "mimetic argument" warrants closer examination.[21] First, the reasons behind the fears of theater extended beyond the moral: Fears of theater's effects on society often had economic and political bases. If we consider the question of mimesis as only a moral issue, however, the question—today as well as for seventeenth-century France—is also double. Ideas about "representation" are linked to what precisely is meant by "good." That is, not only must we ask how we know what good representation and bad representation are, but also we must ask what good violence and bad violence are. Indeed, if "theatricality" is to be taken as the widespread social occurrence encompassing all kinds of play, wherein players and audience are crucial participants in the spectacle's unfolding, then the fear of theater's effects on society is a localized fear of a much more pervasive phenomenon.[22] It is within this dynamic that theater remains a site of rehearsal for the debates that shape a culture.

The issue of violence in theater then becomes one of its adequate expression, and not its justification, elimination, or permission. Already in 1674, playwright and critic Samuel Chappuzeau compared responses to dramatic violence between spectators in Paris and London. Having seen Dryden's *The Indian Emperour* and Boyle's *The Tragedy of Mustapha* performed by the Duke of York's Company, he compares English onstage violence and its audience's reaction, with his expectations of a similar French situation:

> Estant à Londres il y a six ans, j'y vis deux fort belles troupes des Comediens, l'une du Roy, l'autre du Duc d'Yorc, et je fus à deux représentations, à la Mort de Montezume, Roy du Mexique, et à celle de Mustapha, qui se défendoit vigoureusement sur le Théatre contre les muets qui le vouloient étrangler; ce qui faisait rire, et ce que les François n'auroient représenté que dans un récit.[23]

> In London six years ago, I saw two beautiful acting Troupes: the King's and the Duke of York's. I was at two performances: *The Death of Montezuma, King of Mexico* and *Mustapha*, who defended himself vigorously against the mutes who were trying to strangle him, which caused laughter (among the audience), and which the French would have represented only in a description.

For Chappuzeau, this incident seems worth recounting because the audience laughed at a spectacle that should have been treated seriously, because of its nature and its context: a regicide within a tragedy. Chappuzeau's astonishment is not just that for the English, laughter at such a tragic spectacle was apparently acceptable. It is also that a playwright would have deemed it dramaturgically sound to stage something as significant as regicide instead of reserving such events for description. Description in the French style here is seen to preserve, rather than eliminate, the gravity of the violence and therefore its effects.

Theater's increasing performance in the medium of print created another set of problems for violence on stage that had nothing to do with social approbation or condemnation. Print technology shaped theater from the first editions of Terence and Seneca in the mid-sixteenth century, through the works of Racine in the 1670s.[24] The increased availability and importance of print's circulation affected the practices of dramaturges for whom the materiality of print was another arena for the audience for dramatic poems. The medium presented particular challenges for the recreation of a play, and from the mid-sixteenth century, printers attempted various ways of denoting changes in voice, scene division, and complex actions. Printed cues of nonverbal actions, or stage directions, were used to indicate the simplest and the most complex actions, although their parameters were not yet established.[25] Thus Laudan d'Aigalier's 1596 *Horace* uses three different and overlapping depictions of the battle scene. We read what actors say during the battle: "Nous sommes tous ésgaus desanimant ton corps/ Va t'en avec Charon pour vivre sans repos,"[26] (We are all equal in ridding your body of its soul/ Go with Charon to live without rest), and we read an onomatopoeic rendition of their parrying and thrusting: "Ça, ça, tuë, tuë,——, ça, ça, tuë, tuë, tuë, pif, paf." Last, a paragraph-long stage direction with the choreography of the battle follows, as if no single descriptive technique sufficed alone.

By the mid-seventeenth century, these extensive scenic indications had disappeared in all but machine plays, whose highly intricate special effects demanded lengthy accounts of the pyrotechnics, changing scenery, and flying characters which would be seen by the audience but not necessary narrated within the poetry of the play itself. Political tragedies came to have negligible indications beyond what characters could convey through their own speech. In his 1640 *Horace*, Corneille would of course render the battle between the Horaces and the Curiaces through bystanders' reports; the absence of a depiction of the battle along with the divergent reports creates a crucial dramatic tension. The work of the bystanders is woven

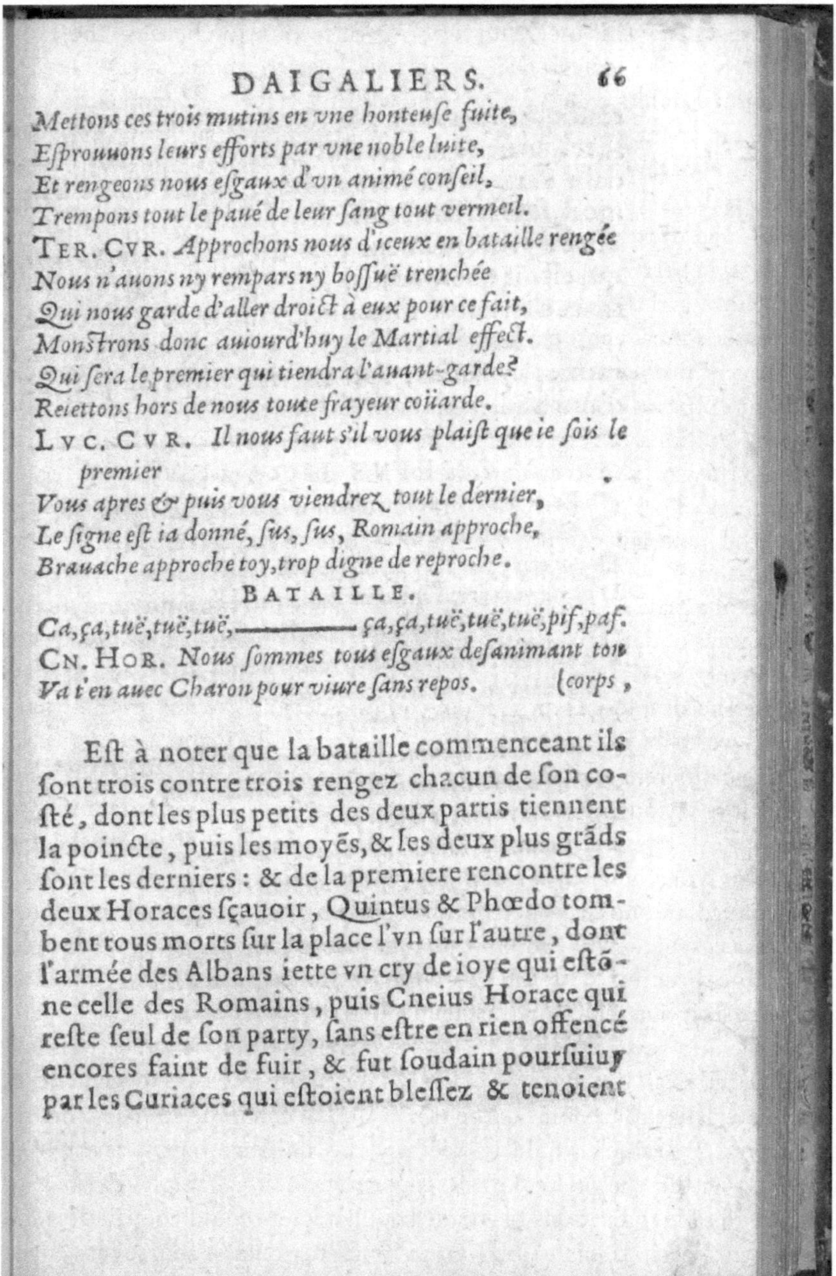

## DAIGALIERS.     66

*Mettons ces trois mutins en vne honteuse fuite,*
*Esprouuons leurs efforts par vne noble luite,*
*Et rengeons nous esgaux d'vn animé conseil,*
*Trempons tout le paué de leur sang tout vermeil.*
TER. CVR. *Approchons nous d'iceux en bataille rengée*
*Nous n'auons ny rempars ny bossuë trenchée*
*Qui nous garde d'aller droict à eux pour ce fait,*
*Monstrons donc auiourd'huy le Martial effect.*
*Qui sera le premier qui tiendra l'auant-garde?*
*Reiettons hors de nous toute frayeur coüarde.*
LVC. CVR. *Il nous faut s'il vous plaist que ie sois le*
   *premier*
*Vous apres & puis vous viendrez tout le dernier,*
*Le signe est ia donné, sus, sus, Romain approche,*
*Brauache approche toy, trop digne de reproche.*
### BATAILLE.
*Ca, ça, tuë, tuë, tuë, ———— ça, ça, tuë, tuë, tuë, pif, paf.*
CN. HOR. *Nous sommes tous esgaux desanimant ton*
*Va t'en auec Charon pour viure sans repos.*     (*corps,*

Est à noter que la bataille commenceant ils sont trois contre trois rengez chacun de son costé, dont les plus petits des deux partis tiennent la poincte, puis les moyés, & les deux plus grãds sont les derniers : & de la premiere rencontre les deux Horaces sçauoir, Quintus & Phœdo tombent tous morts sur la place l'vn sur l'autre, dont l'armée des Albans iette vn cry de ioye qui estõne celle des Romains, puis Cneius Horace qui reste seul de son party, sans estre en rien offencé encores faint de fuir, & fut soudain poursuiuy par les Curiaces qui estoient blessez & tenoient

Figure 6. Combat scene described in Pierre Laudan d'Aigaliers, *Horace*, in *Poésies* (Paris: David Le Clerc, 1596), 66. Source: gallica.bnf.fr / Bibliothèque nationale de France.

into the tension of the play, as the first report proves to be incomplete and therefore erroneous. The occluded battle, then, remains integral to the action, but as a matter of interpretation not spectacle. Bloody scenes disappeared from dramaturgical repertoires, but was it always a matter of propriety? A different issue of representation might have also intervened: Complex movement and dialogue did not translate well to the new theater of print and might have been a factor in their disappearance from plays.[27]

By the 1670s, bodies on the tragic stage did not engage visibly in duels, embraces, or even swoons. The example of Racine's *Phèdre*, the best known of French tragedies, is often taken as exemplary of this disincarnation: In a play about illicit passions and its devastating effects, there are almost no onstage events. What the public witnesses is limited to the halted, frustrated expressions of passion of its major characters, the fruitless verbal schemings and lamenting of its supporting characters, false accusations, and ultimately, in its most astonishing moment, the longest soliloquy Racine ever published, describing the gruesome death of its most sympathetic character, Hippolyte. The play's stage directions are few, in keeping with practices of the period; one the few exceptions, "elle s'assied" (*she sits*), highlights the power of a minor gesture in a stage otherwise defined by physical stasis.

And yet the narratives in *Phèdre* included histories of violence and relationships built on aggression: Phèdre's own heritage is testimony to how even—especially—Racine did not eschew the violent past as frames for his stories. Even in Racine's insistence on *le pathétique* (expressions of passion), we seem to be one step away from passion itself. Perhaps the very division between affect and intelligibility, as Sylvaine Guyot has explored, is what is at stake both in Racinian poetics and performance. The portrait of Phèdre through legible if scientifically obsolete signs of melancholia allows us to read both her corporal shame and her own self-conscious assessment of her guilt.[28] Violence is displaced onto the poetry and manifests itself in concentrated form, as if violence itself operated according to a zero-sum logic. Violence absent from the physical play of the actors appears within their words.

The economy of violence in *Phèdre* might start then with Hippolyte's first non-action: "Le dessein en est pris. Je pars, cher Théramène" (1.1.1), (The plan is set. I am leaving, dear Théramène), a project of great will and no action, which is realized only through the violence of his father's banishment (4.2) and Hippolyte's subsequent death. It also would necessarily include Phèdre's two falls. While the first (1.3.157) seems to shock primarily because it is so unseemly for a queen to drop to the ground, it is most intelligible if we consider it an outward manifestation of her autophagy, fully realized with the second fall (5.7.1622–44). The second fall, clearly from the effects of her poison, is equally a sign of her demise. It is also a form of renunciation and a confirmation that her self-consumption was inevitable and already in progress since the first act, however invisible

These implosive gestures of violence, which perform for the audience what it cannot see, are analogous to the greatest scene of violence in Racine, the "récit de Théramène." This tremendous description of the death of Hippolyte to his father King Thésée by the prince's longtime tutor Théramène, was the longest soliloquy in Racine's oeuvre. Critics derided it precisely for both its lack of *vraisemblance* and *bienséance* as well as its excess: as if it were doing violence to the theatrical experience on the same terms as a murder. Alongside Houdar de la Motte's charges of excessive description, Fénelon too found the premise of such a long account unrealistic and inappropriate:

> Théramène, qui vient pour apprendre à Thésée la mort funeste de son fils, devrait ne dire que ces deux mots, et manquer même de force pour les prononcer distinctement: "Hippolyte est mort. Un monstre envoyé du fond de la mer par la colère des dieux l'a fait périr. Je l'ai vu." Un tel homme, saisi, éperdu, sans haleine, peut-il s'amuser à faire la description la plus pompeuse et la plus fleurie de la figure du dragon?

> Théramène, who has come to inform Thésée of the terrible death of his son, should say no more than these few words, even lacking the strength to utter them clearly: "Hippolyte is dead. A monster sent from the depths of the sea by the angry gods was his downfall. I saw it all." A man in such a state, overcome, grief-stricken, breathless—could he really waste his time offering the most overblown and flowery description of the dragon?[29]

While the récit de Théramène caught critics' attention for its overwrought excess, description in tragedy generally does stand out as the site of intense attention to detail and the concentration of a desired affective response. It is thus under the rhetorical guise of hypotyposis that these descriptions operate, precisely to compel an audience to imagine the scene they cannot see. Descriptions in French tragedy function as more than supplements to the action, or placeholders for offstage action. They expose the violence that is integral to tragedy. They also suggest that violence in tragedy is present not as a tool of expiation but as a mode of politics. We can see this when we recognize why Théramène goes into such detail about the death of Hippolyte, why he betrays his subordinate station and indicts Thésée's refusal to recognize his son's essential innocence. In the description's account of how a peerless young hero might become a mass of unrecognizable flesh, testimony becomes an act of protest, revealing not just the violence in Hippolyte's death but the violence in his father's false accusation, and his subsequent banishment. The crimes of *Phèdre* emerge in Théramène's account, exposing the deep-seated injustice that has shaped the characters from the beginning.

We would be hard-pressed to see Théramène's account, or any violence in tragedy, as merely purgative; critics of the time were uncertain of what catharsis, as the basis for any collective shift, might constitute.[30] In the case of *Phèdre*, there is nothing to expiate: Rather, the account doubles the guilt by exposing Phèdre's own guilt while clearing the way for Thésée to see his wrongs. Even the clemency of Aricie, which Hippolyte requests, feels less cathartic than reconciliatory. What then is the function of violence?

Philosopher Susanne Langer is often cited as declaring that "tragedy is a cadential form. Its crisis is always the turn toward an absolute close." Medean violence betrays such a tragic cadence. It refuses the absolute close and makes bare the very fissures in the form, fissures that allow it to appear and reappear. Langer continued her meditation on tragic rhythm: "This form reflects the basic structure of personal life, and therewith of feeling when life is viewed as a whole."[31] It is here too that Medean practice distinguishes itself, for it does not reflect life lived as a whole—but its truncation or unbearable extension, its overliving, to use Emily Wilson's term.[32] Thus it indicates at once the nearly unavoidable imbrication of our lives with and amid those of others, and the fragility of these connections.

The presence of a certain kind of violence in tragedy—the kind we create by attending carefully to these words, imagining these bloody scenes, fearing the future—suggests that performances of tragedy don't only—or perhaps ever—cure us, lift us up, show us a peaceful future. They might also function to rehearse the impossibility of ever ridding ourselves of violence. I trace the ways in which such a rehearsal is effected through what I call a Medean principle of violence. It is the work indexed to this figure, along with all the freight of the figure's literary and philosophical history, that becomes an organizing principle allowing us to consider violence as an integral feature of literature. Thus, *In the Wake* examines that aspect of tragedy that integrates recurring and unexpiated violence into its architecture.

The Medean principle of violence has five primary features that are interwoven: It is networked or *relational*, and it is *unassimilable*. Paradoxically, it is also *exceptional* and therefore *untimely*. Last, and as a consequence of these features, it is *nonredemptive*. These features might seem familiar to the reader by now, because they are at the core of the Medean story, and they have already each informed this discussion. But it might be helpful to outline them and consider their mutual constitution as a set of qualities. These principles are part of how Medean violence operates, but it is also how we can identify this violence, since Medean violence is not of course the only kind of violence at work in tragedies.

First, Medean violence is relational. Never isolated in one character, it works among the networks which define us. This is first and foremost family, arguably like most of Greek tragedy. But every killing Medea executes seems to underscore and make use of these bonds: She chops up brother Absyrtus so that their father is diverted from chasing her to pick up his son's remains for burial; she compels daughters to kill their father, she makes a king stick to his daughter and burn; she rends her children from herself. Hers is a violence of cleaving, whether to or from. This is also in part why the theatrical form is so important: It is a form that not only examines the joins between the individual and the collective, and stages their fragility, but it constitutes these same fragile bonds among an audience and between the audience and players. The network at stake is performed in multiple facets during the theatrical event.

Second, Medean violence is unassimilable. That is, it cannot be justified or even adjudicated by the dominant order. In many instances this is connected to Medea's occult knowledge or her barbarian origins; Medea is truly a refugee in a land suspicious of her practice. Her violence is so unacceptable not just because it defies local codes of propriety and honor, but also because its origins and power are steeped in an epistemological order that is not native. It is strange, and its exclusion is the only way to understand it. Medea then is paradigmatic of the refugee whom we alternately welcome and fear, who confirms our concept of the social while threatening its integrity. The circulation of Medean violence points to how our sense of justice has already excluded those whose universes are configured differently—the primitive, the colonized, the alien. For these reasons this violence remains outside of the social order, punishable but not effectively, loathed but not vanquished.

Third, Medean violence is exceptional. It is not a cyclical, predictable, or regular occurrence. One might say that even in its near-catastrophic dimensions, its role in a longer history remains nondominant, even minor. Consider the role of Medea in literary history and political iconography: In contrast with other mythological figures in the European tradition, it is never as central to the aesthetic, political, or cultural imaginary as

Oedipus, Phaedra, Hercules, or Apollo. The figure appears, but peripherally, in Aristotelian aesthetics, invoked usually as a limit case for the moral authority of tragedy. Not only a minor player, it is also only an occasional one. This is particularly true in the French tradition. From the medieval period on, Medea punctuates figurative art, poetry, and drama by appearing as a sort of B-grade mythological star for niche performances of passion (whether of marriage or murder), folly, exile, occult knowledge, selfishness, or even self-sacrifice. This occasionality is, however, persistent: an exception whose presence demands an accounting. It is precisely in Medea's intermittent status and the unpredictability of its returns, that another kind of significance can emerge. When traditional scholarly impact measures of a mythological presence do not obtain, whether grounded by ideas of foundational or primary importance (the "first" of its kind) or quantitative importance (the character's impact on culture through the force of sheer ubiquity), something else can emerge. What does it mean when a culture repeatedly exposes and so preserves its exceptional worst? If the story of Medea is also that of an outsider's attempt to ruin the polis, its occasionality seems to underscore how such a threat must be seen as at once contained or containable, yet also ever possible.

Thus Medean violence is untimely. The untimely is that which is improper, inopportune. It usually comes too early, but it can also be too late. Either way, the untimely is characteristic of death and (in the premodern era, sometimes birth as well). Medean violence is untimely in that its calamitous effects occur through a negotiation of time that is disruptive to the present order. In Euripides, Medea asks for a day to prepare her exile, a day that allows her to bring down Creon and his daughter. This exercise of Creon's authority, which takes the form of a kind of grace or indulgence, is also a temporal wedge, affording Medea the opportunity to imbue a gown with poison, which is the vehicle for her assassination of Creon. There is another way in which Medean violence is untimely: Qualitatively it does not belong. Medean violence is seen as primitive—often as occult, unnatural. Medean violence is never modern (even though it is always contemporary). In Medean tragedy the violence is not over; it precedes the action, but it will also constitute that action and, most crucial, ensure its future. The part of the story in which Medea lives to fly off is also the part that threatens or promises her return.

As a consequence of the first four points, Medean violence gives the lie to catharsis or expiation. Corneille himself was skeptical of the efficacy of catharsis and even its occurrence: "Je doute si elle s'y fait jamais" (I doubt that it ever occurs), he remarked.[33] Medea makes it so. Her flight, through which the protagonist becomes the remainder to its very own story, eliminates the possibility of violence as the signature act defining the scapegoat or the self-sacrifice: In Medean violence, Medea always lives on, never sacrificed or eliminated. Medea in this persistence also stands for the impossibility of learning from or resolving certain kinds of violence: The violence might always return. And we expect it.

Medean violence then is the sign of literature's "destructive powers": The idea that the art we enjoy and believe is good for society also repeatedly calls attention to the impossibility of an ideal world, especially and particularly a world at peace. A Medean presence in literature marks how the written word persistently activates our imagination in order to consider how and why we offer ourselves negative lessons, or even lessons that teach us nothing we want to know.

## *The Medean Presence in Premodern Dramatic Poetry*

Performances of *Médée* during the seventeenth century offer their own peculiar understanding of this spreading violence that brings Medea to the fore. In his prefatory note to the first printed edition of *Médée*, Corneille asserted the fallacy of Medea's didactic role and scoffed at anyone who might consider her dangerous to the public: "Il n'est pas besoin d'avertir ici le public que celles de cette tragédie ne sont pas à imiter: elles paraissent assez à découvert pour n'en faire envie à personne."[34] (There is no need to warn the public that those in this tragedy should not be imitated: They are exposed enough to inspire no one's desire.) Corneille here foregrounds the trust he has in his audience to feel no desire for the replication of horrifying acts, putting the burden on the dramaturge to offer a "natural" representation of the ugliness of bad actions. This distinction is part of Corneille's politics of theater and demonstrates the stance he maintains throughout the quarrels on the matter: that audiences are trustworthy judges of good theater. The broader question of theater's proliferation, however, is one that concerns Corneille. He is particularly notable for his assiduous attention to the printed versions of his plays, correcting and recorrecting *Le Cid*, for example, and innovating spelling practices that would affect printing practices thereafter.[35] Corneille was the first French author to supervise the printing of his own collected works, with the first collection appearing in 1644 and the first illustrated edition appearing in 1660. The three volumes of this "monument editorial sans prédécent" also include his dramaturgical essays. In addition to this paratextual apparatus, each play had its own frontispiece detailing a key scene. Signed by engravers

Chauveau, David, or Spirinx these images are part of the editorial apparatus of the work, and represent one way of guiding the reception of the plays.[36] They are also moments where the performance of the play—on the printed page or in the memory of the reader's experience—reproduces itself in untold numbers

What strikes a contemporary reader is the particularity of the moments illustrated. Although they depict events crucial to the play's action, they do not seek to re-create the experience of performance itself. They focus on scenes not depicted at all, but rather recounted. *Horace* is illustrated by a moment during the battle between the Horaces and the Curiaces, in which Horace seemingly fells the last of the Curiace brothers, which in the play never occurs onstage but is recounted by an emissary.[37] The illustration is not terribly violent, and is quite far from the choreographed onstage battle in which, as the directions in Laudan d'Aigaliers's *Horace* account, "L'on tire les corps de part & d'autre" (bodies are pulled [off] from both sides).[38] It nevertheless creates a supplemental function to the performance of the poetics. Larry Norman has suggested that these engravings operate much like effective narration within a play, wherein the primary observers of these images are the characters on stage: "The print illustration is an incarnation of the image that strikes—and disturbs—the characters' minds."[39] Readers of printed plays inhabit not their own perspectives but those of the characters whose words we read. These frontispieces underscore the crucial violence performed by the Corneillian descriptions within the workings of the plays themselves, and rehearse the vividness of their elaboration.

An important exception to these general observations about how the frontispieces function, however, is that of *Médée*. This play's frontispiece does not depict an event missing from the stage and narrated by description. On the contrary, it offers a scene that would be witnessed in performance by both characters on stage and members of the public: the moment of Médée's departure. Below her dragon-drawn chariot Créon's body, a crown marking him as King, is being lifted off the ground. In the background, within the architectural space of the palace, another body is lifted—presumably the bride Créuse. Jason stands in the foreground, as big as the heaven-borne Médée. We can establish nearly the precise moment of this illustration, since while it is clearly the last scene of the play, Jason has not yet uttered the last lines of the play, pledging to end his own life. His sword is drawn and arm stretched out, so he has not yet finished fighting. This is a moment of aftermath but where the work of violence is still visible. It is only a moment of "action" in the modern sense of the word

Figure 7. Illustration for *Horace*, by Louis Spirinx, in Pierre Corneille, *Le théâtre de P. Corneille, reveu et corrigé par l'autheur, II partie* (Rouen and Paris, 1660). Source: Bibliothèque nationale de France.

Figure 8. Illustration for *Médée*, in Pierre Corneille, *Le théâtre de P. Corneille, reveu et corrigé par l'autheur, I partie* (Rouen and Paris, 1660). Source: Bibliothèque nationale de France.

insofar as Médée's flight is crucial to the cycle of violence which she creates.

Another illustrated edition from just a few years later, 1664, drives home this point even more, and also offers an encapsulation of the other problem of Medean violence. This illustrated edition is the "unauthorized" version from Amsterdam, *"reveu et corrigé et augmenté"* (reviewed, edited, and augmented) and "suivant la copie imprimée à Paris" (based on the copy printed in Paris), by the printer and bookseller Abraham Wolfgang.[40] Wolfgang printed many versions of French books, under his own as well as false imprints. This edition has been generally dismissed: Unlike the edition printed in Paris, it was not overseen by Corneille. Its illustrations, unsigned and more crudely executed, are less valuable than those in the Paris editions. Because printed in Amsterdam, it is seen as illegitimate—a charge that, however anachronistic given the nascent status of any idea of copyright in the mid-seventeenth century, has stuck.

Illegitimate, this edition is also an apt figure of Medea's own marginal status: unauthorized, inadmissible to a canon, and perhaps, so far as the images are concerned, more rudely executed. In this edition, each play's illustration functions as a true frontispiece: Each includes the play's title and Corneille's name. The prints are unsigned by either illustrator or engraver. Although they generally depict the same scenes as in the Parisian version, they are not pure imitations. Even beyond the framing fabric that alludes to a lifted curtain, the perspective and layout in the illustration for *Médée* seems to emphasize the idea of a stage performance more directly, with obvious side panels. Within this space of performance, the details remain the same—largely. Jason is still stage right, while further upstage, two bodies are visible. One is being carried off while the other remains on the ground. The forms are indistinct, and so who they are meant to be cannot be determined. Médée is in her dragon-drawn chariot, although this one is drawn by someone else. What is remarkably different in this image is the prominence of destruction: Flames escape the palace's windows and doors; Corinth is shown to be still burning; a skeleton peeks out from the fire above the doorway, as if grinning at the witnesses below who are pointing upward—whether to it or to Médée.

If the Amsterdam edition heightens the portrayal of violence already present in the Parisian edition, it does so by adding elements that likely were not on stage. The flames consuming the palace, for example, bear no traces of any stylization suggesting that they are evoking theatrical effects. Did the skeleton appear on stage, a machine effect whose hands could be moved to express anguish? Or, equally plausible, the image raises the visual

Figure 9. Illustration for *Médée*, in *Le théâtre de P. Corneille, reveu et corrigé et augmenté* (Amsterdam: A. Wolfgang, 1664). Source: Bibliothèque nationale de France, Département des Arts du spectacle.

stakes on the depiction of violence by clearly showing its effects, its damage. This addition also calls to attention the significance of the destruction of the house of Corinth: The dragons of Médée's chariot float just above the burning skeleton, drawing our eye to it.

The Amsterdam image is an icon of Medean violence. A "non-authorized" version created and circulated not just beyond its author's sphere of authority, but outside the confines of the monarchy for which neoclassical tragedy would be set to work, it also figures the scale, scope, and quality of Medean violence, and its legacy in and beyond Corneille. If it affirms that Medean violence did not vanish after 1634, it also emphasizes the work of this tragedy in its aftermath—as leaving a remainder of destruction in its wake.

## Working in the Wake of the Past

Medean lessons tend to stick. About eighteen years ago, I received a newspaper clipping from a former student, reporting on the 2001 conviction of Marilyn Lemak for having drugged and smothered her three children. Apologizing for not having sent it immediately, she wrote, "Just thought I would share this with you," the student annotated. "Lemak struck me as another 'modern-day Médée.'" I've saved this clipping, touched by the gesture and the proof that something from a course on French tragedy had stayed with one of its participants.

It also made me wonder exactly what lingered with the student. What did she mean by "modern-day Médée"? Why did the student append such a qualifier? Did she enjoy the alliteration or was she distinguishing our work from current events for a specific reason? It was not a matter of what is modern about Medea: The qualification suggested, on the contrary, that the figure is resolutely not modern, no matter what era she is in.[41]

The non-modernity of Medea has been emphasized in news media since at least the mid-nineteenth century to describe women who kill their children and survive, exemplified by Margaret Garner. They did so perhaps even before Thomas Satterwhite Noble's 1867 portrait of her capture, *The Modern Medea*, prints of which circulated widely in such journals as *Harpers Weekly*. Even at the time of Garner's trial, the moral ambiguity of her act, and the conditions of her enslavement, her rape by her owner, and the mercy of her act were signaled. Something changed after Noble titled his painting: The ambivalence of Garner's gesture, and those of other "Medeas," faded in favor of clearer assessments of guilt. By the twentieth century, especially in more sensationalist media outlets, being called a

Introduction: Coming after Violence in Literature

Figure 10. Wood engraving after a painting by Thomas Satterwhite Noble, "Margaret Garner or the Modern Medea," in *Harper's Weekly* 11 (18 May 1867). Courtesy New York Public Library, Schomburg Center for Research in Black Culture, Photographs and Prints.

"modern-day Medea" became less ambiguous and far more clearly damning: Lamak, Alice Crimmins, Christy Sheets, Susan Smith, Louise Woodward, and most famously for Americans, Andrea Yates, have all been deemed today's versions of the Colchian witch, precisely because their infanticide did not lead to suicide. What in the time of Euripides, Jean de La Péruse, or Noble was so complex as to escape easy judgment or definitive narrative, had become, by the twentieth century, a barbarism from an archaic past, a decision to choose an unnatural act without self-sacrifice.[42] Medea's violence is itself now not only primitive but other—possible, but not belonging to our time.

What precisely seems primitive? It is the lingering that shocks. The philosopher Isabelle Stengers has said that *Medea* presents "the challenge of a woman who kills her children and yet does not die of it."[43] Both play and character create a double challenge. First, how can we reconcile the fact of a mother who wishes to live after deliberately losing her offspring? How does Medean violence fly off, alive and vibrant, after infanticide? Second, how can we live with the persistence of this violence and its recurrence in our world? In this way Medea is utterly premodern: The figure is an untimely recollection of a past that did not, we hope, lead to our present moment, yet still it subsists. As the mark of unexpiated violence, the same figure is also one of a future to be feared. It is within this double relation to history and futurity that this book operates. This is what it means to be "in the wake" of Medea.

When we are in the wake of something, we inhabit its reverberations, its echoes. Medea, like so many mythological figures, seems eternally to cite its own past iterations. But there is also the future. We know what happens, so the Medea story always anticipates murder and flight. Medea is a rehearsal of violence. Thus to operate in Medea's wake means to come after the carnage but also to linger in it, inhabiting its reverberations while noting the path it has taken and the power of its movement. In French, the *sillage* of a boat's movement through water is also the lingering of a scent remaining on the nose long after the odoriferous object has gone. This sensorial remainder obtains in that other sense of "wake": that of consciousness, of being roused from sleep, of being aware and watchful. And this awareness, in turn, informs the Anglophone use of "wake"—from the Irish, one collective ritual of watchful attendance to a corpse until its burial.[44]

To be awake to the past on its own terms, freeing it of its pressure to respond to today's situation, is not an easy task. Arguing against the historical search for origins, Michel Foucault argued for another approach, that of "effective history," or genealogy. "A genealogy of values, morality, asceticism and knowledge will never confuse itself with a quest for their 'origins,' . . . it is necessary to recognize the events of history, its jolts, its surprises, its unsteady victories and unpalatable defeats—the basis of all beginnings, atavisms, and heredities."[45] Instead of seeing, from the vantage point of our own modern present, the premodern as the past which we have overcome, what if it were the site of unexamined accidents, singular persistence, unacknowledged moments of possibility, however unrealized? Accordingly, what might a theater history of the French classical age offer us if told not from the weight of its dominant forms, but from the nimble vantage point of a minor story? If such violence persists in dramatic poetry, it is not as a precursor, or a start of something, but as a kind of negative eternal return, a live haunting. What would result, then, if we told a theater history starting not from its primitive, first or greatest form, nor from what quantitatively characterizes it, or what it produced, but rather from a starting point of exceptionality and endurance, a persistence that recurs, whose quality and importance lies in its insistent occasionality, in its ability to survive and return? An account this persistent will not offer a new foundation myth. It will not create or alter an intellectual history of any concept, by locating moments of invention, or anticipation of a future that we call modernity. It is perhaps for this reason that the texts examined here disrupt temporal regimes. They trace differences among regimes of historicity, conflicting notions of futurity, or even between premodernity and modernity itself.

Instead of offering a corrective to the grand story of theater, or to the cultural history of violence, *In the Wake of Medea* disrupts them, questioning their sanctity and coherence on several key grounds. First, the history of theater in the seventeenth century is far more diverse, with many more aesthetic experiments, moral trespasses, and accidents of genre than we have previously integrated into the larger story. It must acknowledge more rigorously that if there is something like "neoclassical tragedy" it is a thing whose edges are both blurred and frayed, as they meet poetry, mythology, iconography, rhetoric, performance, and politics. It must indeed be rewritten to refuse a radical rupture between the Baroque and the classical, to consider the myriad sources of inspiration from the Renaissance and earlier. In refusing a positivist march through time, it makes connections across periods and despite generic divisions. And while this rewriting must also refuse a teleological approach to literature that sees it as marching toward a perfect future, it must also investigate the local disruptions of temporality— the ways in which literature's principles of destruction open new temporal structures, experiences of time, and concepts of historical time.

The first task of this endeavor is to reexamine critically the links we have created among mythology, politics, and literature, and to indicate where I think we have strayed. I do so incautiously in a preliminary manifesto, exploring how Western philosophy and thought might be shaped differently if Medea were considered in contrast to the more well known, debated, and celebrated figure of Antigone, multivalent symbol of ethical opposition to an oppressive state, as Judith Butler and more recently Bonnie Honig have examined.[46] My countertheory starts with the idea of Medea as a paradigm of the cautionary tale: that figure against which we must work. If Antigone's allegiances to her brother against the state challenge a certain politics of legacy, family, and duty, Medea underscores the problem not of our origins but of our future: She kills her offspring and creates no replacements. I show how Medea operates at the limits of the moral imperative by virtue of what she knows she can both heal and harm. She is also a Latourian "hybrid": Outside of our traditional categories of knowledge and identification, her actions challenge the integrity of the individual itself, as we have constituted it in society.[47] Medea underscores the relational attachment of the mother to her children, the wife to her husband, and the knower to her forebears even as she undoes these relations. By figuring Medea in our literature, I argue, we rehearse the real problem of the social: the false and fragile divisions that purportedly guard integrated insiders from barbaric outsiders, and modernity from its necessary but primitive pasts.

Chapter 1 serves as the cornerstone of this book, against which all the other chapters can be read. It explores a singular play, Pierre Corneille's 1634 *Médée*. Often read as generic precursor or holdover, as a failed experiment or a primitive attempt, *Médée* is utterly unique for its era in its subject matter and politics: It is a model of theater as a continual vacillation between destruction and endurance, personifying these characteristics in its eponym. I explore how its Médée is framed not by excess, passion, or inconstancy, but by moderation, knowledge, and attachment, in both positive and negative forms. What emerges is a meditation on how we cleave to others, and are cloven from them, indicating the fragile boundaries among our disparate selves. Médée's own "self" is a surface self, existing in contradistinction to the complex self-possessed individual grounded in an interior, the hallmark of the eighteenth century. This surface self is figured in her radiant gown which—in distinction from Didier Anzieu's "skin-ego," the mere "wrapper" of the true psyche—stands both for her history and her knowledge.[48] The contrast between the Medean surface self and the Medean art of destruction, as one of cleaving to and cleaving from, compels a meditation on how the self emerges in relation to others, and what is sacrificed when we see the self as autonomous. Analogously, instead of seeing *Médée* as Corneille's first tragedy, and so a primitive or premature form of what will come after it, this reading positions it at the undisclosed heart of the tragic project, as it reverberates in both its past and its future.

From this cornerstone chapter, readers may turn to any of those that follow. Each contains reverberations and amplifications of Chapter 1. Exploring a range of performance genres, each examines diverse manifestations of Medean violence. Chapter 2, for example, methodologically enacts this forward and backward gaze by offering an account of Medean presence that ties Pier Paolo Pasolini to Ovid in a layering and sutured constellational consideration of literature as an art of destruction. Beginning with an analysis of Maria Callas's performance in the titular role in Pasolini's 1969 *Medea*, I highlight its structural connections to the Medea of Ovid's *Metamorphoses*, connections that upend a traditional understanding of history, influence, and the constitution of character. Through Medea, Ovid aligns destruction with the work of literary creation through the rhetorical figure of description. In a text generally studied and celebrated for its narrative of transformation, and which is often called "cinematic," the vivid scenes of these transformations are also aetiological—they explain the origin of the universe, the deep red of mulberry, why the partridge does not fly, how Icarus gave the island Icaria its name. Medea is an exception: Her transformations are really nontransformative—they leave nothing behind but the story of their violence. Through this Medea story, Ovid exceptionally constructs description as a "monument of destruction." Further, I examine the architecture of the *Metamorphoses* to suggest a link between description and destruction, wherein violence is precisely beyond structural control.

Chapter 3 switches our temporal gaze to a more proximate field. It returns doubly to the present moment of Chapter 1 by exploring the lesser-known playwright Jean Rotrou and his neglected 1634 *Hercule mourant*, performed during the same season as Corneille's *Médée*. Chapter 3 also addresses the present moment of spectacle: what it means to attend to the theatrical presence of violence. It does so first by considering performance strategies that create what poststructuralist performance theorists call "presence": the dynamic system whereby an audience is implicated in the constructed reality of the stage. *Hercule mourant*, a Neo-Stoic play exemplary of a Medean tragedy, exposes a conceptual model of endurance as an experience of tragedy. In this performance of the demigod Hercules' death by his wife's poisoned gift, the hero's slow demise is a major portion of the drama's action. Confined within the envelope of his body, however, the source of Hercule's pain is unseen. Drawing on the play's performance archive confirming its incredible spectacularity, I draw out the tension between the invisibility of burning from within and the audience's poetic apprehension of such violence. This combination of embodied spectacle and poetics, of silent invisible flames and loudly declaimed verse, slows down the moment of crisis to which an audience attends, and whose effects it hopes to experience. In staging such belabored attention to the spectacle of bodily pain and in addressing the problems of expression and communication that pain underscores, *Hercule mourant* provides a potential counterexample to common notions of catharsis that purge the immoderation of the spectacular, by belaboring it instead. It asks audiences to consider endurance as a model of attending to violence.

Further addressing the seeming anachronisms and discontinuities within dramatic history, Chapter 4 returns to Corneille, for his 1660 prequel to the 1634 tragedy, *La Conquête de la Toison d'or*. Traditional readings classify it as political propaganda celebrating the king's marriage. My analysis is the first to consider the play's technological innovations as part of its aesthetic and political work. I show how an onstage Medean presence pits two forms of temporality against each other, each performed by a different stage technology. The production boasted two major innovations in set design and special effects, first in the form of scene changes where new worlds appear instantly, as if magically. It pits this performance of "new natures" against the innovations of ropes and pulleys that allow for actors and scenery, suspended, to fly through the air. This contrast between the instantaneity of scene changes and the suspended experience of watching flight is underscored by the play's contrasting thematics of magic, a form of rapid transformation, and that of narrative suspense. This chapter traces how the play changes the rules of dramatic narrative by challenging audience expectations for what will happen. Eliminating the faithful passion that motivates Medea to aid Jason in stealing the Fleece, and staging a kind of ambiguity about what will happen, *La Conquête de la Toison d'or* creates what modern critics would call "suspense": a futurity of uncertainty and ambiguity, in which violence's evacuation from the stage is clearly temporary. This play offers, contra such conceptual historians as Reinhart Koselleck, an early example of the collision between premodern forms of history and more progressivist senses of temporality.[49] This collision invokes the metaphor of suspension only to replace it with that of suspense, thus effecting a replacement that positions the threat of violence close at hand.

The final chapter turns to the particular nature of a Medean tragedy—that is, the tragedy of what Stengers has called the "challenge" of a mother who kills her children but does not perish. The nature of this tragedy is one paradoxically without issue or finality. In this chapter, the idea of tragedy in the neoclassical age is taken up through this temporal lens, by considering primarily Racine's *Athalie* (1690). Whereas traditional theater history anchors French neoclassical tragedy firmly with Corneille's *Médée*, accounts vary in offering either *Athalie* or Racine's secular play *Phèdre* (1677) at the other end of the continuum, as the great dramaturge's "last" great play. This chapter explores the idea of "lastness," showing how tragedy demands a peculiar reading of our relationship to a temporality we cannot even pretend to control. It considers the changing concept of "catastrophe," originally a theatrical term signaling the final steps of a tragedy's resolution, but shifting, in the eighteenth century, to designate an unpredictable cataclysm. Both within its verse and in its reception *Athalie* is the drama of a shift in temporalities, from one in which we lived history as an unfolding of events in the past, present, and future to one in which the future's devastations are always a surprise. *Athalie* disrupts the temporal structures in which it has been received and through which it has interpreted, in particular, the relationships between modernity and early or premodernity.

The persistent presence of Medea serves not just as a symbol but as an organizing principle of these artistic strategies, revealing literature's "destructive powers": its impulse to refuse a universalizing message, even to resist the idea of creation as its only ultimate goal. *In the Wake* explores how violence, embedded not just in the mythological sources of these tragedies but in their performances and poetics, operates as a force of repeated, persistent temporal disruption. In revising the well-wrought story of neoclassical tragedy's dispassionate, timeless aesthetics, *In the Wake* urges us to let the premodern break free of its paradoxical role as at once our primitive past and our primary source of enduring values. Instead, attention to violence in these plays reveals specific ruptures in their temporal structures, experiences of time, and concepts of historical time. Such ruptures expose some of the persistent accidents of the premodern as they point to ways in which the past did not lead to our modernity—while they also rehearse the impossibility of a peaceful future.

# Medea, a Manifesto

There is good reason to think of Medea today. There is good reason to think of a refugee, of a terrorist, of a nondominant or alternative source of knowledge, of a future that promises much violence and not much resolution. There is good reason to want to find a figure for our times. But I will steer readers away from thinking about a "modern-day Medea" or even a "modern Medea" and instead urge attention to a "premodern Medea," a Medea distinctly not ours, yet who circulates among us nevertheless. This move might not make us feel good—Medea's presence won't offer any answers to our problems. There is no way it could, since it sits so uncomfortably among us. Rather, the premodern Medea denotes a network of relations that belies the attention and hope that we moderns give to the discrete individual and rehearses the nonexpiative role of violence in these relations. If historically we moderns have strived to achieve change through contestation, it is because we are stuck with Antigone, the heroic figure of contestation who resists the tyranny of the polis and dies trying.

Medea is not Antigone. After all, in Medea's presence, Creon, the king, dies.

## The Antigone Impasse

Antigone is a figure on the edge of revolution, at once an icon of political hope and of tragic failure. The construction of this icon, from the initial framing of Sophocles' play, laid a foundation for Enlightenment discussions of individual rights, found new ground around questions of domesticity with Hegel's celebration of family and Lacanian interpretations of the heroine's search for autonomy through death, undergirded Luce Irigaray's feminist interrogation of power, and mobilized Judith Butler's queer kinship claims, which multiplied the liberatory potential of Antigone. In the gamut of contemporary versions—from Marguerite Yourcenar's 1935 Christic prose portrait or Jean Anouilh's 1944 version that was celebrated by *pétainistes* and *résistants* alike, to François Ost's 1999 use of hijab as the vehicle for Antigone's protest, through Seamus Heaney's invocation of her as a critic of the Bush administration's war in Iraq—Antigone offers a multivalent means of interrogating the collision between, on the one hand, a desire to defend and honor the powerless and, on the other, the role of law in creating a peaceful society—the relationship between the individual and the political, the clash between primitive matriarchy and the patriarchy of the emerging polis, or, more generally, the role of kinship affiliation in contrast to obedience to the law.[1] Antigone's fearless conviction that she must do right by her brother's corpse and bury it in the face of an interdiction, her self-imposed peerlessness as she refuses accomplices or partners in right, her truth-telling, "Yes, I am guilty"—all these elements push us to see Antigone as a study of the individual whose allegiances to her particular duties compel her to test the state's power, personified by Creon.

And her death asks us: Who can truly intervene? When moral clarity is obfuscated by the complexity of history, when political actants are themselves multivalent, whose actions can be deemed cogent, pure, defensible? Who, anyway, can ever change the tide pushing against the powerless? Pitting the sacred, familial, private task of burying the dead against the emergent ordering force of the city, this young and unmarried childless daughter of Oedipus has come to represent the power of domesticity and the family against the state, the perils and potential of individual resistance, the power (and powerlessness) of woman in the modern state, and—since debates in eighteenth-century France that took Antigone as their figurehead—a model of the modern individual whose moral judgment indicated the individual's inalienable rights to personhood and political action.

Yet we might pause to consider whether the ubiquity of this figure, and critical perseverations regarding her as a model of action, might all be for naught. Considering where Antigone criticism has gotten us, we might affirm that Antigone emerges in our contemporary moment rather more like a multifaceted model of our inability to marshal a clear and enduring response to the question of what both the morality and the politics of resistance might look like.

I think there are two reasons for this. The first is our construction of Antigone, a kind of paradox we have created out of her. The second reason concerns how our attachment to this paradoxical character betrays some of the significant architectural elements of *Antigone*, the dramatic tragedy.

First, how and why is it possible that the character Antigone, ubiquitous in literary criticism, omnipresent in political allegories and analogies, persistent upon the stage and in rhetorical allusion, remains available to hold all these hopes? For all the reasons she is incapable of realizing them: She is a vulnerable virgin girl. Deprived of political and eventually physical agency, and depriving herself of a future, Antigone is a unique figure for a future interrupted. She maintains historical power from the performance of death as the highest test case for ethical action. But it is this same performance that makes of her a sacrifice, a scapegoat, a martyr: hardly an icon for political action in a liberal society.

One way to consider this problem is to see it as embedded within the nature of tragedy. As Jonathan Strauss has observed, like all tragedy, *Antigone* remains significant to us for the ways the play undergirds one of the hallmark failures, and persistent pursuits, of tragedy: the "difficulty in imagining a living individual. There has a been a strange resistance to the very idea of such a person, as if human thought, indeed humanity itself, formally and constitutionally negated the plenitude of its own experiences—as if at every moment we must deny not only our baser instincts and the crass profusion of animal existence, but our life itself."[2] In Strauss's fine reading, the Greek tragedies are unending attempts to legitimate the city through a reconciliation with those figures whose exclusion the state depended on. Even as *Antigone* "condenses a traumatic moment in the elaboration of individual self-identity," Strauss argues, a careful reading of the play's engagement with the status of the individual can show how tragedy "is a labor not *of* but *against* death, it is the expression of a longing for a meaningful individual life, and it is the attempt to understand what that life would be."[3] Despite this more recent corrective, Antigone's historical power has come in part from her performance of death as the highest test case for ethics.

A simplistic version of the problem to which Strauss alludes is in the rehearsal of death that bookends Antigone's resistance. She may resist because her brother dies; his corpse motivates her. And she herself becomes a symbol of resistance in part because of what she does, as well as what she becomes: In acting (or in saying she has done or will do something), she becomes a corpse herself. Seen this way, *Antigone* reveals a set of other problems folded into the problem of surviving and dying, of mourning others and oneself. It points to the importance of actions as the basis of the performance of politics, as the basis of theater itself.

It is astonishing, then, that discussions of *Antigone* tend to focus on the confrontation between the maiden and her uncle Creon, proposing this duologue—a verbal battle—as a distillation of the tragedy's major tensions. The exchange does have great allure: It captures the moment when a powerless, silenced person speaks and acts in direct challenge to the most powerful. Yet the clarity of this moment is exceptional in the play; its most curious parts are rather all those that elicit the confrontation and result from it: the burial, even burials of bodies. *Antigone*'s tension is not a contestation captured by speech; it manifests through action. And through the question of who did what, *Antigone* reminds us that it is a theatrical performance, a polyvocalic drama with multiple bodies—all living, some also dying—on stage.

One such element that has elicited much commentary is the mysterious "double burial" of Polynices. Although Antigone declares that she had first buried him, she never admits to the second burial and its agent remains a mystery. Antigone's sister Ismene also admits to the burial; this claim as well as Antigone's refutation of it are left unresolved. This second burial bolsters Antigone's claim to righteousness—someone else also insisted on the necessity of burying Polynices—even as it undermines one facet: Antigone is not so singular. Thus the second burial stands as a kind of testimony to action, such as that which Antigone claims and defends, Even as it could also undermine Antigone's own singular stance by indicating that she is not the lone actor, that she is not the single figure of performative defiance, it then further suggests that a single act does not suffice. Either way, the question of burial offers an instance of what all choral theater offers: There is no single figure; there is no single gesture of defiance. *Antigone* multiplies the bodies—Haemon's and Eurydice's deaths follow on Antigone's—but it also multiplies the agents. The central problems are not exposed by a verbal debate between Creon and Antigone but manifest themselves through a network of performed relations within a web of personae.

Yet we remain attached to this paradoxical character, despite how the architectural elements of her tragedy give the lie to her singularity. This attachment to the ethical dimensions of such a remarkable figure can also be located at the root of impasses around Antigone's deployment among critical thinkers. One general point that we may extract from the common chorus of critics who have made of *Antigone* a debate about the emergence of a modern political subject, from Hegel to Judith Butler, Jacques Rancière, and most recently Bonnie Honig, is the status of her defiance. For Judith Butler, Antigone is a model for action toward a queer, nonnormative kinship structure that itself defies dominant authority. For Butler, this model is one of Antigone's "promiscuous obedience." It is a performance of adherence that is also defiance: Burying her brother obeys a tradition while it defies an injunction; admitting her guilt tells the truth but violates the norms of women's nonaction and silence; obeying her brother's wishes, over those of her father's and Creon's, respects his male voice over the much more iconic patriarchal signs of authority that a father and a leader offer.[4]

Even in such a model of an obedience that defies the dominant model—Antigone's claims to a morality beyond that of the polis, a morality that is privately constituted and individually held—the ethical paradigm she exposes has particular limits to it, as her claims emerge in the shadows of a self-possessed individual whose rights are inherent. Insofar as *Antigone* the play exposes a kind of uncomfortable doubling to its instances of trespass—a doubling mirrored by the presence of *two* dead brothers, two possible heroic buriers, and the crucial tension between the tragedy of Antigone in dialogue with that of the even more tragic Creon—it also refuses a single interpretation about the morality of action. Yet when critics embrace the ambiguity of this play, its structural doubling, its multiple moralities, even as they advocate for one interpretation or another, their stances depend on characters who each represent a coherent, singular state or status. And this is where the problem is: How can *Antigone* offer a model for the kind of politics we recognize today when it is also a model for the instability or uncertainty of that model's fundamental unit of validity and expression, the individual? To state the very obvious, Antigone is not *Antigone*; the exploration of the social dilemma and the conflicts that arise therein are the work of a collective. *Antigone* is neither treatise nor duologue but tragedy: a collective work whose "agents," as Aristotle might have called them, are indexed not so much to individuals as to elements within a network of relations and antagonisms, which can then comment on the social.

Among political theorists, the work of Bonnie Honig sees the multiplicity afforded by Antigone as an agent among others. In tracking what she calls the "Antigone-effect," in scholarship, that is, the figure's shift from tracing rival sovereignties to one who is a "humanist lamenter of the dead," Honig instead advocates for a reading that takes up our "responsibility to interrogate the palimpsests of reception that isolate Antigone and make of her a radical individual—something quite different from Sophocles' creation."[5] Honig positions Antigone and her negotiations with Creon, Ismene, and the other players of the tragedy, not just as end-game interruptions of each other, but as informing a theory of democracy that values variable agonisms as generative. Antigone then emerges as something of a community organizer, conspiring to forge a new public through the process of "agonistic humanism." We rally around her on behalf of collective life.

In this reading, Antigone's moves, tone, and performance are not unified, consistent, or defensive, but varied, quarreling, contesting. For Honig, this Antigone is a "community organizer," who might "interrupt our contemporary assumptions that radical politics is limited to dissidence or lamentation. This new Antigone does not only protest and mourn sovereignty's excesses. She also plots and conspires; she quests for power and seeks to infiltrate and claim sovereignty."[6] To effect this reading, Honig refuses *Antigone* as tragedy and interprets it as melodrama. Melodrama suggests an anti-grandiose, pro-democratic landscape in which tones of conspiracy, irony, hyperbole, and overwrought speech are brought out. This reorientation not only demands a certain reading of the play but more significantly compels a specific performance by its actors. In this sense, if Antigone resembles a community organizer, it is because Honig is a dramaturge, offering a reading of a character that inflects its actor's performance.

Antigone is available for these voices, not because she is Antigone, but because she is an acted character in *Antigone*. What I mean by this is that when Honig advocates for an Antigone who "is quite deliberate when she puns, mimics, and parodies," there is a conflation between the changing registers, tones, inflections of performance choices and the deliberate stance of the character.[7] Honig is not wrong to promote an interpretative possibility that would support such dramaturgical choices, but the difference between interpretation and performance is significant. Melodrama here is then a dramaturgical choice that is possible because the play allows it. Ultimately, what makes tragedy and melodrama related forms is that they are theater: They represent a network of relations whose radicality is borne out by interpretations of them in mutual relation and constitution, interpretations that are iterative but temporary, rehearsed but always contingent.

I remain suspicious of our celebration of Antigone, even as theorists have reassessed her drama as a multivalent one with nearly unending models for life in the polis. It is not only that I am suspicious of a politics that holds up—whether for celebration or judgment—the uncompromising actions of an aristocratic girl on the eve of democracy's birth. My hesitation goes further and is twofold. First, as I have said, *Antigone* is theater, not mono- or duologue, so the materiality of its tensions must be addressed, beyond the work of dramaturgical interpretation. And although this tension has implications for models of governance, and for political theory in general, these operations are not the same. If it is possible to argue today, with Richard Halpern, that "the Greeks invented both democracy and theater. And, having done this much, they then invented a third thing—political theory—that allowed them to conceptualize relations between the other two," we should not necessarily understand this conceptualization to be mutually exhaustive.[8] Democracy and theater have had their own lives, and the latter has existed long before and far outside the former. Further, although our ideas about who or what Antigone (or any tragic figure) means for us have evolved, one must recognize that theater's art in the European tradition—at least since the Greeks—has been based not just on a performance of community but also on the tensions between individual and collective signification that constitute it. As Anna Rosensweig has argued, "The physical and emotional interactions among bodies—on stage and off—show us how communal attachments undergird personal claims and capacities. These attachments are integral to the work of theater. Theater holds together the individual and the collective."[9] Current scholarship has moved toward accounting for such dynamism both in performance and historiography, but criticism nevertheless tends to maintain the eponymous character of Antigone as an icon who "stands for" ideals, alone, in duologue with Creon, or in conspiracy with Ismene, and to hold up the power of the singular individual, even if it is to galvanize a collective. Something in the structure of *Antigone* as a model of collective action has generated this impasse, wherein theater works at the hands of an individual. I suspect this is because the model of democracy that it explores has already set the terms for who and what can be at stake: Although *Antigone* questions Creon's polis, its history and future, figures such as Medea have already been excluded from these questions. The time has come to look beyond, or before, a model of political participation that centers solely on the structures of democracy. And if theater remains crucial to this model, it is time to see the multifaceted performance history of theater as constitutive of its politics.

My second concern addresses what *Antigone* achieves for us. Even in her most radical guise, as an advocate for "a (post)humanist politics with agonistic intent," Antigone remains forward-looking, as if the polis in which she "plots, conspires and maneuvers" has always been constituted as such and could never be anything but.[10] Jacques Rancière has offered a way off the Antigone stage and its trauma that is "without beginning or end": through a return to Oedipus.[11] Might we more radically redraw our political family tree, however, by considering the vagaries of geography, conquest, and affiliation? To do so might compel us to reconsider who, and whose stories, constitute the House of Thebes. And who has been excluded from the polis as a feature of its constitution? What then if *Medea* were integral to our genealogy? Above all, we would have to contend with the very conditions that *Antigone*, which starts in the aftermath of war and finishes with regret for a death not spared, elides: the statelessness that war brings home, the problem of revenge, the state's monopoly of force, and the problem of women who kill: in sum, the question of the role of violence in the formation of society.

## Between Futurity and Calculation

If superficially the differences between the two could not be greater, Antigone and Medea do attend to similar problems, albeit with very different outcomes. On the surface: Antigone is a virgin who grieves, contests, and dies; Medea is a mother who ages, kills, and lives on. Antigone wishes to honor her brother with a burial; Medea chops Absyrtus into bits to delay her father's pursuit, compelling him to recover the pieces for burial. Antigone laments her family's curse; whereas Medea carries with her the knowledge bequeathed to her through her house. And although Antigone has been given the uniquely temporally transcendent universal position of being at once a "figure of History," and "identity.... for young girls or women alive today,"[12] Medea is an exemplar of archaism, of a nonidentification. Relatedly, Antigone is a challenge to a certain kind of family and local politics, revealing that the origins of kingship are arbitrary. Medea underscores precisely the opposite logic: the steadfastness of family whether chosen (Jason) or imposed (children). Following this logic, Medea traces the problem not of origins but of the ambiguity of the future. Although the temporality of the Medea myth invites such ambiguity (who knows when her flight will lead her back to the polis?), the act of infanticide poses the problem of a woman who kills her children and creates no replacements. Antigone's death is hers and hers alone: Not only is she alone, but, as

Nicole Loraux asserts, she strangles herself with her knotted veil, emblem of her girlhood.[13]

Appropriate to her final entombment, Antigone's name means, as Ann Carson reminds us, "against birth" or "instead of being born."[14] We might hope that Medea's might mean "against the mother" or "instead of child-bearing," even though it has become synonymous with "she who acts against birth," who denies her own nature. There is a strange parallel here too, in that Antigone's story is of one who, like Medea, leaves no posterity, no traces—as if she had not been born at all. The only monument to her is her contestation. Here again we find a productive contrast, for in Euripides, Medea's last gesture in Corinth is to establish a monument and a festival in her children's memory. But the contrast must be pushed further, beyond a simple opposition. Euripides' *Medea* might be said to be, from the beginning, a meditation on the full potential of Medea as name and as actor.

Medea's name Μήδεια might be said to mean "intelligent planner" or "contriver." It derives from the Indo-European root *med-, which Emile Benveniste defines as "to take authoritatively those measures which are appropriate."[15] From this root developed two verbs and associated nouns: μητιάω, "I deliberate" or "I contrive," from which emerged the noun μῆτις "cunning intelligence," and μήδομαι, or "I plan," "I intend," I contrive," with the noun "schemes" or "plans" having a homonym referring to male genitalia.[16] Medea's intelligent schemes are inflected by tones of masculinity, not least because from her exploits on Colchis through her rejuvenation of Aeson and murder of Pelias, she is coming to the aid of a vulnerable Jason.[17]

David Konstan has noted the repeated sound of the first syllable in Medea's name in the play's opening lines by the nurse through the repetition of a negative, which sounds like *mee*. The effect is not dissimilar, he suggests, to the triple invocation of Zeus in a hymn or prayer. Instead of an invocation of the gods, however, the nurse speaks these sounds in regretting the *Argo*'s journey, wishing the oars had not been built.[18] In this way, the repetition of the first syllable of Medea's name thematically introduces her whole name, and guarantees the full realization of her conniving, planning, measuring self from the very beginning.

This syllable shares the same root as *meditate* or *medicine*; Medea's masculine-haunted careful planning, her careful deployment of knowledge, names the same authoritative care that study or healing does. Medea, of course, is seen neither as a sage nor wholly as a healer: This is why she is portrayed so often as a witch.[19] Medea signals a multivalent but authoritative, measured use of knowledge—knowledge that can be both rejuvenating and devastating.

This ambiguity might explain why the most common visual depiction of her in premodern iconography was of her reviving Aeson, Jason's father.[20] Or is it of Medea killing Pelias? The gestures are similar enough to give one pause, and to make the connection between healing and killing. In this way, she achieves the work of the *pharmakon*: Her philters have both curative and murderous potential. In "Plato's Pharmacy" Jacques Derrida offers the *pharmakon* as the medium for language's undecidability.[21] What interests me is rather its multivalency—it is the circulation of the *pharmakon* and its effects that result in the multiple and even opposing understandings of the term. Similarly, recounts Derrida, the *pharmakeus* ("wizard, magician, poisoner") always meets its homophonal near-synonym *pharmakos*: the exiles, sacrifices, scapegoats sent out of the city and ritually killed as a "purification and a remedy" for the city.[22] Faced with the law, Medea *pharmakeus* is made to be *pharmakos*; her estranged position is geopolitical and epistemological, because what Medea knows comes from elsewhere; it is not part of the Greeks' knowledge order.

Two likenesses of Medea speak volumes about the Medean pharmacological complex. They are both on sarcophagi that depict the story of Jason and Medea from the Golden Fleece to the death of the children. Between the theft of a pelt and the murder of offspring is a kind of amalgam of both these crimes: the death of Creusa. Each sarcophagus depicts the girl in agony, her bearded father distraught, his hand or hands to his face in stunned agony, his emotions a match for her physical torment. Contemplating her compels us to marvel at the undulating silkiness of the fabric and hair that creates the movement in the stone. On the first, witnessed by three other figures who with her father surround her, hands pinned to their heads in a uniform gesture of frozen disbelief and vicariously felt agony, Creusa is as if in movement, her own hand stretched out in front of her: She is running away from the gown that clings to her and that will kill her. Under her bent knee, there is a stool or box, adorned with tragic masks. Even more discreetly, behind the two children to her right, there is another object, a box.[23] Metonym for the absent Medea, it is the case in which she keeps her herbs.

The second sarcophagus lacks the box of herbs. Instead, the power of Medea is expressed through the metamorphosis of hair into flames. The Berlin sarcophagus is less populated than the one at Basel, and so less visually dynamic. The figures are spaced out more deliberately. So the eye is drawn to the Creon-Creusa couple who are even closer together, his

Figure 11. Creusa with case of Medea's herbs. Sarcophagus Medea, Inv. BS 203 © Antikenmuseum Basel und Sammlung Ludwig.

curly beard nearly touching her flowing locks. What is striking here is that Creusa's hair—that symbol of femininity, and often, as it flows before being sheared, youth and virginity—has become enflamed. Part reaches skyward, touching the frame as does Creusa's hand. Medea is absent again, making her mark in the metamorphosis of Creusa's body into fire. Whether depicted as herbalist or arsonist, Medea connects the science of knowing and making with the elemental reality of combustion and destruction.

Unlike Antigone, Medea is not cursed: Even if in some versions she laments her past, she also revels in the inheritance she has received from her grandfather the Sun. It is this inheritance that has estranged her from what Bruno Latour classically called the "modern Constitution," that "agreement" which orders divisions and creates distinctions in the modern world, not only between "Nature" and "Culture," but between humans and others. The "modern Constitution" decides who and what counts as a subject, a "voting member" of the parliament of knowledge.[24] Medea thematizes this precarious stability. Figured as a "primitive," a "barbarian," a "witch," Medea is also a "hybrid," a potent mixture of the natural and the social worlds that intrudes into our society and destabilizes it, proliferating sometimes without our even realizing it. Her epistemological outsider status paradoxically affords her the possibility to revolt—not just by who she is but also

Figure 12. Creusa with her hair on fire. Römischer Sarkophag: Medeasarkophag. Berlin. bpk / Antikensammlung, SMB / Johannes Laurentius.

by what she does and what she knows: It is Medea's witchcraft, her occult knowledge, that empowers her. It is finally her capacity for enchantment that makes of her another version of the *pharmakon*, the one embedded within Bernard Stiegler's understanding of "pharmacology." For Stiegler, technology is pharmacological in that it simultaneously facilitates and debilitates our socialization. Like fire itself, Medea can be said to be part of the very civilizing process that can also annihilate civilization. The technology and art of fire are generally associated with Athena, Hephaestus, and Prometheus, but in its multivalent dimensions, fire belongs to Medea.[25]

It is not just that Medea is a paradox or that Medea is double-edged. There is an occluded dynamic to the role of the *pharmakon*, as both cause and effect, as both root of the polis and its greatest threat, that is also deeply intimate, and corporeal, temporal, and that addresses the problem and possibility of the woman acting in political life.

## The Feminist Anti-Politics of Medea

Consider both Antigone's and Medea's laments. Antigone bemoans her virgin state, that she will never be a mother. In Euripides, Medea's first long speech is a tirade against marriage and motherhood and the pain they cause. To Antigone's regret of a future foreclosed, Medea rages against a past whose future is and will be without any solace. Whereas Antigone is walled up at home, Medea has no home; she is an exile. This means that Antigone will surely die, and Medea will surely live. It might be ironic, then, to follow these terms by affirming that if *Antigone* can be seen paradoxically as a story about political possibility, *Medea* can be seen as one about the failure of politics, not its instantiation, its construction, or its legitimacy.

It might seem nihilistic, then, to argue that Medea offers a different feminist politics based on the failure of politics. Medea is the vehicle for all that we fear, and her inhabiting the role of a woman and mother exacerbates this fear. In Adriana Cavarero's elaboration of a feminist philosophy of vulnerability and care, Medea offers a limit case, which Cavarero elaborates in *Horrorism* (2009) and more recently and with greater nuance in *Inclinations* (2016). The Western imaginary has long assessed the very worst of violence, the extremes that we today commonly call terrorism, by an ontological crime of violence against the helpless: Medea and her sister-in-horror Medusa, because they are women, "are the ancient icons of today's spreading horrorism."[26] In turning the question of terrorism away from what perpetrators do, spread, achieve, and toward "horrorism," what victims of bodily violence experience, Cavarero argues that beyond any reaction to the threat of death, horrorism expresses our "instinctive disgust for a violence that, not content merely to kill because killing would be too little, aims to destroy the uniqueness of the body, tearing at its constitutive vulnerability. What is at stake is not the end of a human life but the human condition itself, as incarnated in the singularity of vulnerable bodies" (8).[27] The germ of horror is set in this alternation between offering care and doing harm, even when killing becomes itself merciful caring. Medea is an icon of horrorism because of her maternal care and of her murderous rejection of this care. In Cavarero's analysis, the violence derives its potency from the vulnerability of the helpless. Twinned with Medusa, whose warrior victims are petrified by the sight of her, Medea offers specifically "the primary paradigm of any discourse on vulnerability," a vulnerability that is proper to every single human. But together, the horror-twins Medusa and Medea remind us that "the killing of uniqueness is an ontological crime" (29–30).

What uniqueness? Mythology's iterative practice reminds us of the repeatability of stories, actions, people. Medea's specific practice calls into question the universality and durability of the value of uniqueness, and asks instead for us to see the bonds between people, not their distinctiveness. A mother who kills her children kills also a part of herself. A comparison to the Madonna and child as portraits of "self-sacrifice" drives home this point. It is "the representation of a maternality that exalts the sole response of care and comes close to the stereotype of self-sacrifice" (27) that makes of Medea a suicide bomber.

There is, as Cavarero admits, also the story of a loving mother. In so many versions, Medea "has nothing in common with the warriors of the *Iliad* and their world. . . . Given that she is a mother, the vulnerable ones whom she terminates . . . are also recognized by her from a standpoint of care" (27). It is this aspect that is particularly unbearable about horrorism, that it can join the face and hands of a mother to the dismemberment of a child. This also raises the question of what whole body Cavarero identifies as the basic unit of humanity: the "whole body" in its "uniqueness"? What constitutes a whole body? Does vulnerability, and the care mandated by it, which Medea's loving yet mortal wounds also symbolize, not also trace the relationship between our imbricated selves, our overlapping and similar beings, our foundational lack of uniqueness that is also at the basis of our relationships? Cavarero begins to explore one dimension of this relationship in her exploration of the notion of "inclination," a critical counterpoint to Western liberal democracy's celebration of masculinist, individualistic "rectitude." The maternal posture of inclination "traces a relational structure," but one that is ethically multivalent, available for realizing both care and harm. Thus "Medea reminds us that care is not an automatic or obvious response of maternal inclination; it is instead the ordinary and indeed desirable side of a violence that is rare and therefore scandalous, but that nevertheless remains equally plausible."[28]

The distillation of the Medean gesture into a single one, a caring-but-dismembering one that is ever in the present tense, must at once acknowledge and then efface the history of this gesture. This history is double. Within the narrative itself, it is no surprise. Medea's killing of her children comes after the slaying of soldiers protecting the Golden Fleece at Colchis, the dismemberment of her brother (a true moment of sacrifice, as she distributes his pieces for their father to find), the rejuvenation of Jason's father, and the emptying of Pelias. And it might not even be the very end: It precedes, in many versions, her attempt on Theseus, son of her protector Aegus. Within literary history, of course, it is well established that

Euripides revised an older story in which Corinthians perform the infanticide as revenge against Medea. Cavarero's own gesture thus occludes both a much deeper relation in which the mother's inclination toward her children is severed by the community, as well as the further scandal of the Euripidean imposition of infanticide upon Medea's narrative.

With and without these narrative layers, Medea seems to also to ask: What if the basic unit of our political life is not the self but something indeed more layered, more historical, more relational, and less manageable? Stiegler observes, "That which is pharmacological is always dedicated to uncertainty and ambiguity. . . . And just as melancholy is essentially the face of dependence, as Freud teaches, so too the *pharmakon* becomes a poison when it provokes dependence."[29] The *pharmakon* that is Medea is also the mother that is Medea; it is the joining of these defining forces, in all their ambiguity and destruction, that lodges the figure of Medea within our imaginary. And so it is perhaps for the very reasons that we find this character abhorrent that the traces of her impact on tragedy should be examined.

What *Antigone* seems to create, then, is what the many versions of *Medea* collectively seek to undo, in perpetuity. Most significant, then, are the differences between the politics of Antigone's stance and the refusal of any such stance by Medea. Antigone may be understood as a lone voice of opposition, who denies the solidarity of even her sister. In contrast, Medea identifies and secures relations. Her work is a meditation on attachment: as both a virtue and a weapon. Medea's violence is, in every example, the work of examining the connections among people. The examples are myriad and punctuate most tellings of her story, including those that appear on these pages. Whether in mobilizing Pelias's daughters to kill their father, or by devising a poison that causes a dress to stick to a princess and her father the king to stick to her, Medea's harm plays with attachments. Even what modern theorists consider to be the most horrendous crime of all, the killing of her children, is another iteration of this operation: It separates kin from kin, as if to mobilize the most significant political power we have: that of relations.

If Antigone appears to be, for so many thinkers, an icon of the politics we wish to realize, it is easy to suggest that Medea represents the world we wish to eliminate. But this would be a mistake. Inherent in the Medean principle is not just the question of violence but of its impossible erasure. In almost every version of the premodern era, Medea is carried away on a dragon-drawn chariot. Sometimes she finds a haven with Aegeus—where she will commit filicide again, murdering her savior's son—other times her destination is unknown. But what she doesn't do is die. She is never expiated. Medea can then be seen as the opposite of a sacrifice—always guilty and yet never to be expiated. Far from an Agambenian *homo sacer*, however, she persists. In doing so beyond the polis, she is ever poised to return.

This recursive, or perhaps more accurately, rehearsive, quality of Medea is crucial to her configuration both on the stage and off, from the Greek reuse of figures from a select number of great houses, to premodern and modern habits of retelling and "reversioning." As Marvin Carlson has so elegantly asserted, theater is based on a choreography of recycling and haunting, not just of characters and narratives, but of spaces, properties, actors, and audience members.[30] Medea's very mythology seems to haunt itself, constituted by incommensurable versions or facets. But Medea does not haunt herself or others—for the simple reason that she is not dead. She returns, revises, and refines, rehearsing her presence.

What would politics look like if we were to accept Medea as its icon? Medea does not offer a lesson—there is no moral outcome to her story. Rather the Medean presence in our imaginary suggests the impossibility of evacuating that which we refuse to assimilate, to recognize the unassimilable as at the heart of some of our most intimate relations. Medea forces us to acknowledge that violence is constitutive of how we protest, resist, gain power, but also love and save ourselves.

CHAPTER 1

# Surface Selves: *Médée*, 1634

Corneille's *Médée* introduces its eponym by way of a singular misunderstanding. The misunderstanding occurs when Jason, reunited in Corinth with his old friend and fellow Argonaut Pollux, announces his upcoming marriage to Créuse, daughter of the Corinthian king. Pollux's response shows his astonishment at this news.

> POLLUX.
>     Quoi! Médée est donc morte à ce compte?
> JASON.                                   Elle vit,
>     Mais un objet nouveau la chasse de mon lit.
>
>                                              (1.1.7–8)

> POLLUX.
>     What? Médée must then be dead?
> JASON.                         She lives.
>     But a new object has chased her from my bed.

Jason corrects Pollux by completing his truncated alexandrine with a three-syllable bombshell. How could Jason remarry, abandoning the wife who secured him the Golden Fleece, killed his uncle Pélie in order to return him to his father's throne, and mothered their children? Médée must then be dead. But, impossible: She lives. This poetic *contre-rejet* works as more than an addendum; it is a kind of necessary remainder: The alexandrine needs it, but it stands alone. The formal sign of both her singularity and her endurance, it anticipates Médée's own continual survival as an obligatory remainder to the wreckage she leaves in her wake.

This concept of necessary survival, of endurance in destruction, is at the heart of Corneille's version. By the end of the play, we have seen the dissolution of Jason and Médée's partnership, the bridal gift of a poisoned gown, the murder of both Créuse and her father, King Créon, the burning of Corinth, and the slaying of Médée's children. It ends with Jason, amid the ruins of Greek society, watching as Médée takes her children's bodies for burial and flies away. If Jason's suicide is predicted, Médée's survival is also guaranteed. The task of Corneille's *Médée* is to justify this survival. In so doing, it offers a model of theater as an ongoing interrogation of the work of forces of endurance amid those of destruction.

To be sure, this is not how *Médée* the tragedy is generally understood. On the contrary, it is seen rather as a first, a last, a precursor, or a holdover. In traditional histories of theater, especially those that value the evolving aesthetics of the form, it marks the "beginning" of the French tradition of tragedy: *Médée* represents precisely the kind of theater that would be overcome just over two years later through the quarrel about *Le Cid*, the public and highly political debate about the role of theater in shaping public opinion, and the role of the public in shaping theater that consumed Parisian dramaturges, moralists, literati, and theater critics. In this narrative, the literary and political controversy over the aesthetic and moral messiness of Corneille's 1637 play would initiate an ongoing process among critics, practitioners, and institutions to elevate tragedy above other dramatic forms through the codification of rules and structures particular to it. This elevation resulted in the banishment of all forms of physical violence to the wings of the stage and the increased use of descriptive reports by character witnesses.

In examinations of the impact of *Médée* on Corneille's own career and sense of authority, the play also occupies an inaugural position, because of its status in his oeuvre as "pre-history" to the quarrel of *Le Cid* and to the politics of the absolutist state, for the ways the eponymous heroine can be seen as modeling Corneille's own sense of poetic genius and his right to transgression against the unities, or in light of its heroine's role as a model for other Corneillian heroes.[1]

However particular a position the individual character of Médée may occupy in Corneille's work, *Médée* the dramatic poem might be said to resist such isolation, attending rather to tensions among the constellation of actors, actions, and histories linking all the tragedy's players. This attention is articulated his 1639 "Épître," the dedicatory letter introducing the first published version of the play. It is elaborated in the "Examen," the short prefatory piece Corneille wrote for this and each of his tragedies that he included in his 1660 complete works, and which served at once as an explanation of and argument for the work. Corneille develops a Medean aesthetic that holds in tension the figure's destructive, excessive passion, and its ethos of fidelity, moderation, and attachment. His dedication and preface confirm how we might read the complex relationships among the play's characters, as well as how we consider the tragedy's specific work within the history of French theater.

## *Médée*/Médée: *The Performance of Print without Apologies*

The "Épître" to *Médée* opens with a gesture as plain as it is perplexing: "Je vous donne Médée toute méchante qu'elle est, et ne vous dirai rien pour sa justification" (I give you Médée as wicked as it is, and will say nothing to justify it).[2] From the first *je vous donne* to the last *justification*, not to mention *Médée* and *méchante*, the phrase brims with ambiguity, ambiguity best confronted by considering Corneille's gift—his version of this play, of this character—as much through theater history as through print and performance conventions, and through the connection between poetry and politics. This grammatical intersection between Médée and *Médée* indicates how Corneille's work on the ancient myth and his work on the theater of his time share an ambiguous status with respect to the generic and moral conventions that shape them. Together with his 1660 retrospective "Examen," the "Épître" exposes a key part of Corneille's politics of theater: the shared nature of moral responsibility that refuses exemplarity and makes Médée, in all her violence, a figure for theatrical possibility. And it is this refusal of exemplarity that leads Corneille to draw a constellation of actions and actors in *Médée* that exposes violence as the heart of the tragic project.

Performed during the 1634–35 season, perhaps in February, by the Troupe du Marais with Mondory in the role of Jason, *Médée* received critical accolades, but there is no trace that it made a significant impression

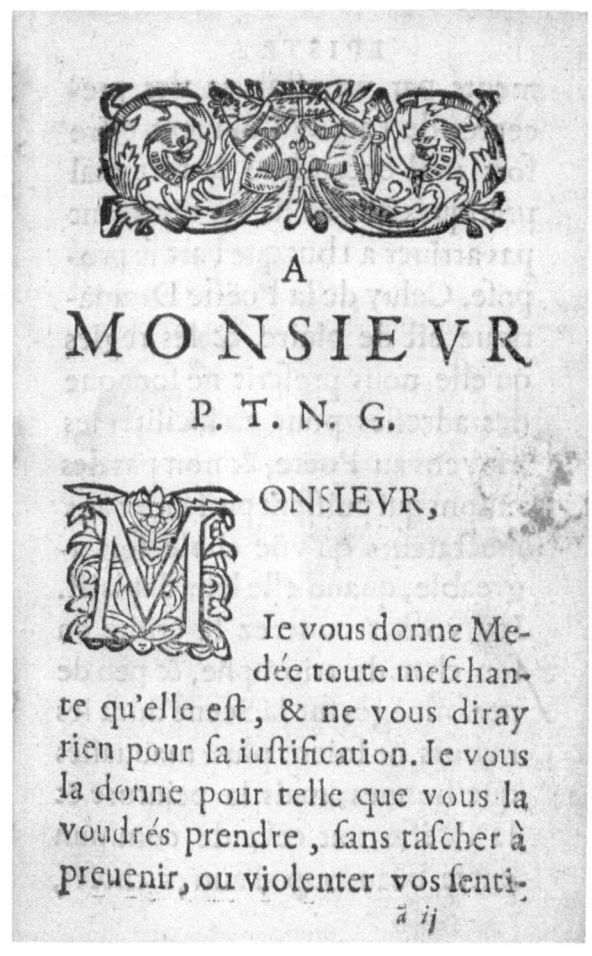

Figure 13. Dedication page, Pierre Corneille, *Médée* (Paris: Francis Targa, 1939). Source: Bibliothèque nationale de France, Département des Arts du spectacle.

on its first audience. Yet in 1639, five years after its début, Corneille had it printed, a quarto edition of ninety-five pages sold by François Targa. This edition would not be definitive; the subsequent version printed by Sommaville in 1644 would include myriad word-level changes. As many scholars have noted, Corneille remained preoccupied throughout his life with the printed appearance of his plays, and supervised the publication of his complete works carefully.[3] It seems more in keeping with this attention, then, to consider this printing a kind of reprise or revival, a renewed staging of a play. Timed, perhaps, to further frame the claims Corneille introduced during the Querelle about what theater could and should do in society, this restaging offered a reason of sorts for its performance in print: *Médée* was the ultimate test of whether theater was supposed to please an audience. It articulates this claim with its "À Monsieur P.T.N.G.," an epistolary dedication whose addressee is acknowledged generally to be fictional. It is thus to this nonexistent *monsieur*, a patron who is not one, that Corneille "offers" publicly the gift of *Médée*.

Or is it the gift of Médée herself? Print conventions of the time did not offer a typographical distinction between title and character, and so although this might seem to be a common point of confusion, Corneille's other letters of dedication contain no such ambiguity—either because the play's title does not refer to a character, or because the dedication specifies the nature of the gift: always the play itself.[4] Here, however, the ambiguity lingers, amid liberal uses of the feminine pronoun, and after Corneille quickly drops discussion of the object of dedication and instead turns to a consideration of the goals of art:

> Je vous donne Médée toute méchante qu'elle est, et ne vous dirai rien pour sa justification. Je vous la donne pour telle que vous la voudrez prendre, sans tâcher à prévenir ou violenter vos sentiments par un étalage des préceptes de l'art, qui doivent être fort mal entendus et fort mal pratiqués quand ils ne nous font pas arriver au but que l'art se propose. Celui de la Poésie Dramatique est de plaire, et les règles qu'elle nous prescrit ne sont que des adresses pour en faciliter les moyens au Poète, et non pas des raisons qui puissent persuader aux spectateurs qu'une chose soit agréable quand elle leur déplaît.[5]

> I give you Médée as awful as she/it is, and will say nothing to justify her/it to you. I give you her/it to take as you like, without trying to influence or pressure your sentiments with a display of the rules of the art, which must be seen as misunderstood and misused whenever they don't lead us to the goals that this art sets for itself. That of dramatic poetry is to please; the rules that it imposes on us are merely some tips to help the poet, not arguments to persuade spectators that something ought to be agreeable when it displeases them.

What is the object of this art: the play or the figure? And which is truly *méchante* or awful? The Académie française would later define *méchante* as "Awful, that which is not good, which is of no value in its kind," seemingly describing a question of categorical fitness, describing a play whose structure and actions violate the very generic conventions that were under scrutiny at the time. Just five years after its performance, a *Médée* published in 1639 might well have been seen as *méchante* "dans son genre," an example of the problem of theater without a form that sufficiently constrains its moral implications: a bad play.

And yet the Académie's second definition puts the concept squarely in the arena of human morality: "That which is contrary to integrity, to justice. *Bad man, bad boy. Bad woman.*"[6] The "Épître" suggests this too, when it offers a comparison between "Médée, toute méchante qu'elle est," and painterly "beaux portraits ... d'une femme laide." This is a good play, a well-executed portrait, but of an ugly woman. But it is also a bad play, in that it makes the same formal transgressions that Corneille's critics decried during the Querelle. Corneille's prefatory letter does nothing to remedy the ways in which a drama about a homicidal, regicidal, and infanticidal woman who escapes with impunity, and about an inadequate king and an inconstant husband, falls well short of either exemplarity or structural integrity. *Meschante* indeed, for Médée's revenge against Jason, Créon, and Créuse through murder, arson, and infanticide is never fully condemned within the play. Nor is it in the *dédicace* itself. To be sure, Médée might be considered as a "méchante femme"; indeed the rest of the "Épître" assumes that she is so horrible that there is no reason even to address the issue of exemplarity, as Corneille asserts at the end of the letter about Médée's deeds, "elles paraissent assez à découvert pour n'en faire envie à personne"[7] (they seem exposed enough to inspire no one's desire).

How does this surfeit of violence and this lack of exemplarity square with how Corneille infamously asserts pleasure as the ultimate goal of theater? As he would repeatedly argue, the goal of dramatic poetry is to please, and rules are there not as rationale for convincing spectators how they should feel, but rather to guide poets in how to achieve what audiences like. If spectators are not to consider imitating the actions they see on stage, what is "pleasing" about the *méchanceté* (awfulness) of Médée?

To understand the particular nature of the this *méchanceté*, we need to situate its performance and publication within the major political-literary controversy of its times, that of *Le Cid*. The play was performed shortly before the 1637 premiere of *Le Cid*, but it was published two years after that run. The printed object *Médée* might be seen as another stone flung into the fray of that quarrel.[8] For the project of the "Épître" is to help Corneille, through *Médée*, take a stand against the exemplary nature of theater in general, while advocating for the crucial role of the spectator as an independent measure of a play, unencumbered by critical debates about the morality of aesthetics.

Corneille's reasoning as to why a play like *Médée* and even a character like Médée need no justification is quite straightforward. First, he declares, evil is so clearly depicted, and so ubiquitous in this play. Second, like painting, dramatic poetry can have the burden not of imitability but of *ressemblance*:

> Ici vous trouverez le crime en son char de triomphe, et peu de personnages sur la scène dont les moeurs ne soient plus mauvaises que bonnes; mais la peinture et la Poésie ont cela de commun, entre beaucoup d'autres choses, que l'une fait souvent de beaux portraits d'une femme laide, et l'autre de belles imitations d'une action qu'il ne faut pas imiter. Dans la portraiture, il n'est pas question si un visage est beau, mais s'il ressemble; et dans la Poésie, il ne faut pas considérer si les moeurs sont vertueuses, mais si elles sont pareilles à celles de la personne qu'elle introduit. Aussi nous décrit-elle indifféremment les bonnes et les mauvaises actions, sans nous proposer les dernières pour exemple; et si elle nous en veut faire quelque horreur, ce n'est point par leur punition, qu'elle n'affecte pas de nous faire voir, mais par leur laideur, qu'elle s'efforce de nous représenter au naturel.[9]

> Here you will find crime in its triumphal chariot, and few characters on stage whose morals are good rather than bad. Painting and poetry have in common, among many other elements, that one often offers beautiful portraits of an ugly woman, and the other beautiful imitations of an action one should not imitate. In portraiture, it is never a matter of whether a face is beautiful, but whether it resembles; so too in poetry one should never consider when morals are virtuous but whether they are similar to the person it introduces. Thus poetry describes good and bad actions indifferently, without proposing the latter as examples. If it seeks to strike horror in us, it does so not by punishing such bad actions, which it strives not to show us, but by showing their ugliness, which it strives to represent naturally.

A good play pleases the audience because it represents the true horror of the bad; how this horror is generated is not through punishment but through "ugliness" presented naturally or plainly. Plays do not create morality; spectators create it in their reactions. Corneille is arguing that plays should *not* offer good examples or scenes of punishment but instead the unmitigated ugliness of "crime in its triumphal chariot." In this way, Corneille's theater is one not of imitation of but apprehension, in both senses of the term: Spectators' pleasure is not in seeing themselves but in understanding the gap between themselves and the awful events on stage. Such exemplarity is nothing without clarity, and the virtue of this play is in the clarity of its portraits of actions that are unambiguously not to be imitated.

Corneille also underscores the major difference between dramatic poetry and "portraiture" to which both Corneille's tragedy and the "Épître" attend: that plays portray multiple people. Neither morality nor pleasure is generally a solitary pleasure. In distinction to the theater, portraits depict individual subjects and represent them by their traits. Although *Médée* portrays the eponym's singular horrors in an unadorned display of crime in all its spectacularity, the collected actions and morals of its cast offer few if any portraits of unambiguous good. What makes this play significant to Corneille is not so much the singular portrait of Médée but the interrelated actions of characters: that embodiment of evil accompanied, even generated, by a network of other morally faltering characters.

For Corneille, then, it is precisely the network of moral complexity that the audience should consider: the connection between Médée, the personification of "crime in its triumphal chariot," and the rest of the characters—Jason, Créon, Créuse—clearly those characters "whose morals are good rather than bad." Glaringly eschewing the basic question about evil's justification or the origins of violence, the play searches not for origins but for associations. It does so first by relying on a system of characterization that releases Médée from being the sole figure of evil, and exposes what is particular about the constitution of horror that is generated in her company.

## Singular Portraits, Poetic Imbrication: Jason and Médée

The play's opening scene embeds its portrait of Médée within an economy of character relations. An opening scene of a classical play must situate the dramatic tension to follow, getting its audience up to speed with the events that have led to the present situation. In dramas such as *Médée* or other stories from antiquity, the exposition serves also to remind the audience of the story and to indicate where in the familiar narrative this particular account will start. This first scene of *Médée* appears initially as simply historical; it provides an account of what has transpired to lead the foreigners in this drama to Corinth. Through this scene's particular strategy of exposition, however, much is revealed, both structurally and historically, about how these characters are bound to each other, how they constitute each other, and how they value each other.

The scene first appears to be a portrait in absentia of Médée. It quickly becomes a far more complex calculation of what could be called the play's geopolitical economy of character. Jason, ostensibly seeking to exculpate himself from any responsibility for Médée, offers a portrait of his wife that both justifies her and involves him in their shared past. And Pollux, at once a plot device to allow Jason to speak out loud and a guarantor of his friend's bravery and trustworthiness, is also an inverted version of Médée, a comparative measure of her knowledge, monstrosity, and persistence.

Bound by his own relations both to wife and to friend, Jason is, from the beginning, an ambiguous agent. He is faithful as a narrator but dodgy as a companion. Structurally, because he offers the context for the play's conflict, he must accurately tell the history of his relationship with her and of their flight from Thessalie to Corinth. A philanderer, a mercenary, an avowed betrayer of Médée, Jason paradoxically is to be embraced by the audience. This trustworthiness is confirmed by the intimate, warm conditions under which his character offers this account—motivated by the unexpected encounter with long-lost friend Pollux, Jason confides in the audience through his honest intimacy with Pollux.[10]

The first line of the play announces the coincidence of two old friends finding each other on foreign soil, and sets a tone of ironic optimism: "Que je sens à la fois de surprise et de joie!" (1.1.1). (How I feel at once surprise and joy!) Pollux is an insertion by Corneille into the Medea story; his presence in the first scene is structurally necessary, Corneille asserts, "pour écouter la narration du Sujet" (to listen to the narration of the story).[11] Corneille's choice of a fellow Argonaut, who continued his adventures in Asia after returning the Golden Fleece, is artful, since as Corneille also suggests in his "Examen" of the play, it is difficult to find a character who is unaware of such major events of history as those forming the background to any great subject of tragedy. Pollux's warm intimacy with Jason allows him to hear the narration as the audience should hear it, rationalizing the exposition. Yet the particular relation that Corneille establishes between them makes of Pollux more than a structural feature of the play, for he plays an active role in both shaping the exposition to which we are privy, and even intervenes later in the play in crucial ways. Michèle Longino has amply explored how Pollux's work in the play extends well beyond the protatic. Underscoring how Pollux's travels inform the narrative also at one other crucial stage, Longino suggests how this "neo-anthropologist" figures a kind of inverse of Médée's barbarian importer of foreign materials and knowledges: Both traveler-savants represent the flow of goods and information in the exchange between "l'Asie" and "la Grèce."[12]

The knowledge of all traveler-savants is not equivalent, however, and the reasons for their travels are not identical. The comparison itself is filled with ironies; Pollux specifies that he is in Corinth on his way to his sister's wedding, a future union that parallels the doomed marriage of Créuse and Jason. Even in this first scene, Pollux's knowledge is doubted and his ignorance is celebrated; it is due to his absence that he needs to be informed by Jason of what has transpired recently. Yet his fears will be borne out by the unfolding of the drama. Pollux acts in this first scene as something of a triangulator of the Médée-Jason relationship, underscoring its complexity and offering the model of an audience who listens faithfully but not naïvely. His position underscores the multivalent nature of both Jason and Médée, and the significance of an audience who must evaluate and even adjudicate their deeds.

Jason's own trustworthiness is immediately undermined by his own account, especially as it is tempered by Pollux. Corneille's poetry richly depicts the kind of mercenary traits that allow Jason to leave his wife for the promise of a throne, and in this regard Jason also portrays each lover as embodying very different kinds of persons. Creating a contrast between himself, with his thoroughly mercenary but highly reasonable ways, and the seemingly monstrous deeds of his wife, Jason's work to distinguish himself from Médée serves rather to tie him to her. As we shall see, this particular feature, a cleaving-from that becomes a cleaving-to, is a remarkable feature of the Medean ethos.

Even before he tells the story of Médée's crime, Jason has established himself as divided from her, albeit by a force greater than he: "Je la quitte à regret, mais je n'ai point d'excuse / Contre un pouvoir plus fort qui me donne à Créuse" (1.1.13–14). (I leave her with regret, but I have no excuse / Against a greater power giving me to Créuse.) Although these lines portray Jason as a romantic mercenary, the seemingly casual appraisal of the imperative to abandon Médée for a "un pouvoir plus fort" is accurate: The political call to become the son of a king is a greater power. Additionally, the divorce from Médée is truly a reconfiguration of his identity, which Jason details grammatically here: From being the direct object of Médée's lament, he individuates himself into a subject ("Je la quitte . . . je n'ai point d'excuse") before becoming the object of a greater sovereign power ("qui me donne à Créuse"). Later in the same scene, oft-cited lines underscore a grammar that is both individual and mercenary:

> Aussi je ne suis pas de ces amants vulgaires,
> J'accommode ma flamme au bien de mes affaires,
> Et sous quelque climat que le sort me jetât
> Je serais amoureux par maxime d'État.
>
> (1.1.25–28)

> I'm not one of those usual lovers;
> I adapt my flames to better my situation.
> And in whatever climes destiny throws me,
> For reasons of State I make this effort.

Portraying a practical cynicism that allows Jason to rise above passions and commitments, these lines also reveal a grammatical insistence on the "je" and the "moi" as distinct, unaffiliated, and unbounded categories of action and possibility. Jason puts himself in the place of a political ruler, whose "maxime d'état," or political policy, guides his reasoning: Adapting to the winds of power in whatever land he finds himself is the best strategy for his political person.

This distinction stands in contrast to the "nous" that unites Médée and him in the aftermaths of their crimes and the troubles they suffered, which led them to the present situation. In his account of the neighboring King Acaste's insistence that they, criminals in his eyes, be handed over, Jason negotiates Médée's banishment instead of her death, while he agrees to marry Créuse. For him there was no other choice than to act in this way, for his own benefit: "Qu'eussé-je fait, Pollux, en cette extrémité/Qui commettait ma vie avec ma loyauté?" (1.1.127–28). (What might I have done, Pollux, in this extreme situation/which risked my life and my loyalty?) But he further justifies his action by repeated references to saving "Médée et moi," with an insistence on the *M* that will later be the trademark of Médée and her self, her "moi." For now, the marital join of "Médée et moi" resonates as the last vestiges of their commitment, which he will soon abandon completely.

If Jason's initial description of Médée mobilizes a monstrous being whose violent ethos appears singularly easy to walk away from, it also allows Jason a self-portrait of someone who has no lasting attachment to his old lover. In yet another way, then, Jason offers a contrasting portrait of himself and of Médée: their regime of attachments. While Jason's commitments are bounded by time and location, that is, by political opportunity, Médée's are far more enduring. This is not to say that Médée is more virtuous—Corneille's project is not to locate virtue within a character—but rather that her politics are based on attachments among people, on locating fidelity and harnessing it. Unlike Jason, Médée cannot betray her attachments, nor can she be assimilated into any larger category: of woman, for example.

This is something Jason cannot understand, for he will attempt to generalize her. He has proven his ignorance of Médée in this regard from the very beginning, with another innocent mistake. When Pollux fears Médée's reaction to Jason's new marriage, Jason does not assert the specificity of Médée but rather the general rule he has experienced with women. He assimilates this current trespass with his abandonment of his former lover Hypsipyle:

POLLUX.
  Dieux! et que fera-t-elle?
JASON.                    Et que fit Hypsipyle,
  Que former dans son coeur un regret inutile,
  Jeter des cris en l'air, me nommer inconstant?

(1.1.8–10)

POLLUX.
  Gods! What will she do?
JASON.                    Well what did Hypsipyle do
  But nurture useless regret,
  Cry out loud, call me inconstant?

Here it is Jason who makes a grave mistake. In suggesting that Médée might follow Hypsipyle's model and react with ultimately inconsequential gestures, he is asserting that Médée will be mired in her tears because she is like most women. The error is twofold: First, Médée does not follow models, but stays faithful to her own histories and structures of allegiance. Second, her passion is never paralyzing, debilitating, or futile.

Médée's fidelity extends to Jason through their matrimonial bond, although after her exile has been issued Médée will exercise her attachment in a different way. She is of course most faithful to herself, exercising what Amy Wygant has called a "kind of Medean cogito," and following the famous declarations from Seneca: *Medea superest, Medea—fiam*, and *Medea nunc sum* (Medea remains; Medea—I shall become her; Now I am Medea).[13] Corneille cites Seneca's formulae repeatedly, in a poetry that privileges Medea in the counter-reject position, the singular remainder completing Nérine's alexandrine:

NÉRINE.
  Dans un si grand revers que vous reste-t-il?
MÉDÉE.                                        Moi
  Moi, dis-je, et c'est assez.

(1.4.316–17)

NÉRINE.
    With such a great upset what is left for you?
MÉDÉE.                                                     Me
    Me, I say, and it is enough.

The construction appears in contrast with Jason's conjunctive fidelity when he describes them as "ma Médée et moi" (1.1.132). The alliterative bond is also one of possession: "ma" symbolizes and secures the bond but also is indicative of its fragility: Possession can be renounced. In further contrast with Medea's Stoic constancy and stability, Jason sees himself as having grown, changed. He has not only overcome, he has also gotten better, and bigger, and more significant: "Et banni que je suis, je leur suis plus qu'un Roi" (1.1.112). (Yet banished as I am, I am more than a king to them.)

In this and many other ways, Médée's sense of self, and the ethos it fuels, stand in contrast with modes advanced by the other authoritative figures in the play, namely, Créon and Jason. Speaking for and as the Law, they use rhetorical strategies of negotiating power that individuate and so isolate Médée, denying her own history of attachments. This stands in contrast to Médée's own politics of constancy. A telling moment in her first on-stage appearance, she rejects Nérine's suggestion that she escape:

> Las! je n'ai que trop fui, cette infidélité
> D'un juste châtiment punit ma lâcheté:
> Si je n'eusse point fui pour la mort de Pélie,
> Si j'eusse tenu bon dedans la Thessalie,
> Il n'eût point vu Créuse, et cet objet nouveau
> N'eût point de nos amours étouffé le flambeau.
>
> (1.4.327–32)

> Ah! I have fled too often. This infidelity
> With a righteous punishment disciplines my cowardice.
> If I had not fled after Pélie's death
> If I had held my own in Thessalie
> He would not have seen Créuse, and this new object
> Would not have extinguished our marriage's torch.

The infidelity that she lambastes can be read as either Jason's or her own. A charge of faithlessness is most easily attached to Jason and his betrayal of her. But syntactically it appears here to refer to her own inconstancy, her lack of steadfastness to her projects of vengeance. Either way, Médée credits it here with compelling her own cowardice and flight. This lament appears as a resolution, for in what follows Médée shows a proof of constancy so strong that it becomes the basis of all her actions, including and especially her displays of force. Her violence can be generally understood as following a logic of *cleaving*: both cleaving to and cleaving from. And this logic demands that she understand and use others' attachments as well as her own. Jason's exposition of Médée's past offers a model of this politics of attachment.

Jason recalls Médée's criminal past, in particular the same gruesome incident when she compels the daughters of his uncle Pélie to kill their father, by demonstrating how they might rejuvenate him by draining and reinfusing his blood through a magical process. They succeed only in assassinating him in the most horrible way (1.1.57–88).

While serving as a kind of justification of Jason through contrast, the account of Pélie's death also introduces the exemplary act characterizing Médée. As recounted by Jason, the death of Pélie demonstrated all that is singular about Médée: the specificity of her occult skills and knowledge, and her peculiar ethos. They are informed, tempered, and sharpened by an engagement with how the human body works—as flesh and blood, and as a social being, a being attached to others. Her power is then in her ability to join families and then to tear them apart.

In the case of Pélie, the uncle who had usurped the throne from Jason and sent the Argonauts on the perilous mission to fetch the Golden Fleece, Médée befriends his daughters, "Malgré l'aversion d'entre nos deux familles" (1.1.57), (despite the aversion between our two families), thus creating intimacy where there should have been repulsion.

Further, she seduces them into wishing rejuvenation for their father by offering them two examples: that of Jason's own father Aeson rejuvenated, and second that of a ram made back into a lamb. The daughters are persuaded by what they see:

Les soeurs crient miracle, et chacune ravie
Conçoit pour son vieux père une pareille envie,
Veut un effet pareil, le demande et l'obtient,
Mais à chacune son but.

(1.1.69–72)

The sisters proclaim a miracle, and, each delighted,
Conceived for her old father a similar desire,
Each wants a similar effect, asks for it and gets it,
But each has her own intentions.

Here we note a play between singular and plural: Enthralled, both cry out in unison, each imagining and desiring the same future for their father: a longer life through rejuvenation. But do they do so together—they both "proclaim a miracle" together—or separately, as "each delighted"? The third-person singular verbs punctuating the coincidence of their desire underscores the singularity of the "chacune" that follows: *veut, demande, obtient*. This play between their parallel desires and unified gestures at first seems to isolate the sisters: each wishing, asking, and getting for herself. Of course, there is no real division between these two sisters, since each is as committed to their father as the other, and so they desire, demand, and act in concert. The singularity is proper to Médée—whose secret intentions are not theirs. The shift is signaled with the change in reference with the second "chacune," which now refers to Médée in distinction to the sisters: "À chacune son but." It is as if Médée inserts her singularity grammatically into their shared desires, poisoning their intentions.

In the real operation upon Pélie, Médée will use not magical but innocuous herbs, whose inert effects will be deadly. In a sense, she kills by omission:

> À force de pitié ces filles inhumaines
> De leur père endormi vont épuiser les veines,
> Et leur amour crédule, à grands coups de couteau,
> Prodigue ce vieux sang, et fait place au nouveau;
> Le coup le plus mortel s'impute à grand service;
> On nomme piété ce cruel sacrifice,
> Et l'amour paternel qui fait agir leurs bras
> Croirait commettre un crime à n'en commettre pas.
> Médée est éloquente à leur donner courage,
> Chacune toutefois tourne ailleurs son visage;
> Et refusant ses yeux à conduire sa main
> N'ose voir les effets de son pieux dessein.
>
> (1.1.77–88)

> Out of pity these inhuman girls
> Will drain the veins of their sleeping father.
> Their credulous tenderness, with cuts of the knife,
> Draws forth this old blood, to make place for the new;
> The most mortal blow lends itself to such a great service,
> Such cruel sacrifice is considered piety.
> And the paternal love motivating their arms

Would deem a criminal act in not acting at all.
Médée is eloquent in giving them courage:
But each still turns her head away;
A secret horror condemns their plans
And refuses to let their eyes lead their hands.

Here, Corneille's debt to Ovid is plain, especially in the contrast of the daughters' "piety" of intentions with the sentiment of "pity" (piété/pitié) that their actions cause, and in the detail of the daughters' inability to watch their hands commit the crime that they believe to be their highest filial duty. The most significant difference is that in Ovid, Medea herself finishes Pelias off; she "slit his throat and plunged his mangled body/into the cauldron full of boiling water" (7.487–88). In contrast, Corneille's Médée removes her own hand from the deed. Pélié is killed only by his daughters.

In what might at first blush seem like a moderation that eliminates violence or culpability, Corneille's subtle revision refines and strengthens Médée's arts of cleaving. What is so scary about this Médée is that she has no actual *hand* in the murder of Pélié: she incites the daughters, is "éloquent à leur donner courage," but never physically touches the victim. The daughters follow Médée's example and think they are going to imitate her rejuvenation of the ram. While she keeps her hands clean, they dip theirs in their father's blood. Médée therefore kills Pélié first by example and second by persuasion, but never by touching.

Daughters using their hands to kill their father is an unnatural family bond—a union that creates a disunion. Here, patricide takes a page from witchcraft, itself the art of disjuncture, mystification, and unnatural unions. Foreshadowing Médée's own act of infanticide at the denouement of the play, the patricide also introduces Médée's tactics more generally: using eloquence and ancient occult knowledge to alter intimate relationships among people. Her method is to make things touch that should not, and to separate things that should be joined.

Jason's telling of this incident at the outset of the play mobilizes it as the foundational event for what will follow. It sets up the horror of Médée's history. The significance of this can be measured against the drama's account of what in premodern accounts is Medea's signature gesture, the theft of the Golden Fleece. Corneille saves the story of the Fleece for Médée to tell in act 2 during her confrontation with Créon, where her actions are works of sacrifice and heroism to save Jason's head, and the occult knowledge behind her cunning is obscured, condensed in a single mention.

Tellingly, Jason does not draw on that originary deed—the theft of the Fleece. As Médée will make clear, its impetus was her bold desire to help Jason and the Argonauts. And here, Jason's motivation is not only to portray her deeds, knowledge, and actions as monstrous but also to distance himself from them, and to obscure the benefits he has reaped from her. When he offers the account of Pélie's murder to his friend Pollux, Jason hesitates at a key moment in it: "La suite au seul récit me fait trembler d'effroi" (1.1.76). (What follows, even just in its telling, makes me tremble with fright.) Testifying to his own trembling in anticipation of the account he must give, Jason styles himself a witness or spectator, apart from Médée—despite being an obvious beneficiary of her crimes. Jason legitimizes his new separation from Médée through historical description as an act of testimony. The slippage between testimonial description and dramaturgical conventions of reporting past events to situate the present action is an easy one here. While historical description serves the dramaturgical purpose of providing the necessary information to understand the play's concentrated scope at one single moment in time, space, and action, it also then motivates history as testimony. Jason becomes the eyewitness for the other side.

Yet Jason also positions himself without totally denying Médée's motivations—her intentions are always to support Jason's political happiness. In the case of Pélie's daughters, Médée seeks to regain Jason's throne from his uncle. In this way, the account also establishes how Médée's passion is a commitment. Her devotion is never in question; her method is consistent with such devotion. In positioning Médée in this way, Jason places himself in opposition to her—and not just politically. Innocent of any violence, Jason is also stripped of any attachment to her.

Jason's portrait of his wife, detailing Médée's exploitation of another parent-child relationship, is the foundational example of what we might call her ethos of *cleaving*: of making things touch that should not, and separating things that should stick. This is a mode of action that seems obviously to refuse, murderously, any notion of the integrity of the self. Yet it paradoxically also defends a relational notion of selfhood, as we shall see.

Through this initial treatment of Médée as being in constitutive relation with others as well as in moral distinction to them, the play offers a meditation on the impossibility of isolating violence or moralizing it absolutely. The changes that Corneille made to the legend elaborate Médée's cleaving mode. In the 1660 "Examen" of the play, a kind of retrospective and apologia for the work, Corneille addresses these changes. Picking up in some ways where the 1639 edition left off in its analysis of the play, the "Examen" further details how his version addresses the problem of Medea as exemplary.

Corneille opens the "Examen" by taking a position against Euripides and Seneca—against the ways they spread Medea's violence across space and infuse it into the chorus:

> Cette Tragédie a été traitée en Grec par Euripide, et en Latin par Sénèque, et c'est sur leur exemple que je me suis autorisé à en mettre le lieu dans une Place publique: quelque peu de vraisemblance qu'il y ait à y faire parler des Rois, et à y voir Médée prendre les desseins de sa vengeance. Elle en fait confidence, chez Euripide, à tout le choeur, composé de Corinthiennes Sujettes de Créon, et qui devaient être du moins au nombre de quinze, à qui elle dit hautement qu'elle fera périr leur Roi, leur Princesse et son mari, sans qu'aucune d'elles ait la moindre pensée d'en donner avis à ce Prince.[14]

> This tragedy was written in Greek by Euripides, and in Latin by Seneca. It is by their example that I have permitted myself to set the scene in a public space, despite how unrealistic it would be to have both kings speak, and Médée plot her revenge, in the same place. In Euripides, she confides in the whole chorus, composed of Corinthian women who are Créon's subjects—at least fifteen of them—to whom she says openly that she will bring down their king, their princess and her husband, without any of them even giving a thought to warning the prince.

Both Euripides and Seneca offer Medeas who perform feats of magic and violence in the same location where the kings pass judgment, and Corneille authorizes his own apparent trespass of *bienséance*, or decorum, by following their example. But under the guise of differentiating himself from Euripides, Corneille draws a curious limit in what is an acceptable onstage violation of *vraisemblance* (plausibility or "realisticness"). When he skeptically wonders how it is possible that a chorus of Corinthian women might hear of Medea's murderous plot against the king and yet do nothing, he suggests that the graver trespass is not a violation of sacred space or of decorum, but of inaction. It is in this way that Corneille announces the heart of the problem of this play: How is it possible that no one stops Médée if she is so criminal, and if this criminality has a long history that is known, accounted for, and shared, and if her intentions are clear and transmitted? One answer to this problem is to eliminate the chorus—which Corneille does. Another is to ask whether it is not just the city—the unity of place, permitting a king's decision and a witch's incantations to be uttered in the same location—that must be rethought but also the question of action itself. Specifically, whose actions? Who is really to blame for the destruction of Corinth? In Corneille's version, the question of action means both the central problem of the play and the actual deeds committed by characters, for the central problem is a problem of deeds, and the relationship among deeds and persons. "Among" and not "between": Deeds are done not by single people but by a complex of individuals; additionally, people are affected by their deeds. Both deeds and people prove to be hardly discrete entities themselves, but mutually constituting networks of consequence, pattern, and affiliation.

In the "Examen," Corneille addresses the problem of deeds and people when he highlights three major changes he makes to the scripts of Euripides and Seneca. Corneille goes to great lengths to balance out the motivations for characters' acts, in order to create greater verisimilitude than his sources, who made Medea too actively wicked to be believable. In outlining his changes, he offers an elaboration of the ideas he presented in his 1639 "Épître":

> J'ai cru mettre la chose dans un peu plus de justesse par quelques précautions que j'y ai apportées. La première, en ce que Créuse souhaite avec passion cette robe que Médée empoisonne, et qu'elle oblige Jason à la tirer d'elle par adresse. Ainsi, bien que les présents des ennemis doivent être suspects, celui-ci ne le doit pas être, parce que ce n'est pas tant un don qu'elle fait qu'un paiement qu'on lui arrache de la grâce que ses enfants reçoivent. La seconde, en ce que ce n'est pas Médée qui demande ce jour de délai qu'elle emploie à sa vengeance, mais Créon qui le lui donne de son mouvement, comme pour diminuer quelque chose de l'injuste violence qu'il lui fait, dont il semble avoir honte en lui-même; et la troisième enfin, en ce qu'après les défiances que Pollux lui en fait prendre presque par force, il en fait faire l'épreuve sur une autre, avant que de permettre à sa fille de s'en parer.

> I thought it right to put things a bit more in balance, by some measures that I took. The first is that Créuse desires passionately the gown that Médée poisons, and that she makes Jason take it from her by ruse. Thus, even though gifts from enemies should be suspicious, this one shouldn't be, because it's not so much a gift that she offers but a payment that is ripped from her, for the clemency that her children receive. The second is that it is not Médée who asks for the one day's reprieve, which she uses for her revenge, but Créon who freely offers it, as if to

diminish some of the unjust violence that he inflicts upon her, about which he seems ashamed himself. And the third is that after all the suspicions that Pollux practically imposes on him, he makes someone else try [the gown] on before letting his daughter wear it.

Corneille's interventions, his "quelques precautions" (few precautions) that will "mettre la chose dans un peu plus de justesse" (put things a bit more in balance) are meant to balance out the responsibility for the calamitous events of the last acts, and to make them more *vraisemblable* for his audience. As if harkening back to the opening sentence of his 1639 "Épître," refusing to defend or "justify" his work, Corneille's attention here to *justesse*—meaning precision, accuracy, and balance—resists any latent form of *justice*, in the classical sense of a "vertu morale, qui rend à chacun ce qui luy appartient" (a moral virtue that returns to each that which belongs to them).[15] Instead, desire and motivation are distributed among characters, creating a kind of network of responsibility, action, and relation. Corneille's changes weave the characters more closely together, making their emotions and futures interdependent. Médée thus offers an ethos for Corneille: She compels him to suture characters' fates to one another. This is what I will be calling her "epidermal mode": her philosophy of action that attends to how people are joined to each other. It becomes a kind of dramaturgical ethos, and it is what sets Corneille's version apart from the others.

Corneille's major changes revolve around what becomes the central moment of crisis, and they highlight Médée's way of acting. The crisis occurs after Créon's decree of banishment is issued, after Médée expresses her desire to have her children spared, and Créuse agrees to protect them. The crisis is Médée's bridal gift of the gown, now saturated with poison, which will burn Créuse to death.

Corneille enumerates three major changes leading up to this crisis. The first redistributes responsibility for the problem of the gown as gift. Instead of Médée simply giving Créuse the dress as wedding gift, Corneille has Créuse ask for it. Thus, instead of being a vehicle of pure revenge, the gown "n'est pas tant un don qu'elle fait qu'un paiement qu'on lui arrache de la grâce que ses enfants reçoivent" (is not so much a gift she gives as a payment torn from her for the pardon that her children receive). Just as Médée creates conditions for Pélie's daughters to desire and demand their father's rejuvenation, thus effecting their own demise, so too does Corneille have Créuse herself require possession of the gown.

Likewise, instead of Médée begging for one more day in Corinth to prepare for her banishment, Créon offers the stay—out of something like guilt: "de son movement, comme pour diminuer quelque chose de l'injuste violence qu'il lui fait, dont il semble avoir honte en lui-même" (independently, as if to diminish some of the unjust violence he is doing to her, about which he seems to feel shame). Just as in the case of Créuse's admiration of the gown, here Corneille redistributes moral motivation to place a great burden on Créon. Without directly concerning the gown itself, this change adjusts the *justesse* of the play's actions, moderating Médée's own cunning and drive, and allowing her to work on the poison, as we shall see. The third change Corneille outlines directly concerns the gown and is another act of redistribution: Créon has someone else try the gift on first, as a matter of precaution. As we shall see, this is a gesture both confirming the politics of *justesse*, and a perverse affirmation of Médée's ways.

Corneille's interventions around the gown highlight the contrast between the law's drive to divide, judge, and conquer, and Médée's own embodied strategy of *adhesion*. In Médée's strategy the gown has immense value. In the Hellenistic tradition, Medea's emotions—love, grief, anger—all "fundamentally involve the assignment of high value to external objects and situations. Her love for Jason, for her children, for her power and position: all these are the mainsprings of her action."[16] In Corneille's version, this external assignment of value is both symbolized and exacerbated by Médée's gown, which is at once an external object and a deeply fundamental part of her self. This alternate understanding of subjectivity has a significant effect on how Médée understands sovereignty and the law.

## Justice *and* Justesse: *The Politics of Negotiated Subjects*

I have been arguing for a particularly Medean understanding of subjectivity and sovereignty, but it is not this version of justice that predominates in *Médée*. As throughout Corneille's corpus more generally, the question of sovereignty is significant to the political thinking in the play.[17] In *Médée* it assumes particular dimensions, with no fewer than three characters—Créon, Jason, and Médée—attending to the idea of sovereignty, and by extension sovereign justice. All three show also its failures.

Most plainly, the thematics of sovereignty are embodied by Créon, whose legitimacy is never doubted. Yet the premise of the action sets sovereignty within its most fragile possible conditions: those of succession, joined with a threat from the exterior. It is also interesting to note that the play doubles both of these conditions: Créon is not only identifying his successor but marrying off his daughter. Additionally, Corinthe is threatened both by Acaste's promised attack and by Médée's presence. We can see from these doublings that sovereignty's domain is established by both territory and time. In this regard, Jason operates to reaffirm Créon's sovereignty in the future, and he does so by separating himself, and his past, from Médée. As we shall see, this is the method of law in *Médée*: to individuate subjects. Both Jason and Créon, speaking by and for the law, use rhetorical strategies of delineating power that circumscribe Médée. In so doing, they endeavor to isolate her from others. In dividing her from the others in the story, these strategies also deny her history of attachments. Amid this refusal, however, Médée emerges with a powerful counternarrative and a particular constitution of the self that refuses such individuation, either spatially (corporeally) or temporally (historically).

Médée's confrontation with the real sovereign, Créon, in act 2, is fueled by an exacerbation of this tension. The language of Créon and Médée's confrontation is a juridical one. Créon's position of sovereignty is tempered by the language of a market economy: of division, forfeit, exchange and worth, of calculated payment. A discourse of negotiated power, it contrasts with Médée's own embodied strategy of adhesion and her refusal to assess worth, history, or affiliation along the law's economic—and therefore divisive—terms. Through this trial scene, Médée reveals how tenuous this division is.

As a sovereign, Créon is not violent; in fact, he does not use force at all. Créon avoids even the most noble use of force, war. Jason offers an early example of how political negotiations to avoid violence effect a division between Jason and Médée. As Jason describes the problem, a war with Acaste, seeking revenge on Jason and Médée for the death of Pélie, is avoided:

> Acaste cependant menace d'une guerre
> Qui doit perdre Créon et dépeupler sa terre,
> Puis, changeant tout à coup ses résolutions
> Il propose la paix sous des conditions.
> Il demande d'abord et Jason et Médée.
> On lui refuse l'un, et l'autre est accordée.
>
> (1.1.117–22)

> Acaste meanwhile threatens war:
> Which would destroy Créon and depopulate his land.
> Then, suddenly changing his resolutions,
> He suggests peace—under certain conditions.
> He first asks for both Jason and Médée;
> Refused the first, he is given the second.

Surface Selves: Médée, 1634

It is upon this condition, that "l'un," Jason be saved in turn for "l'autre," doubly identified and by the feminine rhyme and ending (Médée/accordée), that Créon initially saves his country. This is another instance of a kind of selective attachment: Acaste sees Jason and Médée as joined in the murder of Pélie, while Créon cleaves them for his own purposes. And, in further negotiations with Jason, Créon instead agrees to banish Médée.

Even then with Médée herself, Créon's law avoids the intimacy and physicality of force: It neither kills Médée nor captures her. Instead, refusing to touch her, it turns to the most violent of touchless gestures: exile. Exile as ban is an oral performance of exclusion: To banish one needs only to speak; to utter the declaration is to expel. No force is needed, no contact at all; the exile—now an outlaw—moves herself. Banishment is a rupture, but not a physically violent one. The banished are unprotected because stateless, unmoored because rent from their social fabric.

In the debate between Médée and Créon, banishment is retroactively justified by a quasi-juridical exchange that justifies Médée's elimination, her expulsion without her death. We can see from the very beginning of the exchange, however, that questions of sovereignty, which are at the heart both of the law's ability to ban and of a subject's ability to answer a ban, are the true matter for debate.

It is not without irony that in his first appearance Créon expresses shock at the visible proof of his sovereignty's limits, Médée's very presence before him:

> Quoi! je te vois encore! avec quelle impudence
> Peux-tu, sans t'effrayer, soutenir ma présence?
> Ignores-tu l'arrêt de ton bannissement?
> Fais-tu si peu de cas de mon commandement?
> Voyez comme elle s'enfle et d'orgueil et d'audace,
> Ses yeux ne sont que feu; ses regards, que menace.
> Gardes, empêchez-la de s'approcher de moi.
> Va, purge mes États d'un monstre tel que toi,
> Délivre mes sujets et moi-même de crainte.
>
> (2.2.369–77)

> What—you are still here? With what impudence
> Do you, without any fear, endure my presence?
> Are you unaware of the warrant for your banishment?
> Do you not take seriously my commandment?
> Look at her—swollen with pride and audacity

> Her eyes are but fire, her look—what danger!
> Guards, stop her from coming near me.
> You—go: purge my State of a monster such as you
> Deliver my subjects and me from fear.

His questions seem rhetorically powerful but they also expose a real problem: his ineffectuality. How is it possible that his decree was not obeyed? How is it possible that Médée can be in his presence? His description, as if to his guards or other witnesses, of her anger, her "orgueil" and "audace," her fiery eyes, reads like an internal stage direction indicating the actress's demeanor for this character, but it also marks the transition from one sovereign strategy to another. If at first Créon relies on his sovereign word and status, reminding Médée of his decree and his power, the strategy fails and Créon becomes shocked at the performative failure of his order. He then must act on his own fear—issued first to his guards to protect him, and then to Médée to purge herself from his territory. Ultimately his speech can portray no mastery or sovereign right, but fear and physical defense.

If Créon's initial confrontation with Médée suggests a king who is verbally impotent, physically vulnerable, and politically unstable, Médée will investigate this weakness through an attack not on his body but on his law: "De quoi m'accuse-t-on? quel crime, quelle plainte/Vous porte à me chasser avecque tant d'ardeur?" (2.2.378–79). (Of what am I accused? What crime, what accusation/Is leading you to expel me with such ardor?) Médée through her queries strives to expose the contradictions of a law that lacks process, littering her defense with maxim-like statements: Quiconque sans l'ouïr condamne un criminel,/Bien qu'il eût cent fois mérité son supplice,/D'un juste châtiment il fait une injustice" (2.2.396–98). (Whoever condemns a criminal without hearing him/Even if his crime would have warranted the punishment one hundred times over/Makes of a righteous punishment an injustice.)

Médée continues to accuse Créon of partiality and hypocrisy, of benefiting from a crime while punishing the doer, and so of undermining his own sovereignty: "Est-ce user comme il faut d'un pouvoir légitime/Que me faire coupable et jouir de mon crime?" (2.2.445–46). (Is this how to use a legitimate power? /To render me guilty and revel in my crime?) Through this conjunction, we see shades of an abiding strategy: To seek the joins among people, the relationships that are established through actions. Créon is linked forever to Médée, she suggests, having gained a son-in-law through her deeds. And yet he insists on distinguishing between those who should be seen in the same light:

> Vous faites différence entre deux criminels!
> Vous voulez qu'on l'honore, et que de deux complices
> L'un ait votre Couronne, et l'autre des supplices!
>
> (2.2.452–54)
>
> You make a distinction between two criminals!
> One which you want honored, and so of two accomplices,
> You want one to have your crown, and the other torture!

In contrast, Créon continues to individuate Médée in the most extreme way possible. He separates her interests from those of her husband: "Cesse de plus mêler ton intérêt au sien . . . le séparant de toi, sa défense est facile" (2.2.455–57). (Stop mixing your interest with his. . . . Separating it from yours, his defense is easy.)

Médée sees such division as untenable if not impossible. Her very first line in the play, an apostrophic appeal to authority, demonstrates as much: "Souverains protecteurs des lois de l'Hyménée" (1.3.197). (Sovereign protectors of the laws of Hymen.) What is in the first hemistich a call to the "sovereign protectors" is revealed in the second half of the same alexandrine as not those of the state but of marriage, the laws of union. These powers, sovereign in the sense that they are independent of all other powers, are those that "Dieux garants de la foi que Jason m'a donnée" (Gods, guarantors of the trust that Jason gave me), whose power is jeopardized by Jason's negligence and allegiance to other powers. Their sovereignty is premised on a promise given and a union performed. Médée's vision of marriage is not that of love, or mere contract, but of this attachment. Her fortunes are mixed in with those of Jason, their two lives, their histories, and their crimes are indivisible. If she had not committed her deeds, the Argonauts would not have been successful; if Créon had not given them both safe harbor, Jason would not have appeared in Corinth.

Créon's decree is now willfully amnesiac, a partial erasure of past events. For Médée, Créon has never been a consistent figure of justice. Instead he metes it out as it serves him, which she points out even when the example is in her favor—as when he protected Médée and Jason after the death of Pélie:

> Ma main, saignait encor du meurtre de Pélie,
> Quand dessous votre foi vous m'avez recueillie,
> Et votre coeur, sensible à la compassion
> Malgré tous mes forfaits prit ma protection.
> Si l'on me peut depuis imputer quelque crime,

> C'est trop peu que l'exil, ma mort est légitime:
> Sinon, à quel propos me traitez-vous ainsi?
> Je suis coupable ailleurs, mais innocente ici.
>
> (2.2.477–84)

> My hand, still bloody from the murder of Pélie,
> Was raising all of Thessalie against me,
> When your heart, open to compassion,
> Despite all my trespasses, undertook my protection.
> If since then I might be blamed for certain crimes,
> Exile is too gentle, my death would be warranted:
> If not, for what reason do you treat me this way?
> I am guilty elsewhere, but innocent here.

Médée has done nothing wrong in this land, and she is being punished for past crimes in other states. Even the magnitude of punishment seems out of order, almost lenient: Créon here again offers exile for crimes that should merit death—if his assessment were accurate. Médée strives to show his own vacillations and inconsistencies, and thus to give the lie to this rhetoric of tolerance. A ruse of clemency that spares her life in order to condemn it morally, Créon's decision gives him power over Médée's continuing life and enables him to use it.[18] Médée's arguments call up greater temporal and geopolitical dimensions to address account of the inconsistencies and self-serving negotiations upon which this kind of presentist sovereignty depends, the kind that welcomes a refugee until her mere presence catalyzes a threat from without, transforms her into a monster. Créon's fear-based distinctions dismiss the contradictions between his condemnation of her history and his harboring of her accomplice, his indictment of her violence and his celebration of its effects.

The problem with Créon's manner of judgment is a problem with the Corinthian law. That is, by maintaining a notion of law that is bound by the city and depends on its walls for definition and validation, he must struggle to address Médée as both within the walls of the city and ontologically exterior. It is not just that she is a foreigner; it is rather that the range of experiences and relations that constitute her are cosmopolitan: they transcend Corinth, permeating it through her presence, her person. Thus while he is trying to individuate Médée, to treat her like any other subject of his law, he is also trying to assimilate a barbarian, one who constitutionally stands beyond the law. It is for this reason too that the ban, the declaration of Médée as persona non grata, is a paradoxical one; it is eliminating one who has never been integrated.

Médée's own version of history takes the world to be a much larger, known, and connected place; the Argonauts' work at Colchide is intimately linked with her work at Thessalie. At the same time, she refuses Créon's negotiated, seemingly inconsistent treatment of her person as someone to be expelled and not eliminated. In this debate, then, Créon appears as a weak king, dominated in argument, justice, and power by the outlaw Médée. Médée in turn appears almost reasonable, offering a cogent argument against the legitimacy of a law that cherry-picks the consequences of the past and denies the fundamental nature of bodies; according to her laws, those that are united stay together. Her penultimate words in this scene encapsulate the gulf between her and the Greeks, who have ensnared her in their culture just as they are banishing her from it. Créon's display of tolerance, as he spares her children's lives in deference to his own daughter's wishes, elicits not an expression of gratitude from Médée, but one of contestation:

> Barbare humanité, qui m'arrache à moi-même,
> Et feint de la douceur pour m'ôter ce que j'aime!
> Si Créuse et Jason ainsi l'ont ordonné,
> Qu'ils me rendent le sang que je leur ai donné.
>
> (2.2.493–96)

> Barbarian humanity, which rips me from myself,
> Feigning sweetness to rob me of what I love!
> If Créuse and Jason have ordered it so,
> That they then return to me the blood that I have given them.

The oxymoronic "barbarian humanity" indicts the Greek sense of "tolerance" sparing her children while condemning her to a stateless life of errancy and detachment, a life which is not a life. Positioning her outside of humanity (and so also, following the oxymoron, equally outside of barbarism), it also creates from the second half of the alexandrine a significant critique of the Greek law, "qui m'arrache à moi-même" (which rips me from myself). Separating children from their mother is doing violence to a single body. Using the alliterative signature of the play's ethos, that Stoic citational *m*, it certainly foreshadows Médée's killing of her children, while it is an echo of Pélie's murder by his own daughters. More directly, it seems to refer to the impending deaths of Créuse as well as Créon, for whom the adhesion of fabric to skin causes the ripping of skin from bone. When

Créon offers her the fatal extra day to prepare her departure, her final words, "Quelle grâce!" (What grace!), then, are deeply ambiguous in subject. They seem sarcastically describing her own state, exposing the false generosity of a single day's reprieve. At the same time, they are also perhaps an indication that Créon's act of *grâce* is double-edged for him too: It also opens the way to his own rending.

Médée's reaction to the law's use of tolerance and negotiation speaks again to what I have called her adhesive way of acting. It predicts the deployment of her gown in her demand that Jason and Créuse "me rendent le sang que je leur ai donné" (give me back the blood that I gave them), where the "sang" is at first her children, but might also be returned in the form of their own blood, their own deaths, brought on by Médée's second gift, given after she is forced to leave her children: her gown.

## *First Skins: Médée's Gown*

Médée's gown: Artifact of her own forsaken dynasty and the only object with her from her homeland, "Des trésors dont son père épuise la Scythie,/C'est tout ce qu'elle a pris quand elle en est sortie," asserts Jason (2.4.573–74). (From among the treasures her father plundered from Scythie/It is all she took with her when she left.) As it represents Médée's sense of self and the modus operandi that results, it is also central to this tragedy's apogee. If the gown appears as surface covering protecting her body, it does so while also containing her past. That is, it represents her geopolitical legacy as well as the portability of the knowledge that she carried with her. As such, it is also deeply foundational. It figures the ability to control and moderate violence's deployment.

It should not be surprising, then, that the gown is the point of convergence for Corneille's changes to the legend as he highlights them, and thus is also the hub for the relationships of adhesion and division that the gown weaves and cleaves. Seemingly "external" to her person, the gown's symbolic value is not as metonym for her externalized passions, however. In Corneille's version this surface layer is deeply integral to Médée's sense of self. It functions as at once skin and internal framing.

As both object and subject of material culture, skin can be understood either as surface or as depth. As a surface, we decorate it, scar, mask, or coat it. We have used it as a site of impression—tattoos, scars, piercings, burns—as a display surface, whether on the body (as in jewelry) or off (as in bookbinding). It can appear as a site of eruption or a page for divine markings, as in stigmata. In its anatomical and symbolic functions, it is paradoxical, for the skin can also indicate depth. From object-relations theory, psychoanalysts have explored how the skin is a "containing object . . . holding parts of the personality together."[19] Cultural critics, working from various cultural and historical perspectives, have interpreted clothing and other envelopes as manifestations of complex self-fashioning.

Both surface and depth models presuppose something fundamentally stable—either about the constitution of skin or about its relation to the human it informs, embellishes, completes, or holds together. Models that seek to complicate such stability suggest means to escape from the skin. They account for instability by casting the skin as the site of movement, a Kristevan "no-place of abjection" or in its more social dimensions, as Claudia Benthien suggests, a "cultural border between self and the world."[20] Owing something to Maurice Merleau-Ponty's work on the phenomenology of the self in his chapter on chiasm, Benthien's idea of the epidermal layer as a cultural border also constitutes the skin as a borderlands.

Phenomenological and psychoanalytic considerations of skin and its work and transformations may traverse boundaries between self and society or self and others, but they also seem to reinscribe those same divisions.[21] When Merleau-Ponty offers in his phenomenology a critical alternative to a Cartesian concept of the self as divided into two connected substances, body and soul, the unity he claims makes of the skin merely an envelope.

For psychoanalyst Didier Anzieu, however, the role of the skin should retain its paradoxical qualities, of both static and active force. As he observes in his *Skin-Ego*:

> The skin is permeable and impermeable. It is superficial and profound. It is truthful and deceptive. It regenerates, yet is permanently drying out. . . . It supplies us as much with pain as pleasure. . . . In its thinness and vulnerability, it stands for our native helplessness. . . . It separates and unites the various senses. In all these dimensions that I have incompletely listed, it has the status of an intermediary, an in-between, a transitional thing.[22]

For Anzieu, the skin remains the body's most powerful organ for the multiple ways its superficial qualities render it, paradoxically, the most significant foundation of our selves. The only sense without which we cannot live and "the basic reference point for all the various sense data," the skin is the only reflexive sense—one always feels oneself touching. It is an intermediary in two fundamental senses: It is the primary organizer at once of our sense of the world and of our sense of ourselves. Through our skin we know our relation to others and at the same time we know ourselves.[23]

Anzieu's theory of the skin-ego speaks to so many legends of transformation and becoming in European literature: whether to *Blanche Neige* (Snow White), whose titular character is known for the paleness, purity, and vulnerability of her skin, to the *Peau-d'âne* (Donkey Skin) story, in which a princess hides in a donkey's skin to protect herself from the violent advances of her father.[24] Anzieu's analysis of the skin's functions also demonstrates the multivalent nature of this protection: of the nine main characteristics of the skin-ego, the last is "toxicity."

Médée's gown offers a complementary model to Anzieu's understanding of the skin. Whereas a "skin-ego" model of the self remains confined by the psychoanalytic paradigm of time which is at once mythological and universal, and yet bounded by the experiences of the individual subject, the gown introduces crucial temporal dimensions of history. In doing so, it effects a move away from a developmental model and toward a nonprogressivist notion of the self in relation to others—but one nevertheless deeply imbued with questions of temporality.

The Medean gown is resolutely premodern, in two senses. On the one hand, the gown suggests the archaic and foreign aspects of Medea's character. Linked to her ancestor the sun, it is the sign at once of her very old occult knowledge as well her barbarian status. Additionally, it speaks to a nonmodern relationship between the stuff of one's self and the sense of oneself. For Ann Rosalind Jones and Peter Stallybrass, fabric was "central both to the economic and social fabrication of Renaissance Europe and to the making and unmaking of Renaissance subjects." Fabric becomes a "second skin," much like the double layer of Anzieu's skin-ego. Bearing "quite literally the trace and the memory of its owners,"[25] clothing thus constitutes the self while it retains a kind of dynamism and movement. Here, the skin of clothing at once represents the self as a multilayered subject, shaped by memory and by physical movement, even as it also brings to the self a range of other forces of fashioning, including economic forces and tradition. In this subject-object relationship, objects inform the life of the subject as much as the lives of the subject create the objects.

Objects do figure in this account of Medea's arts of cleaving, which is indeed a kind of artful fashioning—though not always of the self. Rather, the dyadic relationship between skin and skin in *Médée* does not unite to create but rather to destroy. In its destruction, it indicates something about creation, in particular aesthetic, literary creation.

## Coats and Kin

Flirting with her betrothed, Créuse considers the ways Fortune and Amor, having seen her *mérites,* are giving her all—love, a hero Jason, glory, legendary status—and she will give in return. Their love is mutually beneficial:

> Et vous donne au plus fort de vos adversités,
> Le sceptre que j'attends, et que vous méritez.
> La gloire m'en demeure; et les races futures,
> Contant notre Hyménée entre vos aventures,
> Vanteront à jamais mon amour généreux,
> Qui d'un si grand Héros rompt le sort malheureux.
>
> (2.4.555–60)

> It gives you, at the height of your tribulations,
> The scepter which I await, and which you deserve.
> Its glory remains with me, while future generations,
> Telling of our marriage amid your exploits,
> Will celebrate forever my generous love
> Which reversed the misfortunes of such a great hero.

Out of this "amour généreux," Créuse has sought and won the favor of her father in protecting Jason's children from peril or banishment with their mother. But, as Créuse suggests earlier, when Jason asks her to petition Créon, a favor given is a favor owed (2.2.187, 191). And so she admits her "weakness," in a description of a love-at-first-sight encounter. This experience, of seeing for the first time her heart's true desire, is recounted by Corneille as an ekphrasis: Créuse sees Médée's gown and by her own admission, covets it immediately:

> Après tout cependant riez de ma faiblesse,
> Prête de posséder le Phénix de la Grèce,
> La fleur de nos guerriers, le sang de tant de Dieux,
> La robe de Médée a donné dans mes yeux,
> Mon caprice, à son lustre attachant mon envie
> Sans elle trouve à dire au bonheur de ma vie,
> C'est ce qu'ont prétendu mes desseins relevés
> Pour le prix des enfants que je vous ai sauvés.
>
> (2.4.559–68)

> Anyway, you'll probably laugh at my weakness:
> Prepared to possess the Phoenix of Greece,
> Flower of our warriors, descendant of so many Gods,
> My eye was struck by Médée's gown.
> Such whimsicalness affixed my desire to its gleaming
> Without it my happiness is left wanting
> That's how my intentions will be satisfied,
> For the price of those children I saved for you.

Such a minor thing in comparison with the towering Jason, "Phoenix of Greece," and "flower of our warriors, descendant of so many Gods," Médée's gown nevertheless has struck her fancy. It is the "price of those children I saved for you." As Corneille writes it, Créuse's request is a trivial one, a nothing for nothing, as it were—which is what Jason suggests: "Que ce prix est léger pour un si bon office!" (2.4.569), (What a reasonable price for such a good deed!), for saving the lives of his children.

Is such a gown a light price—for children? By Créuse's own description, it is a glittering thing, studded with jewels, strewn with pearls and gold, so dazzling that it brings the sun into the night. It is as bright as if it were aflame:

> Jamais éclat pareil
> Ne sema dans la nuit les clartés du Soleil;
> Les perles avec l'or confusément mêlées,
> Mille pierres de prix sur ses bords étalées
> D'un mélange divin éblouissent les yeux,
> Jamais rien d'approchant ne se fit en ces lieux.
> Pour moi, tout aussitôt que je l'en vis parée
> Je ne fis plus d'état de la toison dorée.
>
> (2.4.575–82)

> Never has such radiance
> Cast the splendor of the Sun throughout the night.
> Pearls embedded here and there among gold,
> Thousands of rare jewels spread on its edges,
> A divine mix dazzling the eyes:
> Nothing close to this has ever appeared on these shores.
> For me, as soon as I saw it decorated so,
> I thought no more of the Golden Fleece.

Corneille's description of the gown's opulence might owe something to Seneca's *Medea*, in which a necklace and diadem accompany the gown. In

Seneca, however, it is Medea who describes the beauty and the power of these precious objects:

> I have a robe, a present to my heaven-born family,
> the glory of our throne, given Aeëtes by the Sun
> as an assurance of his parentage. I have also a
> necklace that gleams with woven gold, and the golden
> [band] set off with bright gems that usually encircles my hair.
>
> (570–74)[26]

The gown traces Medea's family from the Sun; a gift to Aeëtes from his father Helios, its passage to her also inserts her into this male lineage. In Corneille's poetry the power of this lineage is materially present, visible in this "robe sans pareille, et sur qui nous voyons/Du Soleil son aïeul briller mille rayons" (4.3.1135–36), (unrivaled gown, from which we see/From the Sun her ancestor shine a thousand rays). What Créuse is admiring, then, is what are quite literally both the vestiges of Médée's dynasty as well as the source of the power of her occult magics. Indeed, later Médée will call upon the sun her forefather for his help, affirming this lineage.

The power of this gown cannot be underestimated. For Créuse, its effects nearly surpass Jason's over her: "Et dussiez-vous vous-même en être un peu jaloux,/J'en eus presques envie aussitôt que de vous" (2.4.583–84). (And you might have been a bit jealous yourself,/I wanted it nearly as quickly as I did you.) Most important, the gown is so gorgeous and materially precious that, as Créuse says, "Je ne fis plus d'état de la toison dorée" (I thought no more of the Golden Fleece). It eclipses for her the originary object of Médée's and Jason's desire for each other, another precious skin.[27] According to Medean logic and Medean history, Créuse literally wants Médée's hide. She asks her to exchange her own skin for the distant safety of her two children.

From a contemporary perspective, this math is bad. Créuse seems to get both Médée's skin and her children, for the terms of the exchange do not maintain Médée as mother but rather safeguard Jason's lineage. These terms preserve life and lineage but not relation. What Médée gets is knowledge that her children will be safe, but only insofar as they are no longer attached to her. This is a cleaving: of children from their mother.

Créuse proposes another cleaving as well—one that might be properly considered a flaying: the surrender of Médée's gown. Made to give up the oldest and most foundational piece of herself, the piece that establishes continuity with a past that is at once dynastic and epistemological, Médée's pain is not that she must give up something so precious or even that she must give up an object that represents her. Rather, she is asked to renounce a part of herself. When Jason later avers, in light of her newfound exilic status, "Sa robe, dont l'éclat sied mal à sa fortune,/ ... n'est à son exil qu'une charge importune" (3.2.773–74), (Her gown, whose radiance suits her present condition so poorly/ ... is but a bothersome burden for her exile), he confuses the exchange value of the gown's precious stones with their inherent value to Médée alone; since banishment strips a person of all property and social or political affiliation, such a gown is all Médée might be able to take with her in her exile. And Créuse too seems to confuse the gown's visual effects for its other potential. Jean Starobinski has claimed for Corneille a poetry of "dazzled vision" where "the dazzled eye beholds a peerless greatness," a kind of wondrous blindness.[28] Here, Créuse's bedazzlement does not signify a "grandeur insurpassé"; rather, her blindness is a prescient understatement for what will be the gown's effects on her: We are dazzled not only by the visible sight of glittering sun-like gems, but by their effect-to-come of sun-like burning.

"Rivale insatiable," Médée exclaims; "Si la force à la main tu l'as sans mon aveu: /il faut que par moi-même elle te soit offerte" (Insatiable rival, if with force in hand you'll have it without my accord/it will have to be me myself who gives to you). Echoing Seneca's *Medea superest* and her earlier claims of sovereignty, Médée's first tactic is to give the gown before Créuse can take it, to trump force's demand, "sous un faux semblant de libéralité" (4.1.975–77, 983). Médée then alters the gown, impregnating it with poisons.

When she enlists Nérine to be the courier of "cette robe empestée/ Que de tant de poisons vous avez infectée" (this pestilent gown/Which you infected with so much poison), the nursemaid refuses: "C'est pour votre Nérine un trop funeste emploi:/Avant que sur Créuse ils agiraient sur moi" (4.1.1061–64). (This is too deadly a job for your Nérine/Before touching Créuse they'll have their effect on me.) Nérine's explicit fear not just of the "robe empestée" but specifically of the "tant de poisons" reminds us of Médée's adhesive technique, inverted. In the murder of Pélie, she had his body emptied; here, she imbues a skin with poison. In both cases, skins are containers, but porous or leaky containers that can be distinct from the stuff they contain.

Most fearsome are, of course, Médée's potions, which Nérine knows would surely kill her on contact. Médée's reply is telling: It reminds one of another feature of her technique—of combining what I have called her fidelity with what might be moderation. Her science, Médée reassures the nursemaid, allows for an affective fidelity to Nérine—Médée has protected her:

> Ne crains pas leur vertu, mon charme la modère,
> Et lui défend d'agir que sur elle et son père;
> Pour un si grand effet prends un coeur plus hardi,
> Et sans me répliquer, fais ce que je te dis.
>
> (4.1.1065–68)

> Do not fear their power, my incantations moderate it,
> And prevent it from acting upon all but her and her father;
> Before such a great effect find a stronger heart,
> And without answering back do what I ask you.

The word *vertu* here, in its older sense, refers to masculine power rather than to a feminized moral rectitude. But the citation points to the relationship between the two meanings, and indeed renders the virtue of *vertu* subject to Médée's science. This science, Médée's *charme*, finds expression then not just in strength but in the harnessing of strength—in its capacity to tame power. Médée's moderation of *vertu* has the effect of control and targeting, making its effect even greater. Instead of excess, then, Médée imposes herself through a kind of *justesse*.

To not understand moderation as a part of Médée's *vertu* is dangerous. Corneille's last modification of the play toward *justesse* concerns this very ignorance. In the third change Corneille outlines, Créon has a certain "Nise" don the gown first, as a matter of precaution. Amy Wygant notes that this incident is unique in the history of *Médées*. Within the Corneillian universe—where debates about the role of tragic performance in regulating morality focused on the role of verisimilitude as a measure of acceptability—Créon's test of Médée's power emphasizes the extraordinary nature of her witchcraft as it also tests the audience's own capacity to accept such exceptional actions as the stuff of stagecraft.[29] Within the context of the play's politics of sovereignty, it reiterates the division between Créon's notion of sovereignty and justice and Médée's. By treating Médée's work as having the potential of regular political treason, akin to poison in the royal meal, for example, Créon seems to be using a form of prudence.

> Si ce présent nous cache une embûche mortelle.
> Nise, pour ses forfaits destinée à mourir,
> Ne peut par cette épreuve injustement périr;
> Heureuse, si sa mort nous rendait ce service,
> De nous en découvrir le funeste artifice.
>
> (4.3.1166–70)

> If this gift hides from us a deadly trap,
> Nise, for her crimes already condemned to die,
> Cannot die from this test unjustly, [so]
> Will be happy if her death does us this favor
> Of helping us discover the dire trick!

Créon's decision is a fascinating one: Nise, already condemned to die for unspecified crimes, will try the gown on. Should her demise reveal a secret plot to kill Créuse, the death will not be unjust and Nise might even be happy to be of service. We cannot call Créon's use of Nise a sacrifice since this woman is already no innocent; her insertion into this role as experimental subject marks a moment when the sacred is dismissed in favor of a scientific procedure, of what Wygant calls "a curious experiment" that tests the limits of Médée's potions. It does so, however, at the expense of Créon's mercy and along the lines of his ease with negotiated, bargained power. Corneille seems to be signaling this by the gratuitous naming of the test subject and the brief details about her criminality—not to mention that this substitute is a woman. Perhaps a stand-in for Médée, the criminal yet powerless Nise is also a viable stand-in for the innocent Créuse.

In its haplessness, Créon's strategy for testing the garment also confirms Médée's moderating power, and as such is a reinforcement of her system of cleaving. As she explains to Nérine, she decides on whom the poisons work and to whom the gown shall adhere. Créon's futile judgment then highlights the moderation that intensifies Médée's violence: She gets away with poisoning her rivals because she can temper and control the effects of her magic. Créon is helpless to stop her because his imagination cannot reach her image of justice and its refinements, and instead is stuck in expediency.

Furthermore, she ensures her rivals' death by making the gown stick: Créuse takes Médée's skin and cannot get out of it, transformed into a living torch herself:

> Théudas: Cette pauvre princesse à peine l'a vêtue,
> Qu'elle sent aussitôt une ardeur qui la tue,
> Un feu subtil s'allume, et ses brandons épars
> Sur votre don fatal courent de toutes parts,
> Et Cléone et le Roi s'y jettent pour l'éteindre,
> Mais (ô nouveau sujet de pleurer et de plaindre!)
> Ce feu saisit le Roi; ce prince en un moment
> Se trouve enveloppé du même embrasement.
>
> (5.1.1325–32)

## Surface Selves: Médée, 1634

> That poor princess scarcely had donned it,
> When she feels a burning begin to kill her
> A subtle flame is lit, and its scattering sparks
> fly all over your fatal gift
> Cléone and the King throw themselves onto her to extinguish it
> But (another reason to cry and lament)
> This fire catches hold of the King, who in an instant
> Finds himself enveloped by the same blaze.

Théudas's description of a "subtle fire" which spreads first by "sparks" emphasizes at once its incipience, its rapidity and its efficacy—reflecting not just the spread of the fire, but Créuse's reactions, affect, and movements. Even when the flames are extinguished, as Théudas describes, the sticking and burning continue:

> La flamme disparaît, mais l'ardeur leur demeure,
> Et leurs habits charmés, malgré nos vains efforts
> Sont des brasiers secrets attachés à leurs corps,
> Qui veut les dépouiller eux-mêmes les déchire,
> Et l'aide qu'on leur donne est un nouveau martyre.
>
> (5.1.1334–38)

> The flames disappear, but the burning remains,
> And their enchanted clothes, despite our useless efforts,
> Are hidden blazes attached to their bodies;
> He who wishes to unclothe them only rips them,
> And so this new assistance becomes a new torture.

Evoking Pélie's daughters who in wanting to help their father in fact hurt him irreparably, those running to the aid of the king and the princess are part of their torture, since removing the coat—now a second skin—is akin to flaying them. Créon describes it graphically, refusing help from the servants who are grabbing at the garment:

> Loin de me secourir, vous croissez mes tourments,
> Le poison à mon corps unit mes vêtements,
> Et ma peau qu'avec eux votre pitié m'arrache
> Pour suivre votre main de mes os se détache.
> . . . . . . . . . . . . . . . . . .
> Fuyez, ou ma fureur une fois débordée
> Dans ces pieux devoirs vous prendra pour Médée.

C'est avancer ma mort que de me secourir,
Je ne veux que moi-même à m'aider à mourir.

(5.2.1379–88)

Far from soothing me you increase my torment.
The poison is joining my body to my clothes,
And my skin, which your help is ripping from me,
In following your hands is detaching itself from my bones.
. . . . . . . . . . . . . . . . . . . . . . . . .
Run away, or my fury overflowing
In these pious works will mistake you for Médée.
By helping me you are hastening my death,
I want only myself to help me to die.

Médée's art sutures clothing to body, as if it is truly another skin; yet it also flays the real epidermis by gluing it to the helping arms. Refusing the deadly touch of others—an echo of Pélie's own death by his daughters' hands—Créon finally comes into his own self: "Je ne veux que moi-même à m'aider à mourir." In doing so, he also echoes Médée's own Stoic credo, "Moi/Moi dis-je et c'est assez" (1.v), uttered as a declaration of self-sufficiency and strength. In contrast, Créon's position is of infinite incapacity, in which the elusive self-help ("m'aider") is also the name of his murder (Médée). One might see in this final ironic deployment of an overdetermined *M* the Medean signature of constancy to oneself. It is followed by the protracted onstage death of Créuse, joined by Jason, who, without attempting to save Créuse, finds himself just as impotent in his desire for self-immolation:

Et puisque cette robe a causé votre perte,
Je dois être puni de vous l'avoir offerte
. . . . . . . . . . . . . . . . .
Mais ce poison m'épargne, et ces feux impuissants
Refusent de finir les douleurs que je sens.
Il faut donc que je vive, et vous m'êtes ravie!

(5.4.1501–9)

Since this gown has caused your demise
I must be punished for having given it to you
. . . . . . . . . . . . . . . . .
But this poison is sparing me, and its powerless fire
Is refusing to end the pain I feel.
I must then live, while you are taken from me!

The irony of Jason's inability to link himself to Créuse through heroism or death might feel like a macabre parody of tragedies in which characters' fates are linked by love inextricably and through their demise, but it is again another indication of Médée's extraordinary science. Creating a chain of adhesive death that destroys Créuse and her father, eliminating the royal family, but forcing her true enemy to live, Médée uses her own skin not as a layer but as a whole body to alter the Corinthian polis. Now the remainder, Jason, cannot cleave himself to Créuse despite his amorous fantasies of together riding the same boat in Hades. Médée refuses this adhesion and reasserts her absolute commitments: She will not let Jason die united to another; as she has sworn earlier on in the play:

> Tu t'abuses, Jason, je suis encore moi-même.
> Tout ce qu'en ta faveur fit mon amour extrême,
> Je le ferai par haine; et je veux pour le moins
> Qu'un forfait nous sépare, ainsi qu'il nous a joints;
> Que mon sanglant divorce, en meurtres, en carnage,
> S'égale aux premiers jours de notre mariage,
> Et que notre union, que rompt ton changement,
> Trouve une fin pareille à son commencement.
>
> (1.3.237–43)

> You are wrong, Jason, I am still myself.
> As much as my great love did for your sake,
> I will do out of hatred, and I want at the very least
> That a crime separate us, just as one joined us,
> That my bloody rupture, in murder and in carnage,
> Is equal to the first days of our marriage,
> And that our union, which your changing has broken,
> See an end equal to its beginning.

When she rejects the law's bargains, questions Créon's tactics of exile, and his concessions to protect her children, she offers a response that is unregulated by anyone else, and entirely moderated by her own direction. Additionally, Médée is the only one who has an effect, as she alone does anything in the play. Jason recounts, promises, lies; Créuse demands gifts; Créon performs his station in vain (his two sovereign gestures, that of banishment and that of dressing Nise in the gown, are ineffectual). The sole experiential referent, Médée, supplants the social order and its mechanisms of control precisely by wielding her sense of self and the knowledge that undergirds it. When she uses her skin to alter the world, it is a targeted alteration, one not of excess but of *vertu*: of carefully controlled strength.

*Médée* is then all about how the self might cling to its others or cleave from them. Médée's acts ask us to consider the difference between selves whose unity and whose discreteness we take for granted. What separates one body from another—two lovers, for example? What keeps some bodies together—how is a father attached to his daughters, a mother to her children? How can a foreign body attach itself to the domestic? What distinguishes Médée's modus operandi from those of the Greeks is not simply her violence; it is rather her refusal to cleave, whether to or from, in any other way than absolutely. What this epidermal ethos delivers, then, is not a superficial sense of the self in relation to others, but rather a deeply historical and attached one.

The specter of this line of thinking is the scene, in any version of *Medea*, in which the mother kills her own children and then flies away. In Corneille's version Médée does just that in act 5, where, in an echo of Seneca, she announces her own murdering of her children. She does so from her dragon-drawn chariot, as if as a prelude to the play's real spectacle, the machine technology of the chariot's flight. The infanticide is then the denouement to the play, and not the climax. As such, it is the logical conclusion to the events that transpire before it: the cleaving of a father from his daughters; the thwarted cleaving of a wife from her husband, and children from a banished mother; the adhesive cleaving of a father to his daughter, the burning of a city.

When we resist considering the infanticide as if it were the only action that mattered, we can attend to two important aspects of the Medea myth which *Médée* underscores: First, we might suggest such cleaving to and from is part of a pattern of behavior that brings down a city-state, and ends its lineage, but only if we take all the events into account, not just the infanticide. Second, and relatedly, we expand the destructive power of women out of the intimacy of the domestic sphere and into the world.

Corneille's Médée seems to incarnate and so give voice to an epistemological order that directs a person to a set of relations with certain values: that of fidelity to one's history despite all the political challenges that constitute living in a foreign world. The embodiment of this kind of a person is also a model for the conflict that necessarily follows. It is the conflict between a worldview that considers itself whole, moderate, and future-thinking, and what appears to be an interloper into this world. This might be the description of a familiar story in literature: the triumphant, if melancholic, expulsion of a foreign element, and the restitution of a society.

Corneille's version should provoke a reconsideration of these stories. In offering a *Médée* that in many ways "justifies" and prepares an ending without expiation, one in which Médée may always return, it insists on the mutual constitution of inside and outsider, of whole and fragmenter, of certainty and belief. In refusing to isolate and scapegoat the outsider, it indicts such a worldview by showing its partisans to be complicit in the fractures and violences that constitute its wholeness. Going even further, one might even assert that it portrays the outsider as one who considers herself *as such*—unmoored, isolated, foreign. But it is precisely as an outsider, as one with a different history, geography, and set of knowledge and practices, that Médée can be attached, committed, and remembering. This Médée offers a model for the impossibility of eliminating, or even constituting, a world without the destruction that follows such confrontation.

Likewise, Corneille's *Médée* might be a stake set in the field of debates about the role of violence in society, a stake that marks how we reserve a part of our art for the nondidactic, the nonpedagogical. When Corneille revived *Médée* in 1639 to commit it to print, he also seemed to be nourishing the possibility of tragedy to refuse a morally normative role. Corneille's version of Medea asks this question in multiple ways and on various scales, and in doing so it calls to our attention the ways in which this figure of dramatic poetry conveys literature's power to disrupt the moral lesson.

CHAPTER 2

# The Medean Presence: Violence Unmade and Remade

Feror huc illuc ut plena deo.

—OVID, *Medea*

I am borne here and there as if overcome by a god.

The best version of Corneille's *Médée* is Pasolini's 1969 *Medea*. And the best version of Pasolini's *Medea* is in book 7 of Ovid's *Metamorphoses*. As nonsensical as these anachronistic claims of affiliation and intertextuality might seem on the surface, the temporality of the Medean principle resists the march of time as an act of accretion or progressivist notions of change over time, since its destination is neither any end point of modernity or any account of the present moment. One way of putting this is in literary historical terms: The 1634 *Médée* did not evolve from a Euripidean, Senecan, or Renaissance Medea, nor did it beget a twentieth-century Medea. Rather Medean violence folds history and time upon themselves within its narrative, resisting closure and expiation, and inviting recurrence. What follows, then, deliberately refuses a historical account of Medea's work in literary history in a way that is commensurate with her: neither teleological nor simply genealogical. I want to suggest instead that to best understand Medean violence we might follow the structure of its persistence: that of layering, fracturing, suturing, unmaking, and remaking. This rhythm can be seen within the constitution of Medean characters, just as it can be traced through the most fundamental gestures in poetry to apprehend the violence and beauty of the world: description, report, testimony, and ekphrasis.

Let us begin with a figure of unmaking, or a figure unmade. At a key moment in Pier Paolo Pasolini's 1969 *Medea*, Maria Callas's character is nearly undone. The Argonauts, having stolen the Golden Fleece from Colchis and Medea from her father, begin sailing back to Greece. When they stop to make camp, Medea remains on the *Argos*, her profile filled with consternation. Up until this point, the voice of the international operatic diva has hardly been heard; Medea barely speaks. Instead it is her luminous face, huge eyes, and body—made even more regally imposing by the close-ups of her face and also by the apparent weight of her garment and adornments—that create her singular presence on screen. When Medea finally rushes off the raft, it is to warn the Argonauts of the danger they are incurring for making camp so carelessly: "This place will sink because it has no foundation. You are not praying to God that he bless your tents. You are not repeating the first act of God. You are not seeking the center, you are not marking the center. No! Look for a tree, a post, a stone!" Jason and his companions look on bemusedly, their postures casual. A musician among the group responds to her cries with a few strains of music, as if to return her babblings with another form of unintelligible but more melodious sounds. Registering their incomprehension, she turns away, to run across the dry and cracked earth of their camp, as they also turn to light a fire for the meal. The camera panning the scene, the muted colors of the green-gray sky and gray cracked clay of the land fill the frame. Medea's head appears only at the bottom of the image, as uncentered as she feels. The camera tracks her: "Speak to me, Earth. Let me hear your voice! I can no longer remember your voice," she says, breathless and over the jangling of her jewels and chains, unencumbered by her heavy gown:

> Speak to me, Sun. Where must I go to hear your voice? Speak to me, Earth! Speak to me, Sun! Are you losing your way, perhaps never to return again? I can no longer hear what you are saying. Grass, speak to me! Stone, speak to me! Earth, where is your meaning? Where can I find you again? Where is the bond that linked you to the sun? I touch the earth with my feet but I do not recognize it! I look at the sun with my eyes but do not recognize it.

When she finally sits, she does so heavily and motionless with the cracked clay of the camp's land forming her background, as shots of the Argonauts enjoying their meal are intercut. Alone, she has given up on establishing a ground for them. The words in English would be unmoored

Figure 14. Maria Callas in *Medea*, dir. Pier Paolo Pasolini, cinematography by Ennio Guarnieri, 1969.

or unanchored. Are nautical terms appropriate?—given that Medea feels a disconnection from the land itself. She might seem *dépaysée*, *déracinée*, or uprooted, perhaps *déboussolée*—her compass is broken; she is disoriented. Yet she recognizes the basic elements of the world: The sun, the earth, the plant life appears the same as in her land—she sees it well enough—but it does not communicate in the same way.

This sequence of shots conveys Medea's particular kind of alienation. Having given up her homeland, she has not only abandoned familiar territory, people, and culture, she has severed her ability to understand the world. This is particularly striking for a figure whose knowledge base is from the physical world: the plants and chemical interactions that create her magic, whose lineage derives from her grandfather Hyperion, the sun. Pasolini also evokes the depth of this knowledge through the diva's own presence. Callas was in her mid-forties at the time of the filming, and instead of this Medea appearing too old to be a young girl in love, she appears literally to embody a very old culture. The actress's maturity becomes a kind of deep groundedness. Attached to the earth and its minor-chord resonances, she has the experience of a whole culture's knowledge.

In the scene of the encampment, Medea's urgings appear primitive, even archaic in the way others' superstitions tend to seem; the Argonauts do not feel unmoored and do not sense or fear the lack of connection of which she warns. Of course, this contrast underscores the tensions between the sacred and the secular upon which Pasolini draws elsewhere in the film: opposing Medea and her world to Jason and his world, and contrasting the young Jason, who believes in the mythological histories of his centaur tutor, and the grown, disenchanted Jason. In this scene, however, we know Medea is in a sense right to consider that the world has come undone. The Argonauts shall not be rewarded, and Medea's life in exile has begun. The acknowledgment that the ground is unstable, that the things of this world are disconnected from each other, and that the speaking earth is now mute suggests that her disconnections are not just physical but even epistemological.

It is again in this sense that Pasolini's Medea is deeply Corneillian, just as it is deeply Ovidian. In both Ovid and Pasolini, the Medean personage is constituted by her sense of allegiance to the world around her, the command she can have over the world and the knowledge it provides, and the gap between this sense of self in the world and that of a dominating sociopolitical structure that comes to see her as alien and threatening to its constitution. Both Ovid and Pasolini trace the perdurance of her violence and its particular constitution.

### *Layered Medeas: Pasolini, Corneille, Ovid*

Corneille was not the only adapter of the Medea myth to freight the gown with critical significance. Pasolini's *Medea* might be also considered a premodern adaptation of the myth, for the ways it strives at once to elucidate, expand, and validate the presence of an archaic past, and to challenge how we see our relationship to history as a thing we leave behind. Also like Corneille's *Médée*, Pasolini's filmic version intensifies the crisis by reiterating it; Pasolini tells the story of the deadly gift twice. The first version follows the mythological story. The camera lingers on Creon's daughter Glauce—as Creusa is known in the Latin—as her attendants dress her carefully in Medea's gown, her heavy jewels and diadem weighting the princess's slight body. She gazes at herself in the mirror, and then cries out in torment, running out of the palace. As she runs past the palace, we see an image of Medea superimposed over the scene, looming above Glauce engulfed by fire. As Glauce runs outside of the city, her father follows. The girl's burning body running past the city walls, in the borderlands right near Medea's refuge, is a metonym for the burning city, a version of the 1664 Amsterdam frontispiece of Corneille's *Médée* discussed earlier, in the Introduction. The king catches up to her, and his deep red robes catch the flaming contagion, confirming the concomitant demise of his sovereignty. They die together in a pile of fire.

In the second version, the mechanism by which Glauce is murdered is rendered invisible, as is the Medean presence. After the princess dons the gown, she looks at her reflection in a mirror, cries out, and runs to the city walls. She leaps over them to her death, and Creon follows, landing on top of her. Cleansed of the occult's fires, Glauce's torment is internalized, perverse perhaps. Does she feel regret? Guilt? Has she gone mad? In both

Figure 15. Medea overlaid on Glauce on fire. *Medea*, dir. Pier Paolo Pasolini, cinematography by Ennio Guarnieri, 1969.

versions, the devastation is the same, however, as are the consequences—Corinth is deprived of a future.

Or is Glauce somehow imbued even more deeply with a Medean presence, by virtue of the dress? When Creon banishes Medea just after the first burning, he specifies his reasons. In distinction to the Euripidean model, it is not simply out of fear of the barbarian, "but rather out of love for my daughter, who feels remorse for you. She knows what you are suffering, and she suffers too." Whereas in ancient models, Creon banishes Medea out of fear of what she might bring against the kingdom, here Creon is worried about the effect she is having specifically on his daughter: Creon wishes to end Glauce's compassionate suffering, stopping the affective contagion that Medea threatens. It is not clear if Creon is concerned for his daughter's pain or for the actions it might compel her to take, but Glauce's second death seems to answer this fear: What might Glauce do if Medea stays? Is Glauce's second death then a revision of the first, a correction to a fantasy, or rather a sign of Medean proliferation?

These layered stories, retellings that are neither entirely corrective nor divergent, are a part of Pasolini's poetics. Early on, the movie offers us an analogous way of reading through the centaur Chiron, Jason's tutor, who tells the first story of the movie and will assume two different forms over the course of the telling. We see Chiron's metamorphosis from a bearded centaur into a clean-shaven human, as Jason grows from a baby to a man.

As centaur, he tells the baby his origin story, one firmly grounded in the complexities of myth. Then, as Jason transforms into a boy, Chiron laments: "Everything is holy. There is nothing natural in nature.... Everywhere you look gods are hidden. But the gods that love at the same time hate." With regard to the human response to this religious interpretation of the world, Chiron goes on to say, "For ancient man, the myths and rituals are concrete experiences which include him even in his bodily and daily existence. For him, reality is a unity so perfect that the emotion he experiences before the silence of a summer sky is equivalent to the most intimate personal experience of a modern man." Pasolini's doubled Chiron, who evolves from a mythic beast to a civilized man, a "desecrated" one who, as he says when he reappears at Corinth, tells the cautionary tale of our forsaking the mythic complexity of the world for one that is linear, disenchanted, and mastered. The mythic lives within the civilized permanently, he says; it is never gone: Thus, Chiron the man will later appear next to himself as centaur. The centaur is silent now, for "his logic is so different from us that [it] is incomprehensible."

The implication is that as he grows, Jason sees less and less the mythic, hidden powers of the world and its histories. Jason's origin story as told by Chiron, the centaur himself, and Glauce's death by burning are aspects of what Noa Steimatsky has called the "archaic" aspect of Pasolini's cinematography, an archaism evoked for the very ways in which it permeates the contemporary: "The presence of the archaic within contemporary life complements in Pasolini's oeuvre a vision of the present in an allegorical projection of the past."[1] In *Medea* one cannot choose between the archaic and the contemporary, or between the past and the present. Even if the narrative begins with the "archaic" and ends with a "cleaner" version, it cannot be said that the sanitized version of Medea's murder, transformed into a suicide, effaces or disarms the violence of the first. Rather the archaic remains as a layer: the first iteration of multiple versions, just as Medea is layered over images of Glauce in the first version of the princess's death, but also just as the shadows of Chiron as centaur and as fully man reach out to each other, never completely touching. The filmic editing underscores how the epistemological suture is never invisible. The desire to reveal the endurance of the mythological results in a cinema that is deliberately "contaminated," to borrow Pasolini's own term, one that is layered, that offers variations not in a dynamic of alternatives (we cannot choose between them) but as one structure—whether sutured or constructed through palimpsest—with a frame of externalized violence that undergirds the cleaner, self-disciplined suicide of the second.[2]

Figure 16. Chiron's two versions (Laurent Terzieff). *Medea*, dir. Pier Paolo Pasolini, cinematography by Ennio Guarnieri, 1969.

Through this layered, reiterative architecture of narrative, character, and history, Pasolini constructs an Ovidian Medea, composed of seemingly multiple sources and incommensurable qualities: a Medea who does not evolve by moving and improving from one state to another. Rather, she continually encompasses the past as she moves. Her significance is in an endurance at once powerful and nonmonumental. It is through this structure of layering that she is also an agent of nonmonumentality, leaving behind her nothing but the effects of her violence. Fragmented, rehearsed, cleaved, repeated, the Ovidian Medea is a courier of destruction.

Paradoxically powerful and yet fractured by multiple story lines, Pasolini's Medea is like the centaur in Jason's Corinth: at once at the mercy of the Greeks and in the end always majestically in command of each crisis she meets. Pasolini's Medea takes up an Ovidian tradition that emphasizes the staying power of this destructive force. Both Ovid and Pasolini constitute this figure as at once layered and fragmenting. Like Corneille, they trace the role it plays in shaping and limiting the contours of the social.

So it is to Ovid that we must turn in order to understand how Medea lingers on to sow the seeds of destruction in the premodern dramatic imagination. If Pasolini provides key images of this constitution, the poetics of Ovid's Medea offers a model for renderings of her in tragic forms and elsewhere. That said, I am not arguing that Ovid should be seen as a source for Corneille any more than Pasolini could have been in the traditional sense of influences and intertextuality. Ovid was indeed a "source" in the traditional literary-critical sense of this word. That is, if we count verses and other textual allusions in *Médée*, book 7 of the *Metamorphoses* is "cited" within Corneille's poetry—but in a minor way, quantitatively much less than either Seneca or Euripides.[3] This is one way to measure influence: the tracing of a progressive accretion of erudition infused into authors by schools (Ovid was the single most read author in premodern educational programs) and diffused by their writing. But this model of transmission and inheritance is not Medea's, a figure whose narrative history has never followed one trajectory, since it incorporates and shifts over time and according to cultural-political context. Like the figure, the story itself vagabonds for its survival, never dying but always remaining ancient.

By underscoring how Pasolini's creation seems to work with the same Ovidian pieces as seventeenth-century tragedy, I wish also to trouble—from the outset—any clear sense of historical accretion or development. Doing so will highlight affiliations that eschew this originary story about the transmission of ideas, and underscore how certain constructions frame and permeate the elements that constitute a figure. It is not so much that the Medean presence is transmitted from author to author like a citation. Rather, this presence is embedded within the poetics, political stakes, dramaturgical demands of this figure. So it is that twentieth-century poet, novelist, cinematographer, philosopher, and political thinker Pier Paolo Pasolini is exemplary of what I'm calling an premodern Medean presence. That is, his Medea is a sign of the endurance of a kind of violence that refuses to be assimilated into a dominant moral order, an endurance that takes its force from its aesthetic principles. The Medean presence occurs, recurs, reshapes itself, and returns anew, as an index of literature's reliance on violence.

And in the same way that Pasolini's Medea is premodern, so Ovid's classical Medea evinces the same structures. Ovid's *Metamorphoses* offers one of the clearest expressions of a specific architecture structuring the Medean narrative and its reception, wherein harm and destruction are acts of creation insofar as they are embedded within the poetics of the text. Ovid's *Metamorphoses* offers then the most basic template for the Medean presence as a performance of destruction. Keeping the layers and sutures of Pasolini's archaism present, I will explore how the poetics of this presence takes definitive shape in Ovid through the art of description, and how the poetics helps us reconsider the work of description as a principal tool of Medean violence in literature.

## *The Politics of Description: Lessing, Timomachus, and the Ekphrastic Impulse*

Perhaps the one thing scholars of Ovid agree on is the capital importance of narrative in his oeuvre, and within the *Metamorphoses*, the specific narrative form of description. Description: that rhetorical device so integral to premodern tragedy because it must convey all off-stage action, including whatever precedes and even follows theatrical action. It also is the very impetus for the *Metamorphoses*, whose proem begins, "My mind leads me to speak now of forms changed/ into new bodies."[4] To "speak now of forms changed" is to relate transformations that have occurred: It is to *describe* them. At the heart of the *Metamorphoses* is the act of description as an account of a past we can no longer see, feel, or experience. If we can say that Ovid's stories of nature in evolution deploy description in so many ways as to demonstrate its fullest range, the story of Medea at the beginning of book 7 of the *Metamorphoses* occupies a specific place.

Within the framework of the project of the *Metamorphoses*, the story of Medea's becoming and her deeds works as a particular limit case as to what narrative description can bear witness to. That is, within all of these stories of *becoming*, Medea's stands out as a narrative of destruction. That is not to say that its account is as gruesome as that of the flaying of Marsyas, who loses a music contest to Apollo and is punished, crying, "Why do you deconstruct me?"

> The skin is stripped from his body
> until he's all entirely one wound:
> blood runs out everywhere, and his uncovered
> sinews lie utterly exposed to view;
> his pulsing veins were flickering, and you
> could number all his writhing viscera
> and the gleaming organs underneath his sternum.
>
> (6.551–60)

Nor does violence punctuate Medea's story as much as it does that of Procne, her husband Tereus's rape of her sister Philomela, and his removal of her tongue, "its stump throbs in her mouth, while the tongue itself/ falls to the black earth trembling and murmuring" (6.803–4), and the feast Procne makes of her own son to feed Tereus as revenge. On the contrary, the basic details of Medea's violence are kept to a surprising minimum. It is rather within the mobilization of description itself that we shall see destruction emerging as a value; vivid description becomes itself an act of violence.

If we speak of an "act," we must speak of an actor or agent, and perhaps an object to be acted upon as well. The aesthetic stakes of vivid description generally have been constrained by a rhetorical formulation that, placing the emphasis on oratorical virtuosity, resists any question of agency or examination of its ability to wield power, its politics. Yet the notion of vivid description as a gesture full of power relations, full of a consciousness of the self's ability to apprehend and therefore change the world, is already embedded in one rhetorical term for description: *ekphrasis.*

As the literary representation of visual art, ekphrasis describes one facet of the interplay between the literary word and visual art and has come to refer narrowly to poetic description of a work of art. But we should not rest on this definition, which is in any event a product of the impact of aesthetic theory on eighteenth- and nineteenth-century poetry. Furthermore, if description from one medium to another cannot be said to be a simple transfer, additionally the history of ekphrasis as technique or genre is quite a bit more complicated.

The Greek refers to a notion of "telling in full" or of "speaking out," and therefore seems to encompass all descriptive power, but by the third century C.E. it referred more particularly to the description of visual art. Theorists of the modern era sought to untangle the complexity of such transmutation of the visual to the verbal. We still retain G. E. Lessing's 1766 meditation on it in his essay *Laocoön*, which emphasizes the loss of experience in this transformation when poetry is faced with the dimensionality of art.[5] Lessing distinguishes between materials: between the presentation of marble, stone, or pigment, the variations that allow visual art to present us with a multiplicity of effects, gestures, and forces in space simultaneously, in contrast with the limitations imposed on poetry by language itself and the act of reading, restricting our access to a line-by-line experience, one word or syntactical unit unfolding only after the other has been apprehended.

One might join in the scores of critics who have considered this "ekphrastic fear" and the attendant debates about the relative value of media. Within such debates, the key question of the ekphrastic process occurs at the moment of transfer: How does the poet wrestle dimensionality away from the object and capture it in the diachronic experience of the sentence? And yet even Lessing knew that ekphrasis was a good deal more complex a procedure than this, as his examples suggest. Perhaps the most famous one is that of Achilles' shield, which in Lessing's argument is not actually an ekphrasis at all: It recounts the action of the shield's making, not the action of a spectator apprehending it. As W. J. T. Mitchell has observed, Homer's description of the shield, as it undermines "oppositions of movement and stasis, narrative action and descriptive scene, and the false identifications of medium with message," offers two different functions: one for characters within the *Iliad* and one for its readers.[6] The very idea of this as ekphrasis is pure fiction anyway, Mitchell notes, since "the blind Homer of course can't claim to have seen it. He is just repeating what he has heard from the muses."[7] In pointing to its absence, Mitchell identifies a crucial component of the ekphrastic gesture: It is an act of testifying to the apprehension of a work of art. Homer's ekphrasis of the shield breaks his own audience into two, just as it reveals the importance of testifying not simply as individual apprehension but as transmission—ekphrasis is always relational and never originary.

Lessing doesn't address the issue of apprehending or witnessing art, but he knows that the question of transmission is crucial: Another example he offers is Timomachus's *Medea*, a painting lost to us and known only through visual and written descriptions. What Lessing praises, in this Medea he never saw, is the way she is depicted in a moment prior to her violent action, when hesitation, uncertainty, the weight of the decision, have stilled her. For Lessing, the visual can depict these moments of silence, of stasis, as moderated indications of the storm of violence that has passed or will befall the subject. Like Homer, Lessing was inspired to comment on the visual blindly: Having never seen this work of Timomachus, he apprehended it by other means: other paintings and poems, especially ekphrastic epigrams, brief verses derived from the Hellenic tradition of inscription but which include an expression of the writer's reaction to artwork.

One ekphrasis begets another; one experience engenders the desire to account for it and for the weight of history that informs any accounting. Lessing did know that the key moment in action is that time just *before*: In theater it would be the *peripeteia*, that moment before decisive action takes place and there is no turning back. I think this moment is also key to the power of ekphrasis and is the core of its definition: Ekphrasis is not simply the rendering of visual art into poetry, or the translation of one artful experience into another, but a record of the *process* of that translation, indeed the *experience* of effecting that interpretation. As Valentine Cunningham has suggested, the ekphrastic gesture is "that pausing, in some fashion, . . . before, and/or about, some nonverbal work of art, or craft, a *poiema* without words, some more or less aestheticized made object, or set of made objects."[8] This gesture of pause, of beholding, seems to return to Lessing's notion that the best works of art capture those moments of pause around a grand and violent event: "that point or moment which the beholder not so much sees as adds in his imagination, and that appearance which does not seem so transitory as to become displeasing through its perpetuation in art."[9] If we return to his example of the unseen painting of Medea, rendered through descriptions, it seems that unseeable paintings are made accessible by a beholder who "adds" the moment "in his imagination"; art worth talking about is art that demands that the beholder create art in response, art that accounts for the experience of art.

As minor as it is for Lessing's argument, this example encapsulates the work of ekphrasis not just in the transmission of story or image but as a moment of mediation between the artifact and the beholder: the artist, the critic, the historian, the spectator. The creator of that ekphrastic gesture is always first a witness, whose experience, intuitions, reaction—whose very body—is embedded within their rendition of the work of art beheld.

There is something particular to the Medea myth that makes it uniquely suitable to, and troubling for, arguments about ekphrasis, as if the myth's internal framing demanded not just an audience but a moment of assessment. As Kathryn Gutzwiller so elegantly explores, in reading ekphrastic epigrams on Timomachus, "It becomes increasingly difficult to know whether the subject remains Timomachus's Medea or whether it has been replaced by an altogether different painting."[10] In one by the Julio-Claudian poet Philip, Gutzwiller shows, the poet's reader is asked not to imagine a painting or a figure, but the reaction of the viewer of art. As the epigram ends, "Still wet with blood is her sword. Flee the destructive mother, / still murdering her children even in wax."[11] The poetic form becomes a comment on the ethics of violence in art, and the power of the beholder to accept or reject its presence.

Such a reaction also is a part of the Medea legend. So often scholars must perform their own ekphrasis of the myth: I suspect inserting one's own clear moral standing into one's work performs a necessary retreat from the object, as if there might be a danger of complicity through silence. With particular regard to scholars of the Ovidian Medea, arguments about its lineage, affiliations, and contours are not just debates about intertextuality as erudite citation. The consideration of this figure is consistently imbued with commentary, with a reaction. Our history of Medea is that of beholding a story, a sculpture, a bowl, a *cassone*, a poem, a song—and bearing witness to one's experience of that beholding: Medea's "pregnant moment" before she kills her children is thus also the viewer's moment, and the reader's silence, as we understand what is about to happen.[12] The history of Medea, then, is an ekphrastic one. What is compelling about this story is not simply that it happened but that we feel something of it, have an opinion about it, one worth assessing, crafting, and sharing. The history of Medea is as much about her actions as it is about our preconceptions about what a foreigner is, what a mother should do, where a lonely exile can go, what a witness to violence can do and should think.

## *The Ekphrastic* Metamorphoses, *the Ekphrastic Medea*

Among the voluminous scholarly understandings of the *Metamorphoses*, the strain situating the work as a text that comments on its own literary history, and on the possibility of understanding any literary history as such, suggests that a key way of understanding the impact of Ovid is not through a traditional linear literary history but through a model of reverberation and fragmentation, of which Medea is a paradigmatic figure.

As Stephen Hinds has suggested, there is no one figure of Medea. Ovid wrote at least three: one in his *Metamorphoses*, one in the *Heroides* (an Ovidian Medea that is deeply embedded in questions about what or who "Medea" is), and the lost tragedy *Medea*. Although I focus on the *Metamorphoses*, the Ovidian Medea emerges in literary history amid its own multiplicity, commensurately, within the complex debates of Ovidian composition and the values revealed therein.

One version of this history would be to investigate origins: how Ovid takes the Medea story first from Euripides, who may have taken it from Neophron. Both of these might also have been inspired by mentions of Medea in Hesiod, Pindar, and Herodotus—or did Euripides inspire Neophron? And did Ovid find greater inspiration from Apollonius of Rhodes? Moving beyond the great tradition of *Quellenforschung*, countless classicists have examined Ovid as writer and rewriter, through his techniques of rewriting his predecessors (specific authors such as Virgil, certain techniques of comparison and contrast). Richard Tarrant asserts, "For Ovid all writing entails rewriting; all reading, rereading. In contemporary critical parlance, Ovid recognized the inherently intertextual element of literary meaning."[13]

There's something particular about the figure of Medea within this poetic-critical tradition, however, as Hinds avers, "It will always be possible for a suspicious reader to fragment *any* given Medea into some or all of her predecessors and successors. Medea is an intertextual heroine: every one of the limited number of moves in her story is multiply determined in literary history."[14] While one form of literary history will take as ultimate goal the certain establishment of sources and their derivatives, another might look upon the fragmented, uncertain literary history of a figure like Medea and see how such fragmentation is absorbed into the figure itself, into its telling and retelling, and into the political, philosophical, moral, and epistemological questions raised by continual reinscription through new interpretations. In this regard, Hinds's Ovidian Medea—developed from readings of a range of Ovidian texts—is one whose story is not linear;

thus Hinds is conscious of the problems of a history that is read purely on the basis of causality, whose fate is intertwined not just with that of Medea's husband and children, but of the wife and even wives who came before her.

With regard to the *Metamorphoses* in particular, the adaptation of earlier versions of the stories emerge through myriad linguistic strategies (repetition of certain words, use of particular grammatical forms, and so forth), and particularly through an insistence on retelling as *rewitnessing*. Many of these stories include either the presence of the narrator or, even more vividly, the reader as spectator to the event. The *Metamorphoses* has been considered a deeply visual text; so as Ovid is a re-writer, rhetorically speaking he is also a seer and re-seer. This is precisely the dynamic relation to which Dan Curley calls our attention when he asserts both the theatricality and the metatheatricality of the *Metamorphoses*: its spectacular visuality, as well as the way in which the self-consciousness of the text as theatrical implicates its audience in the changes Ovid makes to the dramatic form.[15]

In a literal way we might see these points of hypervisuality as another mode of citation. Classical scholarship acknowledges that Ovid's predecessors include poets as well as visual artists. And of course, for so many of the tales from which Ovid's stories derive, they appear in statues, murals, vases, some of them visible in Ovid's time, some erased but recalled from other beholders or artists whom they inspired. It might seem obvious to say that classical myths are conveyed as much through language as through visual artifacts, but such an assertion challenges one to reconsider the role and contours of such notions as "intertextuality" and "literary history." Asserting this multimedial legacy insists on the intermediality that might be embedded in such narratives: poets are borrowing from and commenting on other texts and language forms and also on the visual arts.

As witnesses to the work of art, either as makers or as beholders, the agents of intermediality are the links between works of art. They are inscribed in the transfer. A linear or progressive history of the evolution of a figure is made impossible. Within the context of Ovid's *Metamorphoses* especially, this non-accretive quality is not unique to Medea. Ekphrasis, at least in the minimal sense of "vivid description," defines this text, condensing all the interplays among media, between artist and spectator, into a continual meditation on that moment of beholding. The *Metamorphoses* is a compulsively ekphrastic text, first because the stories at its foundation were depicted previously in the plastic arts and because the text seems to suggest that deeds themselves can be *poiema* without words, before which we might pause.

If this "pausing before" an object of description is also at the heart of the Ovidian aesthetic, the *Metamorphoses* also seems to comment on such pauses as moments of ambivalence, where we see the difficulty of depicting certain of its stories in art at all, whether in a statue, a woodcut illustration, a narrative poem. Unendingly ekphrastic, then, as if beholding were the motor of intermediality, the *Metamorphoses* calls out for a beholding of its own stories, and a reinterpretation of them. Thus a text such as the *Metamorphoses* can use the ekphrastic gesture, the beholding of an aestheticized moment, as a moment of meditation on creation and re-creation, but also on the limits of such creation, and on a possibility of no re-creation—or even of destruction.

This might be an inherent feature of metamorphosis itself. Tim Bahti has suggested that ekphrasis—in its fullest, most etymologically fundamental sense of "giving voice to"—may present Western literature's "most cosmic ambitions": the motivation of the literary imagination to tender something into words, or rather to turn one thing—person, object, or experience—into another, a text.[16] As I alluded to earlier, Ovid's text begins by articulating three related components of the idea of metamorphosis, that define his text as having an ekphrastic charge of cosmic dimensions:

> My mind leads me to speak now of forms changed
> into new bodies: O gods above, inspire
> this undertaking (which you've changed as well)
> and guide my poem in its epic sweep
> from the world's beginning to the present day.
>
> (1.1–5)

The mind and its tales of new bodies, the poetic work of art, the world over time: These are the three components of the *Metamorphoses*. The first five lines of Ovid's text thus suggest the interrelation among description, art, and world history. The mind compels the speaker to bear witness to forms changed: Once one shape, they are now "new bodies." The translation underscores how this syntax is reiterative (nearly redundant) by suggesting three iterations: the moment of speaking, the forms, and their new bodies. The small work of the speaker, its offering up of a single perspective which gives way to the multiplicity of "forms changed into new bodies," gives further way to the enormous dimensions of the project: a poem of "epic sweep" that will cover the life of the world. The connection between the instances of change and the epic dimensions is one of continuous shifting and change: World history is made by tracing the transformative relationships among beings. Some of the most beautiful and memorable parts of the *Metamorphoses* offer an account of this ontological continuity: Daphne's change into a laurel does not erase the girl's passion or fear:

> Her supple trunk is girdled with a thin
> layer of fine bark over her smooth skin.
> . . . . . . . . . . . . . . .
> her head becomes the summit of a tree;
> all that remains of her is a warm glow.
> Loving her still, the god [Apollo] puts his right hand
> against the trunk, and even now can feel
> her heart as it beats under the new bark.
>
> (1.756–62)

The beating heart opens the question of whether the change into a laurel tree has been incomplete at the same time that it reinscribes Apollo as the witness to that transformation, whether continuous or incomplete, of life. Other stories also account quite directly for what Marina Warner calls "the principle of organic vitality as well as the pulse in the body of art," such as that of Pygmalion and Galatea (book 10).[17] Pygmalion has been the myth of choice for meditations on the overwhelming power of artistic representation, from Ernst Hans Gombrich on, as a story about the often dangerous triumph of representational skill, measured by its ability to arouse passion.[18] Transformation is then a key word for both the connections among objects and for our appreciation of these objects; we are transformed by the objects we transform.[19] It is finally Pygmalion's gentle assault of her, laid on his bed, that brings Galatea to life (10.353–60), she is "aroused" from inertia to sexual heat. Here too, transformation indicates not just the movement between objects but the impetus for this shift: Galatea's transformation occurs first because of Pygmalion's regard of the work of art. Pygmalion's vision is what identifies life in art; so no wonder art historians embrace this story as their own.

We witness the mutations of the world, we apprehend them, we might even cause them or compel them. Our art is the stuff of these encounters, and this is the matter of the *Metamorphoses*. Such an assertion seems self-evident; the back-and-forth between one art and another is a core definition of *metamorphosis*, and our appreciation of it is a key step in that back-and-forth. Offering a new form to an older body, a form that contains a pause before, a commentary on, a revision of the older body, this ekphrastic gesture is fundamental to the *Metamorphoses*, and why the metamorphoses are not just vivid aetiological descriptions. Whether a witness like Pygmalion or Apollo is named or not, these stories as witnesses to the long history of nature as transformation contain within them layers of objects of past descriptions, and among those layers the presence of a maker, an artist, a critic, a witness, and from that description a generative, creative will to incite more such transformations.

The ekphrastic account insists on history, an object's past, as well as on the present moment—the time of beholding, the time when a spectator or auditor confronts an object and grapples with its impact. Vivid descriptions of all kinds call on the reader or auditor to imagine on his or her own terms the scene described. Ekphrasis has the special burden of mobilizing three key features: the fact of witnessing as implicitly one of judgment or assessment; the artfulness of such apprehension, and the inquiry into making.

Having moved well away from the simple definition of ekphrasis enshrined in the nineteenth century as a poetic genre whose subject is a work of art toward an understanding of ekphrasis as the poetics of how we aestheticize what we witness, we can better understand the politics of description in the Medean legacy, for it is precisely this role that ekphrasis plays in Ovid, and it is through ekphrasis that Ovid shapes the Medea story as one about the unavoidable necessity of destruction.

To start, a simple question can be asked: Why has Medea endured through ekphrasis, and to what effect? Put another way, why was Timomachus's Medea so fascinating, why was it available for, even demanding of, a subjective and artful response;? In turn, why did these ekphrases shape theories of the word-image relation, such as that of Lessing? I think that this has to do with the peculiar way in which the narrative of Medea embraces the problem of moral assessment as one that can be posed but not solved by art. Unlike but like the shield of Achilles—or closer to home, Jason's own gown described in the *Argonautica*—Medea is not an object one apprehends, she is a figure of a woman; it is not her body but her skill that is attested; and it is not merely her history but her future that is at play. Thus, the "artfulness" of the Medean ekphrasis is triple: that of the artist, that of the beholder, and that of Medean knowledge itself. Ovid's Medea works with all these facets to create a powerful narrative of literature's destructive principle.

## *Ovid's Medeas:* Metamorphoses, *Book 7*

Given all of this, the narrative of book 7 works in multiple ways to undo the relation between description and transformation as creative enterprises. It does so through ekphrastic techniques that recast the stakes of metamorphoses as they relate to the power of description. First, Ovid's rendering of sources, his "pause" before prior models—the innovations that he achieves through these redeployments—offer a commentary on how to consider the Medean tradition. Second, the narrative's structure itself can be considered antitransformative: It belies the power of creation by showing the undoing of transformative powers. Last, and as a result of these first two features, the Ovidian Medea comes to stand not for transformation—whether of loss or gain. Rather, it is a story of travel and movement, movement marked by epistemological and historical inquiry, marked not most significantly by passion and corpses, but rather by a series of botanical names and place-names.

Situated among a series of stories in the middle of the *Metamorphoses* that features women exposing their feelings (often monologically), book 7's heroine is not alone in her meditations on the impossible situation her passions have created for her.[20] But she is uniquely structured. Carole Newlands has argued that book 7 is the conjoining of at least two separate traditions in the history of Medea. Before Ovid, Medea was identified either as the youthful princess who falls in love at the sight of Jason when he arrives at Colchis to take the Golden Fleece back, dedicates some of her magical arts to his success, and, after killing her brother and betraying her father, runs away with him. Or Medea was seen as the master of occult knowledge. She is a wise woman whose fury, after Jason's rejection of her, causes much death and destruction, including that of her own children.[21]

If Ovid is the first writer to piece together these two very separate traditions, they remain just that—pieced. There is no amalgam of the two Medeas. Rather, book 7 juxtaposes them in the story: The younger Medea comes first, and then gives way to the older Medea. Although this suggests a development over time, the two sections of this story bear no marks of relation or gestures toward development, continuity, or evolution. The two Medeas are quite different. The first is focused inward yet exposed. She is expressive and reveals her feelings, whereas the second is silent and oriented toward action. The narrative of the first is motivated by her current turmoil and future hopes, whereas that of the second is a response to the past. The younger Medea offers a naïve self-portrait of her ardor as she falls in love; the older one barely says a word as she travels about the world. There is no explanation of how an ingenue might become the vengeful woman. Rather the Ovidian Medea is presented in all her contradictions, sutured as if to expose such a lack of continuity.

Ovid's first descriptive gesture, then, is to juxtapose two prior Medeas. He does not transform them at all. Rather, he places them side by side, joined in a straightforward way by time: The young Medea cedes to the older one. This sutured Medea may be seen as the functional inverse of the Pygmalion myth, in which the sculptor Pygmalion creates a statue so real he falls in love with it. The first Medea is a real woman who falls in love with a man attempting to craft himself into a hero; she helps him achieve this through her magic arts. Medea here is the artist, Jason the product—though Medea falls in love not with the finished product, but with the rough Argonaut whose heroism must be revealed through her arts of transformation.

But this is also, as the second Medea confirms, an artist of annihilation, of flight, of knowledge, of passion: not of metamorphosis. The structure of Ovid's story affirms this anti-transformative power of Medea, as it uses these juxtaposed Medeas to undo the artful creative effects of Jason's emergence as a hero in the first part. In the second section, it offers up the power to make anew only to quickly and sacrificially undo it. The narrative presents a kind of narrative mise en abyme in which transformation is followed by its negation, with this reversal nestled between two extended moments of travel description.

Book 7's particular framing of the question of transformation—its conditions of possibility, its dangers—is announced from its very beginning through the introduction of an unexpected recurring theme: the transformation wrought by aging. The connection between books 6 and 7 would appear to be the Argonauts' quest for the Golden Fleece, for book 6 ends with the birth of the twins Calaïs and Zetes, who will accompany Jason on his voyage. At the beginning of book 7, the voyage is well under way: The Argonauts have already seen Phineus and saved him from the Harpies. There is an irony to the phrasing in which King Phineus "was seen" by the Argonauts; his blindness allows the Harpies to torment him and steal his food continually. Ovid doesn't say that Phineus is blind, but he does say that the Argonauts can see him, emphasizing on the one hand the Argonauts' heroic strength and power in the situation, and on the other Phineus's vulnerability. Just alluded to here, but thematically developed throughout book 7, is the other great contrast defining the relationship between Phineus and the Argonauts: the former's old age in contrast with the Argonauts' youth. Phineus is vulnerable because he is both blind *and* old. The tension between young and old, between the strengths and passions of the youth and the helplessness of the aged, structures the sections of book 7 concerning Medea, for the Argonauts' voyage leads us to Colchis and to Medea.

The manner in which Medea herself comes to structure this section picks up on this tension between states of life, between vitality and decline. As I have said, this Medea of book 7 is really two: a young Medea and an old Medea. Young Medea falls in love with Jason, commits to give him the means to steal the Fleece, and sails with him back to Thessalonian Iolchos, where he intends to secure the throne from his uncle. Old Medea is passionate as well, but her passions are neither directed inward nor expressed verbally; the old Medea is silent.

Arguably age constitutes the major realm of questions in this section of the *Metamorphoses*: What is the difference between a person in youth and that same person aged? How does one change? What is the role of experience? In Ovidian terms these questions might be expressed in the physical changes of a body as it withers and becomes fragile, or by the journeys on which life takes a person. In Medea's case, however, the differences, are not expressed physically. Medea's body is only an accessory to the question. The major difference between the two Medeas is that the youthful one is outwardly expressive in her passions: full of voice, self-questioning, hesitation, reasoning about her impending betrayal of her father and kingdom. The old Medea is inward, virtually silent; her self-explorations are ceded to the trials of experience.

It is remarkable, then, that the difference between young and old Medea is not delineated by the changes in her own body but rather by those of other bodies: Young Medea may be seen to create youth and strength, whereas old Medea destroys it. Knowledge of the external world emerges as a link between the two Medeas. Young Medea exercises her knowledge of plants and of occult practice to help Jason. Old Medea also uses similar knowledge extensively. We can see how the narrative highlights this tension through the division it creates, despite the continuities that form it.

The narrative of these two Medeas divides her story neatly, with an important join marking and linking the two. In the first, Medea falls in love with Jason and helps him overcome the obstacles to securing the Fleece. In the second half, Medea befriends Jason's usurping uncle and successfully directs his daughters to kill him, compelling the couple's flight to exile in Corinth and the events there.

Between the two is an episode of crucial importance. Narratively it is the join, a kind of hinge or suture between the two halves, and thematically it is a powerful amalgam of the Medean techniques highlighted in both halves. Having fled Colchis and arrived at Iolchos, Jason asks Medea to help him save his aging father Aeson. Medea rails against his request that she help him trade his life for his father's, and suggests another way: that of Aeson's rejuvenation, which she achieves. This same scene would become a mainstay illustration for commentary on Ovid.[22] Crucially, Aeson's rejuvenation is the only positive transformation in the Medea story. It also creates something material and tangible that is a testimony to Medea's power: a young Aeson, a first version of Jason.

The narrative insists on the goodness of this change and even prepares for it by indicating minor signs of the potion's power: An olive branch that serves to stir the potion emerges from the cauldron heavy with leaves and fruit; splashes of the liquid fertilize the ground and cause grass and flowers to appear. When Medea then drains Aeson's blood and replaces it with the potion, the detailed description of his body returning to the man he was forty years ago is the culmination of a narrative of abundance, strength, and vigor reappearing. This remedy for old age is so effective, and so good, that Dionysus obtains it for his nurses, as the conclusion to the section adds. But it also offers a structural analogue to the great murder by deception of Pelias which dominates the second half of Ovid's version.

In the second half, Medea herself transformed—out of both her youthful passion and the conviction of her own arguments—acts seemingly on her own, with less speech and no introspection at all. The transition Ovid uses is rich for what it both presupposes and omits: "Neve doli cessent, odium cum coniuge falsum/Phasias adsimulat Peliasque ad limina supplex/confugit."[23] (Now, so that guile might not go out of fashion, / Medea feigned a breakup with her husband/and ran off as a suppliant to Pelias.) This transition assumes the reader's knowledge about why Medea would target Pelias, Jason's uncle who usurped his place as king, sending the Argonauts on their mission for the Golden Fleece, the price established for the return of the throne. Ovid never qualifies the motivation any further. Appearing also without explanation, Medea's "dolus"—artifice, guile—has no context within a plot of revenge, perhaps even a justified one. Rather it relies on a kind of continuity within the acts mentioned. Any sincerity motivating the earlier act of Aeson's rejuvenation appears retroactively also as contrivance or scheme, and not the reluctant act of a devoted wife. In this way Ovid naturalizes the treachery to come.

Thus, the only moment of reluctant goodness in the Medea story, the rejuvenation of Aeson, is paired with her use of this same magic to do the very opposite. Persuading Pelias's daughters that their father too may grow young through her art of replacing old blood with new, she incites them to kill him, telling them, "drive his old age off with your sharp weapons, / let his blood out by plunging in your swords!" (7. 472–73). Every element of the Aeson episode is counterbalanced negatively in the slaying of Pelias: Just as vividly as the narrative details Aeson's transformation into a younger man, so it offers the gory details of Pelias's death. And just as she sends her spouse and attendants away from the altar where Aeson is lying, so she incites Pelias's daughters to kill; his astonished pleas to his daughters to stop slaying him compelling them only to look away.

That this power to make a new body is altered quickly to make a dead body, is further highlighted by a narrative frame that contains these twinned episodes. The frame consists of descriptive details of the two voyages that Medea takes. These hypotyposes, rich with detail, meet the ekphrastic insofar as they beg theatrically for an audience to behold the events they chronicle. Her first trip is a quest for the magical herbs she will use to rejuvenate Jason's aging father. We follow Medea over various lands to gather what she needs:

> below her lay
> Thessalian Tempe; she set her dragons for
> those regions that were sources of her herbs:
> and she descried below plants found on Ossa
> and lofty Pelion, on Othrys, on Pindus,
> and (larger than that last one) on Olympus;
> the herbs that pleased her she took, root and all
> or snipped off leaves with her bronze pruning hook.
> . . . nor were *you* exempt,
> Enipeus, from her provisioning.
>
> (7.319–30)

As many scholars have noted, Medea's travels follow a clockwise tour of the mountains and waters surrounding Thessaly. We can see this as the expedition of a herbalist expert in local flora, including the precise techniques of gathering each plant. Her prowess is truly transformative: At the end of her journey, all herbs gathered, her dragons feel the rejuvenating effects, and they shed their skin for greener scales. The voyage has a transformative effect on the herbalist too: A wife no longer, she returns as a virtuosa about to perform her greatest act, having gathered her props in preparation.[24] Just as significant is Medea's knowledge of her terrain: The description emphasizes geography in order to underscore the knowledge of place and plants informing her voyage. We can then see in this stage of her performance also that of the anatomist's preparation prior to dissecting a body.

The second voyage occurs as she escapes after killing Pelias. The voyage echoes her first one in its emphasis on her itinerary. It too describes the territory over which she and her dragons pass. This time, however, the sites are identified not by the flora found there, but rather the metamorphic events that had occurred in each locale, as recounted by the monuments that remain:

> On her left she passed Aeolian Pitane
> with its gigantic serpent made of stone,
> and Ida's grove where once the son of Bacchus
> rustled a calf; in order to protect him,
> his father changed the boy into a stag;
> she passed the site where Helen's love lies
> beneath a meager monument of sand,
> and passed those fields which Maera terrified
> with her strange barking; flew above the city
> of Eurypylus, where the Coan women
> . . . . . . . . . . . .
> she passed the ancient city of Carthaea
> on the Isle of Cea, where Alcidamas once
> would find himself astonished by the strange
> metamorphoses of daughter into dove.
>
> (7.499–519)

Medea's flight continues: giant stone serpents, sand dunes, animals once human are followed by mothers whose tears dissolve them into lakes, incestuous sons, mourning fathers.

The first difference to be noted between this and the description of Medea's first voyage is scale: The description is longer because the territory covered is vaster. Extending beyond Greece into Asia Minor, it is, for Curley, a "one-woman Argonautica in its scope."[25] Additionally, the second itinerary is described not by Medea's own knowledge. The places noted have no consistent relationship to the woman in flight. Rather, the path of Medea's flight is significant because it is marked by sites of legends echoing the Medean work of violence and flight: Infanticide and avian flight abound.[26] It is fitting that these legends have their monuments, lasting memorials to the tragic events that shape most landscapes.

Taken together, these voyages bookend and give reason to Medea's own works of transformation. In the first place, knowledge of the earth and its life can transform an old body into new; such knowledge can then reappear to create out of an old body a dead one. In the second place, the earth records these creations and inscribes upon the land and its fauna monuments to violence. Together, then, the first description creates the means by which the monuments in the second description might have come to be. At the same time, however, what these descriptions encapsulate is Medea's own work, which leaves no monument at all. Pelias is not transformed; he is killed. And his daughters do not change after their deeds; we never hear from them again.

Without monuments to the great transformations it has wrought, what remains of Medea in Ovid? We might say the story itself, but the absence of remains, of any monument at all, points to a different thread than that of nature's ongoing metamorphic pulsing. What then occupies the Ovidian version of Medea is not the central tenet of vitality in the *Metamorphoses* but rather the pulse of knowledge in the world—whether botanical or geohistorical—and its continuity, which allows for accounts of such deeds.

If we take up the reconsideration of ekphrastic description as one that gives full voice to our apprehension of the world, we might consider these descriptions as having a certain ekphrastic weight; they witness our apprehension of Medea's voyages of knowledge as they shape our understanding of the world. Taken with all its elements together, however, the narrative frame that allows for Medean transformation to occur—a transformation that is negative, a transformation that is an undoing—highlights the very disruptive, disjointed, and even sutured status of description's power to transform the arts into words, qualifying such power, in this instance anyway, as one that causes as much pain and suffering as it does monuments to life. The arts of this world are often as deadly as they are enlivening. And description, as a literary tool to create, make visual, bring to life an experience of art, can also be the means to secure the vitality of deadly force alongside that of creation.

Since the majority of ancient and modern sources take up the figure of Medea insofar as Euripides made her a killer of her children, we might then wonder why Ovid elided this episode so strikingly when it is the primary issue of debate and concern among philosophers. Scholars have given a variety of reasons; a persuasive one is that this was the very subject he treated at length in his tragedy *Medea*. One of the surviving fragments is understood to treat her vacillations before the infanticide: "Feror huc illuc ut plena deo" (I am borne here and there as if overcome by a god). This fragment appears in Seneca the Elder's *Suasoriae*, with a reference to Virgil serving as an example of intertextuality. Scholars assume that it is part of a speech by Medea sung just prior to the infanticide. As such, it would likely be a reference to that monologue hesitating between shame and remorse in Euripides and may also have influenced Seneca the Younger's *Medea*.[27] It is also a configuration of Timomachus's missing Medea, and it also fairly represents Lessing's fascination with the portrait he never saw and experienced only through fragments and brief poetic interpretations of that moment of indecision and of crisis where any outcome could follow but only one will happen.

If we are to read this fragment in the context of its assigned plenitude—that is, as a part of a missing whole whose contours seem to be detectable through a linear literary history that takes shape through traditional strategies of intertextual allusion—then it encapsulates both Lessing's "pregnant moment," where Medea knows not which step she will take next and the audience is captured with and even beyond her in this critical juncture, as well as the Stoic dilemma of a divided heart and mind. This is what Helene Foley has called in the Euripidean Medea a "divided self" struggling amid "a clash between two positions in which reason and emotion unite on either side of the argument."[28]

In the context of an Ovidian Medea of book 7, one also might read in the "huc" and "illuc" physical, or geographic, indications as much as psychological ones. Medea was also truly borne by a god from one place, her home, to another and another. The multiple meaning of *plena* might even be extended away from "overcome by" toward a more powerful "full of"; infused with a god, Medea is borne from one land to the next. The Ovidian Medea is less a figure of hesitation, vacillation, and succumbing than one filled with and moved by the knowledge of the gods, acquainted with the geography of occult herbs, ready and able to fly away.

Perhaps, then, Ovid's book 7 Medea does not take up the infanticide in anything more than an incidental fashion because it is not core to this figuration. What is fundamental, instead, is the full force of a Medea at once fragmented and fragmenting, yet nevertheless always surviving. Fragmentation is not here the rejection of either a core identity, or of history in general. Rather it is the refusal of dominant narratives that accrue with no regard for what is hidden or eschewed by their domination. When we prioritize these very marks of persistence over the fissures, differences, and ruptures, we are acknowledging the real staying power of this story.

The first poet to combine two very different Medeas and present them alongside each other, Ovid folded into Medea's relation to tragic discourse certain contours and imperatives. That is, the tragic Medea shaped by the *Metamorphoses* is one who insists on tragic art's lingering, recurring questions, not its resolutions or its reconciliations. The relationship to the archaic that is so integral to Pasolini's *Medea* is not the same as the meditation on a surface self that Corneille elaborated. Through their lingering attachments to the Ovidian Medea and alongside one another, these Medeas suggest how tragic questions are asked, if never resolved, by the performance of the physically devastating and politically debilitating, of the morally irrecuperable.

Eighty years later, in 1634, another drama will also attend the violence of real-time passions on the stage. The same year as Corneille's *Médée*, Rotrou staged *Hercule mourant*, another play about a burning body. This time, the audience must witness the burning on stage. We will see how violence permeates a play in which there is no Medea but there is Medean violence.

CHAPTER 3

# Staying Power: Performing the Present Moment of Tragedy

Alongside Medea is Hercules. They do not seem to have much in common thematically, this barbarian witch and that physical giant of a hero. Yet they stand next to each other in at least two ways. Quite literally and historically, the season 1634–35 included Corneille's play and that of Jean Rotrou, *Hercule mourant*, which will be the primary subject of this chapter. Further, they perform a similar kind of tragic violence, characterized by burning bodies: In *Médée*, Créuse and Créon burn and die, and perhaps all of Corinth is set afire, while Rotrou's play follows the legend of Hercules, who too dons a poisoned cloak to first burn from within before creating his own funeral pyre. Here then Médée and Hercule stand alongside each other in surprising ways: After the burning, each lives on, as Médée flies away and Hercule ascends to immortality among the gods. Both *Médée* and *Hercule mourant* ask the audience to consider what it means to witness the fire of Medean violence. *Hercule mourant* offers particular insight in that experience by rendering it the defining condition of spectatorship.

## The Present Moment of 1634

The appearance of *Hercule mourant* on stage in 1634, likely in February, may be understood in the context of a theatrical revival of religious themes that culminated with *Le Véritable Saint Genest* (1644). The year 1634 was also Paris's year of the Imperial Stoics: three of the city's best-known dramaturges introduced plays drawn from Seneca during that season, including *Médée* and La Pinelière's *Hippolyte*. *Hercule mourant* is drawn in large measure from the Senecan *Hercules Oetaeus*, and also includes some elements from Seneca's *Hercules furens*.[1] Neo-Stoicism, a philosophical inquiry into the Christian understanding of such Imperial Stoic values as fortitude, constancy, prudence, and resignation, crystallized in the late sixteenth century around Justus Lipsius's *De Constantia*, and was elaborated through the seventeenth century in France by poets and Christian philosophers alike. Rotrou's interpretation of a Stoic hero's ultimate trial in particular has been described as a "dramatic *mise en évidence* of the analogies between the mythological and the Christian" or as a "Christianization" of Stoic motifs.[2] Honoring both its sources and its cultural context, Rotrou's play exhibits both the traces of the Stoic order of nature as well as those of the Neo-Stoic consideration of the human in relationship to the divine.

The tension between Stoic source and seventeenth-century revision is obvious from the first lines of the play. In *Hercules furens* Juno opens the play with her vengeful promise finally to bring down Hercules; only in act 2 does Amphitryon recount Hercules' labors; Hercules himself does not appear until act 3.[3] Rotrou's audience did not necessarily need an extended account of these deeds or their origin in Juno's wrath, since Hercules' legacy preceded him and was well known by these audiences. The sixteenth- and early seventeenth-century imagination, whether aesthetic or political, confronted the myth of Hercules in all its dimensions: philosopher, hero, and kingly figure, the embodiment of a masculine ideal of strength embraced by Renaissance Stoics.[4] One version of this fortitude as a political idea was particular to France: The *Hercule gallique* figure, leading a crowd by delicate chains attached from his lips to their ears, embodied the ideal civic leader whose power to unite and lead was derived from his eloquence. From Charles IX on, Hercules leading such chains symbolized speech as a strategy of peace.[5]

It might seem that Rotrou's Hercule conforms only ironically to this ideal of Herculean eloquence, since *Hercule mourant* is truly about one thing: Hercule's dying. From the beginning of the play, where Hercule prepares for and is disappointed by a promised apotheosis that is not granted, through his poisoning and slow demise, to his eventual Christic ascent, his departure from his earthly trappings dominates. And yet throughout his moments of hoping to die, of dying, and of after-death deification, he speaks. The poisoned tunic will burn Hercule from within for the rest of act 3. He will not fall until act 4.2, with the report of his final demise in act 5. As Hercule smolders through something like 545 lines and seven scenes, his eloquence accompanies his dying and even fortifies it. Speech becomes the ultimate mark of Hercule's strength.

First, however, his own words are a mark against him. In the first scene of the play, we meet Hercule ready for his promised ascent to the realm of the gods. Instead of an expository scene in which another character reminds the public of our hero's status as demigod, of the trial and accomplishments of his twelve labors, we hear and see Hercule himself. A portrait of arrogance, he praises his own deeds and extols his own virtues. The long-awaited apotheosis promised by the gods doesn't happen. He's outraged. He goes to find solace at the knees of his new love, the slave Iole. His wife, Déjanire, is furious until she remembers how to recapture the "first flame" of their love; she drops some blood from the centaur Nessus onto Hercule's coat and gives it to him as a present. The centaur tricked her into exacting his own revenge; Hercule will die from the coat that sticks to him. We watch him fight invisible flames, beat off an enemy not beside but within him, go insane, and run off to kill a scapegoat. We then watch his ongoing queries, finally his acceptance, his mother's mourning; we hear tell of his death upon a pyre he builds himself; we see him, finally deified, descend from the heavens—probably in a basket rigged to ropes and pulleys. He forgives those whom he had condemned; the lovers he had separated are delivered to each other's arms, and his confidant Philoctète offers a final charge to those remaining:

> Ô favorable sort,
> Qui de deux innocents a diverti la mort;
> Qu'en plaisirs éternels votre douleur se change;
> Bénissons ce Héros, publions sa louange,
> Rendons à sa vertu des honneurs immortels,
> Et d'un commun dessein dressons-lui des Autels.
>
> (5.4.1483–88)

> O favorable destiny
> Who from two innocents has diverted death
> That into eternal pleasures your woes change

> Let us bless this Hero, let us publish praise of him.
> Let us offer to his virtue immortal honors
> And together let us build him altars.

"Let us bless this Hero, let us publish [or hear tell] praise of him." These last words create a cycle: They circle back to the beginning lines of the play, where the hero publicizes his own praises in the name of his desired deification. They also suggest the fate of the "poème dramatique" (dramatic poem) that spectators have just witnessed: its repetition—the next performance will take up this very charge. In the context of premodern material culture, it is also a cue to consider "performance" and "publication" as the broad and overlapping categories that they were. Just as print publication is today a kind of public "performance" of a text, the print culture of theater influenced theatrical performance in very specific ways. How plays were printed, and the fact that they became destined for print at all, influenced what playwrights wrote.

Furthermore, dramaturges like Jean Rotrou or, more strikingly, Pierre Corneille actively used print as another—sometimes primary—stage, carefully considering the use of stage directions, offering important prefaces, developing protocols for punctuation and capitalization that would indicate how certain lines were to be delivered. The dramaturge's text—our primary archive—contains the text's declamatory poetry, also external stage directions, and internal indications of players' gestures and stances. So there is a tension at the heart of seventeenth-century drama: Both poetry and performance, interpreted as at once published/pronounced text and memorable spectacle, became a handbook for future performances. *Hercule mourant* is an especially incarnated poetry, appealing both to verbal persuasion and corporeal performance, and attending to the tension that emerges from this dual appeal—and it is within this tension we locate a question of *endurance* in early modern performance, a notion that might be analogous to what performance-studies theorists have called *presence*.

## Performance Studies and Presence

It might seem terribly retrograde or wrongheaded to consider the staying power of early modern theater by appealing to contemporary performance studies theories, for presence is in a key way precisely the opposite of what much of contemporary performance studies seek to trace. I want to briefly rehearse some of the key concepts used in performance studies to consider the spatial and temporal dynamics of attending to spectacle, that is, the elaboration of and debate over what might be called the concept of *presence*. Although I will borrow this complex idea from performance studies, I hope to return it with a renewed sense of how and why theater works with violence as a radical context for such presence.

How it is that an actor inhabits what we call a character, which in turn is received by spectators as both real enough to warrant consideration but not so real as to be mistaken entirely for anything but spectacle, has been considered through the question of theatrical presence. Thus one of the founders of performance studies, Wallace Bacon, saw at work in an actor's performance two selves—performer *and* text—who both negotiate delimited but permeable boundaries separating them. It was by animating a text to the point of agency that Bacon saw the complexity of this notion of "presence" emerge, as a production of negotiation.[6]

The art of theater—the aesthetic regimes it mobilizes to contain these multiple levels of presence—and the problems this art confronts, have been deeply informed by philosophy's intervention into the ontological status of "presence." Jacques Derrida asserted that ontology raises the question of absence. If being, being here and now, finds its coherence and its contours by presupposing another—another place, another time (before or after the "not" of being)—the primacy of being as the major philosophical question of the Western tradition has thus been destabilized, forever tempered by Derrida's "trace" of that which "being" presupposed: absence, but also the prior, the future, the there, and the shuttling among these modes.[7] In Peggy Phelan's classic analysis performance is that which "becomes itself through disappearance;" its "only life is in the present."[8] Philip Auslander's examination of the ever-mediatized condition of "liveness" becomes pertinent here.[9] Arguing that there is no real ontological distinction between live forms and mediatized ones, Auslander allows us to consider that the sense of "here" and "now," the idea of an spatiotemporal immediacy that is the condition and impetus for a shared experience, may be generated through the fact of mediation, not its absence or erasure. Jon Erickson seems to take a completely different tack when he argues that "it is not the case that performance is somehow based or grounded 'in' time: rather performance actually produces time (or, if you will, a sense of time) for the audience."[10] However, I would wager that because this production of a specific *sense of time* is effected precisely through mediation, the *sense* produced is an affective response to and investment in the medial apparatus.

What kinds of "sense of time" can performance produce, and how do we apprehend its production? What precisely is the experience of this production? Gordon Coonfield and Heidi Rose suggest that presence is "an experience of 'thisness,'" an affirmation of the materiality and coexistence of the thing created in performance with those witnessing and therefore participating in that creation, however momentarily, however much cordoned off from the rest of life it may be. It is a *sense in time* of the "liveness" of even the unliving or the never-lived.[11] In this "post-postmodern" theatrical sense, the presence of performance is not disappearance or absence but the effect of the dynamic relationality created among perceivers and perceived that results in an object, a situation, a moment—the material, affectively defined "this" we have all experienced.

It is precisely based on this material connection, this "thisness" of performance, that I wish to consider how a play from the past might *persist*—not through an afterlife of its universal values, nor through any other form of death and return, or haunting, but through the ways its performances create a sense of ever-presence, or endurance. I also hope ultimately to offer, and I think this is the most interesting and useful part of this paradigm, a different way of understanding *what* and *how* we get what we get from theater; so I offer a different mode of both experience *and* interpretation.

It matters very much that my example is premodern, because this theater places particular demands on its audiences. It is by virtue of those demands that an audience gets something, experiences something. The particularity of premodern theater is not, however, in either the universality of its timeless values or its formidable distance from us. Rather, it is the way the constellation of epistemological and ontological structures (including, in the case of *Hercule mourant*, Neo-Stoicism and the function of the passions in creating shared affective ground) creates a certain temporal theater-going experience in which the presence of the drama is experienced in a particular way. The terms by which we generally think presence (the magic of "stage presence," the "miracle" of "transport" to different times and places, or conversely the notions of "vanishing, disappearance, and absence") belong to temporal regimes of both experience and interpretation that can be categorized under the rubric of suddenness. I will be advocating for something much slower—what I will be calling "endurance." This value, as a value of theater and of interpretation, might find its home in early modern theater in particular. But nowhere is the tension that creates endurance more paradoxically productive than in the burning moment—a paradox heightened by the ways in which invisibility and silence define that productive conflict between performance and poetry.

## The Enduring Hero

The key scene of *Hercule mourant*, the true crisis of this play and the reason why I think this play is exceptionally paradigmatic of a model of endurance, is also a moment of shock. It feels at first like an instance of epiphany. At the beginning of act 3, Hercule prepares a sacrifice intending to honor his father, Jupiter, secure his own deification, and compel an era of universal peace: effects to which he believes himself entitled.

Kneeling alongside his men, he begins to utter the invocation. Suddenly he must rise, thus interrupting his own prayer: "Mais quelle prompte flamme en mes veines s'allume?/Quelle soudaine ardeur jusqu'aux os me consume?" (3.1.645–46). (What sudden flame in my veins lights up/What quick heat consumes me to the bone?) In reaction to the internal assault, Hercule stands to counter the attack of this unanticipated foe, a gesture that will prove to be the last show of physical strength against his ultimate enemy. His assailant is nowhere to be seen, however: His torturer is a gift, the tunic offered by his wife, Déjanire, in an effort to reclaim his love. This critical state will last for nearly the rest of the play. From here until his fall in act 4, he will question the heavens, query his own body, seek a scapegoat, and—as reported in act 5, build his own funeral pyre. His protracted demise not only is the setting for his own laments and changes of heart, it is the catalyst for his actions and those of all others in the play. And because this is a Roman play made Christian, this protracted demise and the suffering it exhibits is also the basis for Hercule's ascension to the heavens, reminiscent of the ascension of Christ's resurrected body.

We can observe here briefly how integral the Christian story of the resurrection has been to a foundational habit of European theater, which has been to repeatedly offer versions of itself—repetitions of characters, reuse of stock scenes—to recycle its past; we have here again Carlson's "haunted stage" or theater as "memory machine."[12] Perhaps any play produced in a Christian context operates with this paradox of presence. A theatrical character dies and lives again, ascending to the heavens for eternal life. Furthermore, this same character is played by an actor who dies, lives eternally—and then does it again the next day. I think this play complicates even that story of revival and reliving through its practice of endurance.

## To Live Longer Than Forever: Enduring and Immortality

The author Jean Rotrou addresses this very issue in the dedication of this play to the kingdom's primary patron of the theater, the Prime Minister the Duc de Richelieu. In this dedication in which he announces the problem of presence as a form of endurance, Rotrou speaks on behalf of his protagonist, acting as a kind of translator:

> Il aurait été avantageux à Hercule que vos gardes lui eussent dénié l'entrée de votre cabinet, ils lui auraient épargné la honte de trembler; et de rougir, tout déifié qu'il est, lui qui n'étant encor que mortel ne sut jamais connaître la peur. Il s'oublie soi-même à l'abord de Vôtre Eminence, et reconnaît, Monseigneur, que vous faites aujourd'hui l'histoire dont Il n'a fait que la fable; mais vous l'avez flatté d'une espérance capable de le rassurer, . . . il préfère à son immortalité l'honneur qu'il va recevoir de vivre chez vous.

> It would have been advantageous to Hercule if your guards had denied him entry to your study; they would have spared him the shame of trembling and blushing, as deified as he is, he who mortal never knew fear. He forgets himself in your presence, Your Eminence, and recognizes, Sir, that you make the history of which he only made the fable; you have flattered him with a sense of hope capable of reassuring him; . . . and he prefers over his immortality the honor that he will receive of living with you.

Hercule is so nervous about appearing among the books in the cardinal's collection that he would have been better off having been denied entry than to suffer "the shame of trembling and blushing, as deified as he may be, he who, mortal, never once knew fear." The game of flattery is evident: Even immortal he knows more fear in the face of the great cardinal than he did as a mortal. Rotrou here mobilizes theatrical presence and simultaneously undoes it: Hercule is both an immortal character and a trembling visitor to the cardinal's palace; he is a deity with human traits; he has performed the play but is about to be part of another performance, one encased in stamped leather, for what happens inside the cardinal's doors? The ultimate apotheosis: Hercule will be shelved in the cardinal's vast library.

Lest we read this dedication as only a rehash of the poetry-as-immortality saw, which it is, partially, I should emphasize that in this ascent to bibliophilic greatness, Hercule is not ascending to another kind of immortality. No. This transformation of a deity into an object of collection appears so great an end to Hercule that "he prefers to his immortality that honor which he will receive of *living* with you." In other words, living is better than immortality—if I get to do so in Richelieu's library. This powerful invocation of "vivre" leans toward mortality as it evokes a comparison to the immortal, while it also puts pressure on another contrast: between the ceaseless nonlife of a character and the brief, albeit reiterated experience of the human actor who incarnates him. Rotrou then is imagining a moment in which Hercule is being received and honored, as if he were both a god stepping out of a fable and an actor at the hôtel de Bourgogne called on to visit His Eminence, when indeed, he is a character from a play in print. There is no separating actor from deity from fable; the difference between living and ever-living, or never-living, should not be discernible.

Through this performance in and of print, Rotrou is reaching for a model by which his character lives *even longer* than he would as a deity, something beyond immortality: an ongoingness that emphasizes vitality and not lack of death. The gesture's constitutive parts are intimately related to the subject of Rotrou's play about Hercule: transformation, apotheosis, strength, humility, and most important, living—or not living. Accordingly, the incarnated poetry of *Hercule mourant* stages, during the course of its unfolding, an endurance test. It is not without irony that this staging occurs through the protracted performance of dying.

## *The Burning Hero*

Appropriate to the play's title, Hercule's dying is not just the longest event of the play, but also its primary subject: Dying is the point of the play since the hero Hercule must die to become the deity Hercule. Yet dying is so important, and so protracted, that as a form of transformation it has a particular mechanics and a related logic that appear together in the first lines of the assault as a moment of reanimation: "Mais quelle prompte flamme en mes veines s'allume?" Before they become the first sign of death, the flames "light up" his veins, intensifying his physical action. Additionally, they cause him to move again, reorienting him away from the still, kneeling command of the sacrificer and toward the active and upright stance of the combatant. Instead of felling him, then, the poison urges him to move. These flames thus work within a logic of paradox, of revealing the stillness within life (the kneeling sacrificer), of interrupting speech to urge more speech, of infusing life as a way to indicate the end of life.

Although the legend from which it derives would indicate that what is truly stunning about Hercules is his apotheosis, this version turns that on its head by underscoring the event of dying as a process. It does so by turning his assailant, these slow invisible flames, into a kind of actor—who gives cause to Hercule to express his experience, to explore its significance, and even to alter his perspective on it, an actor with whom an audience must contend. This whole tragedy depends on the protracted presence of the flames and the power they have to generate understanding, an understanding that is only slowly unleashed. The temporality of tragedy, as Stanley Cavell has written, "demands a continuous attention to what is happening at each here and now, as if everything of significance is happening at this moment."[13] In *Hercule mourant* the tragic moment is concentrated even further and doubly so: It is one thing that happens, and to one character. Crucially, there is no moment of decision. If there are moments of action, these are the result of attending to a kind of literal interiority in an extended fashion. Hercule's dying is inevitable, yet at the same time he dies because he attends to his dying.

The flames lapping at him then allow for this death in two senses: They kill him, and by mobilizing him to feel their excruciating pain, they compel an extended poetics of query, doubt, self-examination. Their persistence even creates the conditions for his self-interrogation. But this is not an understanding from revelation, as in the moment of striking and rapid confession to which Phèdre is compelled by her self-administered Medean philters, which "j'ai fait couler dans mes brûlantes veines" (5.7.1637), (I let flow through my burning veins), and which we might witness during the few minutes of her dying tirade. That Hercule's pain lasts for so much of the play sets another rhythm entirely, and another relation: The flames become something like a character in the play.

For Hercule, the extended presence of the flames means that they repeatedly interact with their victim, compelling both speech and act. That said, there is no dialogue; the flames never speak. If there is no conversation between executioner and victim, the flames speak their piece as it were, they make their mark by forcing an acknowledgment that they are there even if they cannot be seen or heard. It is then the silent persistence of this killer within Hercule that allows for Hercule's confrontation and gradual understanding of his death. Rotrou's particular rendition of Hercule's death, then, compels us to measure the tension between Stoic reference and Neo-Stoic culture, between poetry and performance, and, as a product of those tensions, the work of the experience of tragic performance with and upon audiences such as ours today, schooled in the spectacularly ephemeral, and no longer in the enduringly invisible.

Unlike plays that begin at a moment of aftermath (Corneille's *Rodogune*) or at a time prior to a monumental event (Racine's *Iphigénie*), or those that begin *in medias res* (*Horace*), in his eponymous play Hercule arrives in limbo. Existing in a moment between his past heroism and his future deification, Hercule is astonished that his apotheosis has not occurred yet. The reason for this state soon becomes clear—Hercule's love for the slave Iole and

Déjanire's fury at this newest infidelity has angered Hera. But Hercule's status on stage is from the first scene highly ambiguous and ambivalent. It is not so much that we do not know what will happen to him—Hercule's fate was inscribed in history—but rather to what we will attend during the spectacle—how we will get to an apotheosis. Accordingly, the first act characterizes Hercule by his heroic deeds, the greatness of which are tempered by his foibles and unpredictable disposition. A philanderer, Hercule's passion for Iole hovers just at the edge of violence; there is a thoroughly bizarre tableau scene in this act in which Hercule has his head on Iole's lap as she is working on a tapestry and lamenting his murder of her family. A braggart, Hercule's deeds are transmuted on his tongue from triumph over adversity and rational harmony with the forces of the world, to proof of overweening pride.

The first acts of the play also suggest poetically that such excess of flames—of passion, of pride—are contagious. Hercule's troubling pursuit of Iole is matched by the uncontrolled fury of his wife, Déjanire, in the next act. Her fury against his infidelity is articulated through a vocabulary of raging fire. If the first act of the play exposes the precarious moral position in which even a legendary hero can find himself unwittingly, the second act exposes the extent of this problem: Passion is contagious, and so affirms the problem of moderation for Stoics. Accordingly, Déjanire's language is that of ultimate harm and limitless pain: "Si mon forfait est grand, mon mal est infini" (2.2.388). (If my crime is great, my evil is infinite.) Any assertions of limits are themselves ruses: Déjanire's nurse Luscinde expresses fear of the consequences of Jupiter's reaction to Déjanire's murderous desires. But her suggestion of moderation is precisely what will lead to Hercule's downfall. Déjanire demonstrates this when she invokes one of the dominant figurative topoi of the play, that of the flame, as another multivalent figure of passion, one signaling both the eternal energy of love and the power of destruction. Prior to deciding to use Nessus's poisoned gift to revive her husband's passion for her, she furiously declares her revenge on him: "J'éteindrai de son sang avec ses sales flammes,/Les torches de l'hymen qui joignit nos deux âmes" (2.2.393). (With the cursed flames of his blood, I will extinguish/marriage's torches which united our two souls.) While the "sales flammes" are clearly metaphors for Hercule's illicit passion, the obvious materiality of fire signals the contagion of love's passion as well as that of revenge.

This contagion is further underscored when Déjanire turns instead to the power of enchantment and the magical blood of the centaur Nessus:

> Là de ses fortes mains une corne il s'arrache,
> Et pleine de son sang; tiens (me dit-il) et tache
> Un de ses vêtements de ce sang précieux
> S'il est jamais blessé d'autres que de tes yeux.
> Il aura la vertu de te rendre son âme,
> Et le fera brûler de sa première flamme.
>
> (2.2.473–78)

> At that, with his strong hands he tears out his horn
> All full of blood; here (says he to me), as he stains
> One of his garments with this precious blood
> If he is ever struck by eyes other than yours,
> It will have the strength to return his soul to you;
> And will make him burn with his first flame.

Déjanire's account of Nessus's oracular instructions in case of Hercule's straying depends on the multivalent vocabulary of burning as both physical harm and deep passion. Her misunderstanding of this pronouncement—confusing amorous passion with real flames, mistaking Nessus's dying act of apparent sympathy with his last will for revenge against Hercule—will lead her to poison her husband. Her drive to alter the order of things without quelling her passion is a direct consequence of Hercule's own confusion of *virtu*—strength—with the unbridled force of passion. In this way, and up until act 3's sacrifice, *Hercule mourant* remains indebted to its Imperial Stoic roots in offering no solution to the very Stoic dilemma of how a hero's political, civic *virtu* may be contained and so transformed into moral *vertu*.

What changes, then, in act 3? What allows for Hercule's apotheosis? The crisis of the play is the transition of Hercule from sacrifice-giver to the sacrifice itself, a sacrifice who attempts, *as sacrifice*, in the middle of being sacrificed, to achieve a kind of mastery over himself before giving that self up to the heavens. The play does not seem to propose a moment when this transformation occurs, an alexandrine of revelation. Instead, the move from Hercule the hero to Hercule the law-giving Christic figure is staged as an experience and condition of burning. So if this play meditates upon this dying, this transformation as not an instant conversion, if it retains our expectations—of an ascension—quite clearly, it also allows an accompanying experience of witnessing such duration and depth.

Again, the sacrificial moment presents itself as a rehearsal of this transformation. It is worth quoting this moment in its entirety here, since Hercule's performance of pain operates on several levels, including in the printed verse:

> Qu'une éternelle paix règne entre les mortels,
> Qu'on ne verse du sang que dessus les Autels;
> . . . . . . . . . . . . . . .
> Et que le foudre en fin demeure après mes faits
> Dans les mains de mon père un inutile faix!
> *Se levant, il dit:*
> Mais quelle prompte flamme en mes veines s'allume?
> Quelle soudaine ardeur jusqu'aux os me consume?
> Quel poison communique à ce linge fatal
> La vertu qui me brûle? Ô tourment sans égal!
> Ouvre Enfer à mes cris tes cavernes profondes,
> Prête contre ce feu, le secours de tes ondes;
> Souffre Alcide là bas, non pas comme autrefois
> Pour désarmer la Parque et ruiner ses lois,
> Mais Alcide souffrant d'insupportables peines,
> Et qui porte déjà les enfers dans ses veines;
> Quoi ? Ce linge brûlant, à mon corps attaché,
> Par mes propres efforts n'en peut être arraché?
> De moment en moment ce poison devient pire?
> Ô rage! Ô désespoir! Ô sensible martyre!
>
> (3.1.639–58)

> May an eternal peace reign among mortals,
> May blood only be spilled over altars;
> . . . . . . . . . . . . . . .
> And may lightning remain, after my deeds;
> In the hands of my father, a useless burden!
> *Standing up, he says:*
> What sudden flame in my veins lights up
> What quick heat consumes me to the bone?
> What poison endows this fatal cloth
> With the strength to burn me? O matchless torment!
> Open to my cries, Hell, your deep caverns
> Offer against this fire the succor of your waters
> Suffer Alcide down there, but not like before

> To disarm Fate and destroy her laws
> But an Alcide suffering from unbearable pain
> Who already carries hell in his veins
> What? This burning cloth, attached to my body,
> By my own efforts cannot be ripped off?
> From one moment to the next this poison worsens?
> Oh rage! Oh hopelessness! Oh undeniable suffering!

The sharp pains that shock Hercule out of his prayer also change the spatial and temporal scope of his address. From a hero's benediction articulating universal and eternal peace, he shifts focus radically inward, to his body and to the moment at hand. Eschewing the heavens, and quickly apostrophizing the underworld, he beseeches it to open its doors and receive him, ending his present pain. Already a different person, he apostrophizes even himself—"Alcide souffrant"—Alcide being Hercule's birth name.

From this moment, the key words *ardeur* and *flamme* shift from metaphors of affect and passion to their most material designations indicating heat, burning, and destruction, a shift that signals a turn toward a new order, in which the Stoic becomes the Neo-Stoic, the Christian whose faith will ground his fortitude. The Neo-Stoic self's moral ability to overcome the problems of the passions is expressed in some of the key words of the play, in a semantic field whose transformation operates through the moment of interrupted and transformed sacrifice. In the play, the passion that so worried the Stoics becomes the Passion of Christ, but only through a manifestly physical transformation. "Ardor" initially denotes the vivacity of a great hero destined to realize godly feats, before emerging on stage as the index of carnal desire on the verge of its inevitable turn toward violence. It is only in act 3, when Hercule feels the first effects of the poison, that ardor veers away from the metaphorical, to denote the physical sensation of burning. Similarly, the use of "flames" is informed at once by the poetic and philosophical tradition: They represent love (both corrupt and uncorrupt), passion, and the uncontained heat of fire that burns bodies. Flames themselves, constituting a primary essence of the world, are of course a Stoic topos. By the end of the play, however, this essential element is forged into a theater of Hercule's grace. He has fully embraced the physical pain of his state, even going so far as to prepare his own *bûcher*, or pyre. Hercule's move throughout the play, away from the Stoic cautionary tale of the hero whose passionate *vertu* was never fully in his control, and toward the subject who is resigned and therefore full of grace, represents a Neo-Stoic exemplum.

## Burning as Spectacle

This Neo-Stoic order is characterized by a turn toward the material and the physical, an attention to the stuff of ourselves that does not endure. To that end, Rotrou's version depends on a crucial revision to the structure of *Hercules Oetaeus*. In the Seneca-era drama, Hercules' suffering, his killing of a servant, and his attempt to quench the fire by jumping into the sea are all described by his son Hyllus. In Rotrou, these elements are rendered as embodied and spoken events. Hercule's realization that he is being attacked by an invisible enemy is an echo of Hyllus's quotation of his father acknowledging the source and meaning of his pain: "Non furor mentem abstulit,/furore gravius istud atque ira malum est:/in me iuvat saevire." (Madness has not stolen away my senses;/this evil is graver than madness or wrath;/it delights to rage against me.)[14] Rotrou not only puts Hercule's words back in his own mouth, he also makes what Hyllus reports of his father the very matter of Hercule's work on stage throughout his dying; the Senecan Hyllus reports his father's insane murder of the servant Lychas, whereas Rotrou's Hercule actually chases him offstage, "une massue à la main," his massive wooden club in hand, thus serving as a metonym for his violence, and so as a spectacular promise made to the audience of murderous brutality occurring beyond their sight.

The spectacularization of Hercule's physicality in Rotrou is confirmed by the play's performance archive. In constrast to Rotrou's sources we know that *Hercule mourant* was designed as an ornate and elaborate visual and auditory feast for its first public. A description of it is in Laurent Mahelot's *Mémoire des décorations du théâtre de l'Hôtel de Bourgogne au XVIIe siècle*. Mahelot's account begins succinctly: "Le théâtre doit être superbe" (The theater should be superb).[15] The objects enumerated and decor described are either integral to the action or they contribute to the symbolic landscape of the drama, including one side of the stage where there is a hidden "temple de Jupiter, bâtit à l'antique et enfermé d'arcades autour de l'autel, et que l'on puisse tourner autour de l'autel" (Temple of Jupiter, built in the ancient stule, with an altar surrounded by arcades so that one can walk around it), as well as "une cassolette et autres ornemens" (cassolette and other ornaments), a statue of Jupiter and four small pyramids painted with flames. On the other side, Mahelot designates, "une montagne où l'on monte devant le peuple et descendre [*sic*] par derrière . . . dessous la montagne doit être une chambre funèbre remplie de Larmes, le tombeau d'Hercule superbe" (A mountain which can be climbed up facing the audience and down in the back . . . under the mountain is a funereal room filled with Tears,

Hercule's superbe tomb). On this side too, we find "trois Pyramides, deux vases où sortent deux flammes de feu, en peinture tous les travaux d'Hercule y doivent paraître, le dit tombeau doit être caché" (three pyramids, two vases from which flames shoot, all of Hercule's labors must be painted, the aforementioned tomb must be hidden). The machinery of the play's final scene is described in detail, with "un tonnere," to make thunder-like noise, as well as a basket for Hercule's descent as a deity that was likely equipped with some pyrotechnical capacity.

The many objects enumerated and the decor described indeed seem integral to the action or they contribute to the symbolic landscape of the drama, and any surfeit seems also in keeping with the thematics of the play.[16] There is an important tension, however, between the drama's central problem and its setting as Mahelot records it. That is, Hercule's burning both conforms to this spectacularity and deviates from it. There is the remarkable stage direction that interrupts Hercule's prayer, which the play's first printed edition materializes by centering it among the verses, in contrast to most that appear in the margins. As we have seen, this gesture of rising is a terrific rupture, going even so far as to halt the initial primary gesture of this scene: Hercule's sacrifice. The sacrifice begins fourteen lines prior, with Hercule "*se mettant à genou*," kneeling, as a marginal stage direction indicates. His rising in the middle interrupts the sacrifice but also undoes or rewinds the ritual. Further, in a move opposite to that of another self-sacrifice in a tragedy performed forty years later, where Racine's Phèdre will also burn from within from a poison coursing through her veins, Hercule rises instead of falling. Also in contrast with Phèdre, who falls twice (once because of her passions regarding Hippolyte, once because of her death), Hercule rises once here as prefiguring his apotheosis and assumption to the heavens as a deity.

Thus, Hercule's rise in recognition of his pain is symbolically linked through performance to his apotheosis. Both bodily actions, accompanied by verse, draw on the way the body's performance to a certain extent makes sense of the words, and even renders them redundant. Here, actions are not just central to the meaning of the poetry; they indicate the poetry's force and its limits. Because Hercule does not simply expire but indulges in a protracted and verbal dying—uttering more than 275 lines while aflame, the tension between performance and poetry is put into relief more significantly.

Arguably, burning on a seventeenth-century stage would likely be the opposite of spectacularity: No actor would be immolated; there would be no visible flames real or feigned. On stage, the actor's rhetorical perfor-

Figure 17. "Hercules on his funeral pyre at Mt. Oeta." Engraving by Gilles Rousselet after Guido Reni. Marsh Collection, National Museum of American History, Smithsonian Institution.

mance of suffering would bear the burden of conveying the effects of the fire. Similarly, premodern images of Hercules generally effaced the power of the flames, as in Gilles Rousselet's engravings after Guido Reni's paintings of Hercules. These works emphasize the hero's phenomenal physique, not his demise. Rotrou's verse and dramaturgy play with the invisibility of the flames. Hercule's epistemological dilemma is one he shares with the audience: the problem of identifying something that he cannot see. The invisible assailant renders both gesture and language more urgent, and compels a greater complicity between them. We can see here why Hercule's presence exemplifies quite the opposite of what has been identified as the "baroque" trend of questioning appearances, of veils. Whereas Eugène Green asserts that "the baroque body has no reality in itself, existing only insofar as it renders visible a heretofore hidden reality," Hercule's body is all he can trust.[17] Witnesses to his devotion to the knowledge and experience of his body, we are called on to believe that which we cannot see. Behind the veil of the hero is a man transforming into weakness. If paradoxically this confirms the rift between appearance and essence, between mind and body, note that Hercule's discourse reverses the poles of these values. What we see—a healthy body—is not what we get. And yet it is the body we should trust, not the racing mind, stunned by such corporeal rebellion and openly ignorant of its causes.

The state of wasting from within permits full functionality on the stage—unlike death by sword, drowning, monster, or battle. Up until the moment of succumbing, there are no physical gestures that signal this failing, and so the dying person may continue to ponder, investigate, and articulate the very state of dying. It is a perfect way to die philosophically in public since its gradual and invisible nature invites and even demands introspection. Hercule's transition from unstable hero to madman to resigned and finally Stoic sage occurs through the display of this attention to the instability of the self and the confrontation of failure. The first recognition is of the impossibility of knowing or responding to the enemy in the way of a warrior:

> Pour sauver du mépris ma constance abattue,
> Je ne puis exalter l'ennemi qui me tue
> Je combats sans effet d'invincibles efforts,
> Et ce n'est pas un mont qui m'écrase le corps.
> Je me sens étouffer, je rends l'âme, et ma fosse
> N'est pas sous Pélion, sous Olympe, ou sous Osse.
> Je doute de quel trait la mort touche mon coeur

> Je me trouve vaincu sans savoir mon vainqueur,
> Et je meurs, ô malheur ! sur tous incomparable,
> Sans pouvoir en ma mort faire un coup mémorable.
>
> (3.2 717–27)

> (Even) to save from contempt my constancy felled,
> I cannot even praise this enemy who is killing me:
> I combat with no effect invincible blows
> And it is not a mountain which is crushing my body
> I am suffocating, I give up my soul; and my grave
> will be neither on Pelion, Olympus, or Ossa.
> I know not in what aspect death is touching my heart.
> I find myself vanquished without knowing my victor,
> And I die, oh affliction! Worse than everything:
> Unable, upon my death, to deal a memorable blow.

There is no enemy to address, there is no target of wrath to attack. Expressed through a grammar of negation and a lexicon of absence, death, and impossibility, this unknowability is first what allows Hercule to come into his own body as the site of his mortality. This can occur because, in a fundamental way, he has nothing but his body. The essential Neo-Stoic value of "constancy," that inner strength which allows one to be unaffected by external accidents, is "felled," yet Hercule does not know by what. He must become and remain an object of his own inquiry. The force of this rhetorical performativity is amplified by the accompanying apostrophe personifying pain. With pain a subject, he becomes object: "Ô tourment sans pareil! Ô désespoir ! Ô rage !/Ô mal plus fort qu'Alcide, et plus que son courage!" (Oh torment without equal! Oh despair! Oh rage!/Oh evil stronger than Alcide, and greater than his courage!) (4.1.925–26). When the *moi* can be retained, it is as a frustrated source of knowledge; the divorce between past self and present condition is so total that he is unable to understand his body's predicament beyond the material state of its combustion: "Moi-même je m'ignore en ce triste accident,/Et ce qui fut Alcide est un bûcher ardent" (4.1.939–40). (Even I myself do not know myself in this sad situation,/He who was Alcide is now a burning fire.) In many ways this introspection is of a piece with Neo-Stoic theater's attention to "the subjectivity of the victim . . . [in an] attempt to generate a new evaluation of violence by looking at both the commonality and the irreducibility of the pain it inflicts."[18] Hercule's introspective meditation is particularly attentive, however, not just to the pain but to the epistemological quandary it causes.

The more Hercule questions the connection between his past history and his present decay, the more the brutality of his pain turns him toward himself. But the more his physical presence becomes the object of his inquiry, the greater the cleavage between the speaker and his body, underscored through demonstratives exposing the difference:

Mais je sens par le feu ma voix même étouffée,
Et ce corps dénué de sang, et de vigueur
Après tant de tourments succombe à sa langueur,
(*Il tombe comme évanoui.*)

(4.2.1043–44)

But I feel now even my voice suffocated by the fire
And this body drained of blood, and of vigor
After so much torment succumbing to its languor.
(*He falls, fainting.*)

Here, in his last appearance onstage as a mortal, Hercule appears as a body emptying itself of its essence, its "blood" and "marrow" leaving merely a "speaking shadow." By offering a firsthand account of that experience which we witness but cannot actually see, Hercule produces through performance his own presence as a presence on the other side of life from us, the living—not death but dying as a form of mortal endurance.

Because Hercule's own demise is a twofold mystery (the mystery of the body's undoing and the mystery of what is killing him) the resolution of one part—the discovery of Nessus's curse and Déjanire's mistake—allows Hercule to resign himself, almost entirely, to his end. In so doing, he also recedes into silence and absence, two self-erasures that nevertheless underscore the power of his body in its act of persistent decomposition.

He leaves the stage at the end of act 4, returning only in the form of description by Philoctète in act 5. This hypotyposis of Hercule's last moments is a vivid depiction of action, action (not passion) *spreading* from Hercule's own body to those of his associates. As he fells trees for the pyre, he enlists his men to work as hard as he. Echoing references to Hercule's past labors, Philoctète portrays a singular labor using multiple verbs that together convey the physicality of its realization:

Quand il eut résolu cette mort inhumaine,
Il fit nos propres mains complices de sa peine.
. . . . . . . . . . . . . . . . . .
Lui-même le premier travaille à sa ruine,

Il coupe, arrache, rompt, jusques à la racine.
La forêt retentit à ce trouble nouveau,
L'un frappe sur le chêne et l'autre sur l'ormeau.

(5.1.1205–12)

When he accepted this inhuman death,
He made our own hands accomplices to his end.
. . . . . . . . . . . . . . .
Himself the first [to] work toward his ruin
He cuts, pulls, breaks, down to the root.
The forest echoes with this new commotion,
One chopping the oak; the other the elm.

In the final portrayal of a forest and its denizens being consumed by a phoenix-like hero, rising up to his last challenge, Hercule's unspeaking role in this tableau is defined by eloquent action. Hercule's ultimate silence—his death—becomes a sign of his redemption. In doing so, however, it is first lodged as a sign of his endurance. It is a corporeal persistence that works beyond the word, yet is expressed only through the fiber of poetry.

## Endurance and Epiphany

When we are called, as readers and spectators, to "bless this hero," to "publish his praise," we are aware that such publication demands the reliving of this suffering, of the hero's and perhaps of ours, as recent witnesses to this spectacle of suffering. Our attention to how theater, through its combination of poetics and embodied spectacle, *might slow down* the moment of crisis, deserves attention for the ways it asks us to attend to and interpret theatrical action differently. I think of Hans Ulrich Gumbrecht's development of an approach to hermeneutics that tempers the "meaning-oriented" culture that our intellectual world has become, in which the work of interpretation is something performed upon our objects of inquiry. "If we attribute a meaning to a thing that is present, that is, if we form an idea of what this thing may be in relation to us, we seem to attenuate, inevitably, the impact that this thing can have on our bodies and our senses."[19] In his reorientation of aesthetic experience to what he calls "an oscillation (and sometime interference) between 'presence effects' and 'meaning effects,'" Gumbrecht embraces a material, even embodied, and decidedly premodern approach. He even aligns it with the mind-set, if not the era, of the medieval period. And he suggests that "presence effects" take the form of "a knowledge acquired at once through one's mind and body." It is a question of a suddenness, an "intensity of feeling," even "an epiphany."[20] The epiphanic moment—the moment of revelation—is the experience we also associate the most with that very old justification for theater's utility, *catharsis*: that quick, sudden purgation of "pity and fear," as we think Aristotle wrote, a possession that is driven through terror or horror, like an exorcism.[21]

This mode of apprehension takes up almost no time or space; it is in this regard most closely aligned with revelation in the material sense: an unveiling. The compaction of time is structural, as Paul de Man observed: "Strictly speaking, an epiphany cannot be a beginning, since it reveals and unveils what, by definition, could never have ceased to be there. Rather, it is the rediscovery of a permanent presence which has chosen to hide itself from us—unless it is we who have the power to hide from it."[22] De Man raises the question of our role in creating the epiphanic revelation, whether in our willful erasure of "what, by definition could never have ceased to be there," or in our potential to hide ourselves. Either way, the idea of a "permanent presence" suggests a paradox within our Gumbrechtian model of a "production of presence." How does one *produce* something that was already there? De Man might wish to point us toward an ontological quandary regarding our or the object's constitution, but his observation unwittingly signals an important dimension to the production of an already existing presence: its temporal and iterative qualities. Why must discovery, or rediscovery, be sudden? Why are revelation and unveiling always considered instantaneous? Why must the temporality of coming to change be conceived as a quick one? What if epiphany, and other forms of transformative understanding, occurred through a slow unveiling?

There are some models for this kind of slow understanding. Jennifer Roberts, in a short but influential article, suggests a pedagogical approach to art history that might be called "slow looking," in which patience for observation is achieved through hours of examination of one object. In T. J. Clark's exemplar of this approach, *The Sight of Death*, he offers a record of several months' near-daily visits to observe two Poussin paintings side-by-side. The record—part diary, part palimpsestic revisionist ekphrasis—is a testimony to how painting's complexity both calls for verbal engagement and resists any clear narrative of its work, and how the pictorial is irreducibly material.[23]

These models contrast to the traditional modes of academic understanding, which generally follow a discovery model—what Michael Chaney has archly called the "surge of eureka," in which scholars all of a sudden comprehend the essential truth embedded in an object.[24] I don't think it's a coincidence that these critiques of the epiphanic mode of understanding come from art historians, whose discipline developed around an overwhelmingly visual and place-based notion of aesthetic experience. Like theater historiography, the scholarly principles of art history emerged in the nineteenth century. So it's no surprise that a nineteenth-century regime of aesthetic experience has come to define and dominate both disciplines, upset perhaps in the late twentieth century by the art and theory that emerged from poststructuralism and developed in performance studies.

If theater is a medium that is particularly well-suited to exposing the multilayered nature of temporality, then a theater criticism and history that foregrounds the ways in which an audience—spectator, auditor, reader—participates in these various layers, confronts them and lives with them, must be developed. Indeed, one might say it is this very space of confrontation that is the "present moment of theater." Then what if the "presence effects" of theater, its cathartic impact, were experienced, and interpreted, as a slow, insistent process whose material and epistemological dimensions must work upon us as we on them? Rotrou surely never meant to propose an alternative form of theatrical experience, catharsis, or a different mode of interpretation, nor did he pretend to see in *Hercule mourant* a justification for the theater, but our witnessing of Hercule's death even in print—all two acts of it—can suggest to us how the theatrical scene is an imperfect but singular locus for this kind of experience. It compels us to constantly measure our reactions against those of our company, while accepting that the affect we experience is ours alone. Derived perhaps from a solitary experience, neither catharsis nor humanistic interpretation is ultimately, finally, anything but a slow and collective—sometimes burning—experience.

CHAPTER 4

# Flying toward Futurity: Spectacularity and Suspension

As we have seen, as it is a feature of the Medean paradigm to refuse the march of time as either eternal or progressivist, so it is also a feature of Medean theater that the violence it necessarily performs contributes to the interruption of temporal continuities. Nearly thirty years after *Médée*, Pierre Corneille returned in 1660 to the originary Medean myth—that of the Golden Fleece. We might recall that the 1634 tragedy—the first Medean moment of the seventeenth-century theater—elaborated Médée's gown as the centerpiece of a dramaturgy of violence that elaborated a self neither self-generated nor isolated from others but embedded in the inescapability of a network of forces: those of history, knowledge, and politics.

It might be tempting to consider this examination, then, of the Golden Fleece as a kind of prequel, a return to something not explored in *Médée*. But this would be to privilege a linearity of narrative and a progressive sense of history, which—as discussed in Chapter 2—seems not to obtain in the case of Medea. The Medean force of theater refuses both of these in favor of a temporality that, spiraling out from its 1634 moment of crystallization, seems to return back to itself, touching upon similar preoccupations with different dimensions and outcomes. Refusing any progressivist narrative of figures, concepts, and aesthetics is also historically sound—perhaps paradoxically so, for a modern reader. Such rejection of a progressivist history supports current understandings of the nature of temporality and historicity in the premodern period, whether we consider it as cyclical, recurring, providential, or even without a discernible pattern.[1] Such a nature informed the Medea myth itself in specific ways, Accordingly, *La Conquête de la Toison d'or* appears to stage a return of *Médée*, but it warrants an examination of the much greater complexity of temporality which it presents.

Written in the late 1650s, *La Conquête* was retrofitted a few years later at the end of the Thirty Years' War to celebrate Louis XIV's marriage to the Infanta of Spain (known as Marie-Thérèse in France), as stipulated in the Treaty of the Pyrenees ending the war. After a Prologue allegorizing the established peace and the ensuing marriage, the play recounts the familiar story of Jason and his Argonauts' conquest of the Golden Fleece at the end of the world: the faraway kingdom of Colchis, ruled by King Aeëtes with his witchy daughter Medea. The play repeats familiar elements: the princess Médée's love for Jason, her help for the Fleece's theft from her father Aète's kingdom, and their flight aboard the *Argos* toward Greece. The narrative is embellished both with pastoral-like explorations of the vagaries of love and also a great number of displays of current technological innovations to stage machinery, allowing for such special effects as scene changes, flying, aerial battles, celestial thrones, and a giant moving shell.

The usual story about this retrofitting suggests that Corneille was enlisted by the marquis de Sourdéac, an amateur engineer enthralled by the marvelous potential of the period's innovations in stage machinery, to mount *La Conquête* at Sourdéac's château de Neufbourg, in honor of the royal marriage. In this version the play's authors are willing propagandists in the machine of Louis XIV's state-fashioning.[2] Corneille would have carried this will to Paris, where it soon took three initial forms: First the Théâtre du Marais staged the play again and second Corneille published the text of the play, as was his strategy. But he also published the *Desseins de la Toison d'or*, an account of the production that detailed the poetic events of the play but, more significantly and at great length, the marvels of the stage machinery. Published in an octavo and a more impressive folio edition, the *Desseins* follows print conventions for theater. Beyond even its subject matter, the play has structural echoes to Corneille's *Médée* while, in the machinery it uses to create its spectacular effects, it is the heir to his 1650 *Andromède* and an important precursor to opera.[3] Overlapping with the play but itself a distinct artifact, the *Desseins* suggests that the perfor-

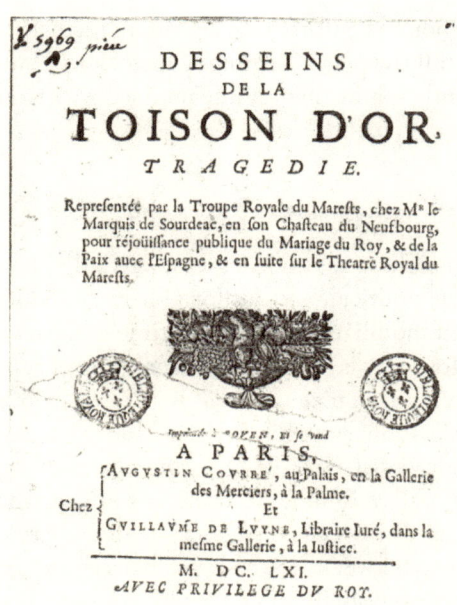

Figure 18. Title page, Pierre Corneille, *Desseins de la Toison d'or*. Source: Bibliothèque nationale de France.

mance of *La Conquête de la Toison d'or* exceeded that of a regular theatrical production.

Interpretations of *La Conquête* acknowledge this excess, by signaling variously the multiple historical contexts it invokes: Greek history, the play's immediate political context of a royal marriage, and Corneille's own theater history. Can a play address all of those contexts? How then do we understand the various planes of experience, or history, influencing our interpretation of *La Conquête*? We can't seem to help but place it some twenty or thirty years after Corneille's *Médée*; we understand it to be contemporaneous with Louis XIV's marriage to Marie-Thérèse; we might see it as treading on a threshold to lyric opera's full blooming in the next decades. We also consider how it creates rupture or continuity relative to other temporal markers: how it is in harmony with other propagandist elements of the postwar period in which it was presented, how it picks up the story of Jason and Medea before the events at Corinth, how it seems to break with the tragic discourse of sovereignty in Corneille's oeuvre, and how it seems a tellingly odd choice for a marriage play. All of these markers create a story about the evolution of this spectacle and therefore determine and undergird its value. This value is determined, then, not just by what the play says about its culture's own sense of historicity—what François Hartog might call the play's "regime of historicity" but—and perhaps even more importantly—how that regime intersects with our own relation to the past, present, and future.[4]

## The Past's Future: Theater and Allegory

How might it be possible to set aside, at least partially, these progressivist narratives of literary, political, and authorial history to look more closely at how the play itself mobilizes questions of time as a part of its story and its performance? How easy is it for us to discern what a rupture or disruption is within an premodern text and what is rather part of a local concept of temporality? Philosophers of history have long debated the extent to which our "modernity" distinguishes itself by virtue of a specific shift in perceptions of temporality. Reinhart Koselleck's understanding of modernity as "future oriented" depends on a contrast with a premodern temporality in which any gap between "the space of experience" and the "horizon of expectations" was very small indeed.[5] This understanding of modern temporality is interesting for what it says about a premodern *mentalité* and how it locates such a mind-set.

Koselleck's paradigm for understanding premodern temporality is a painting, Albrecht Altdorfer's 1529 depiction of the fourth-century BCE Battle of Alexander at Issus. In Koselleck's reading, two elements in particular suggest a double conflation of historical time. First, flags carried during the battle, recording the eventual dead of each regiment, suggest that the battle's outcome is already known at the moment of its crisis. Second, while the Greek Alexander fought the Persians, the painting figures his enemies in Turkish dress, and the Greeks in sixteenth-century European dress, pinning the battle to a conflict more local in both time and place: the defense of Vienna against the Ottoman Empire by Maximilian in 1529, the year of the painting's creation. As Alexander and Maximilian's campaigns "merge in exemplary manner," according to Koselleck, such anachronism indicates not a resistance to or elimination of historical time, but of a particular experience of it: "Present and past were enclosed within a common historical plane."[6] In Koselleck's paradigm, the historical time of the subjects of Altdorfer's painting was not just double—the past of Alexander, the present of Maximilian—but triple: Those spectators of the painting who knew the outcomes of both battles occupied what we would consider the future. The battle "thus is not only contemporary; it simultaneously appears to be timeless."[7] As Koselleck argues in the same essay, up until the 1700s, the eschatological hermeneutics characteristic of Christianity also dominated temporal conceptions of what was to come: The future, in the form of the rapture, literally was known. In this cultural mind-set past, present, and future as experiences are not distinguished by notions of progress, evolution, or primitivism. Oracles, astrology, and the like, popular at the time, also attest, for Koselleck, to the knowability of the future in the temporality of the now.

Might the topics which drew premodern dramaturges, and are so characteristic of seventeenth-century French elite culture, be available for some of the same analyses as Altdorfer's painting? If we bracket Koselleck's particular interest in meditating on the contours of futurity as it defines modernity, and instead turn our attention to how he sees in the premodern artifact a temporal sensibility that warrants a particular kind of interpretation—one that allows for the past and the near present to occupy the same plane of experience as that of the future—we can consider how the past was often deployed in concert with something like an eternal present.

Taken generally from ancient history and mythology, figures of *histoire* and *fable*—like Tamerlane, Sophonisba, Cleopatra, Hercules, and Achilles—belonged both to the historical past even as they were embedded in the contemporary culture. Prefatory material to plays featuring these characters asserts the historical context, while the themes explored validate contemporary notions of sovereignty, virtue, and the like. Arguably such "exemplary merging" could be seen as characteristic of *grand-siècle* royal aesthetics in general, producing the figure of Louis XIV as Apollo, the Roi-soleil, or of France as the New Rome. In this way, the political-aesthetic program of the seventeenth century seems to complement Koselleck's understanding of its temporality; interpretations of complex figures admit the past and present in order to inform a future that is utterly knowable and secured.

In some visual arts, and in certain forms of literary production, that sensibility is expressed through the idea of allegory, which, in Angus Fletcher's classic formula, "says one thing and means another,"[8] though it often does so through a complex system of signification, creating a network of meanings and interpretations. Allegories "lead us to imagine a set of meanings of the other side of [a] hermeneutic wall. In political and cultural terms, these meanings lying on the other side of the wall comprise parts of the whole of an ideology—its commentary and interpretation." Premodern allegories in particular seek, despite and even through their complexity, to stabilize meaning.[9] Koselleck's premodern temporality is that of allegory. The temporal relationship among Altdorfer's signs is a kind of stable unity, where the signified can be understood only by accepting the single and therefore simultaneous horizon of temporality along which all the events—and their meanings—can be situated. The future of the premodern allegory is a flat one; it is embedded in the problem uniting the figures that constitute the allegorical complex. Layers of signification do not change the outcome, or the resolution of the allegorical problem. This flat futurity is particularly striking in the theatrical genre of the allegory, wherein conflicts among personifications of abstract values or states reiterate those very values; an allegory's outcome is never at stake. Just as in Altdorfer's painting, where the joining of the figures of Alexander and Maximilian into one, leading one army, confirms the outcome of both battles and indeed of the as yet unfought ultimate battle of Christianity, allegorical art's ideology is visible in the interplay among its layers of signification and performance, not in the resolution of any conflict.

Through such multiple layers, certain aesthetic forms deploy the distant past productively alongside references to a contemporary political or cultural context. The genre of allegory in drama exacerbated the potential for these temporal planes to inhabit the same spaces, as well as for them to collide, creating a crisis. And in addition to the particularity of the theatrical medium, the specificity of the Medean myth offers new dimensions to an inquiry into premodern temporality. *La Conquête de la Toison d'or* exacerbates the tensions in allegory. It stages the confrontation of these temporal structures and embodies their crisis through its performance of technological innovation.

## *Between Propaganda and Performance: The Action of the* Conquête

Even interpretations of *La Conquête* that eschew progressivist historiographies are faced with a dilemma regarding the play's relation to the moment in which it is performed, with which it engages. Namely, what kind of propaganda was this? How did its first public witness its presentation of its events, and how should we read a marriage play celebrating the end of a terrible war that uses technology to return to the stage a mythological figure which, the same dramaturge has already established, is barbarically seditious and infanticidal? The mild shock that some criticism evinces concerns more than historical anachronism or allegorical complexity. Rather the tenuous exemplarity is astonishing. Did Corneille want to suggest that, in his bride Marie-Thérèse, Louis XIV had chosen to wed a Medea?

Even the possibility of such a question overlooks the specificity of premodern uses of historical and mythological time and their avatars. For example, it overlooks the significance, since Ovid and especially during the Renaissance, of Jason and Medea as symbols of the passion of marital union. Their likenesses appeared on dowry chests, in murals offered as part of a marriage home, on wedding goblets and other decorative art pieces. Medea and Jason together embody passion as a motor for union. Assuming a conflict between this figuration and that of the violent Medea also seems to assume that mythological characters were stable, whole figures who bore, at all moments, the entire burden of their narrative. Premodern allegories and histories executed the "exemplary merging" of temporalities, but also what we might call the "exemplary divisions" of figures, which allowed writers and artists to embrace exclusively one element of such a figure's history (to the exclusion of others) and to magnify its reverberations over time.

This practice is abundantly clear in the paratextual materials to tragedies, where authors justify their dramaturgical choices by citing their sources, sometimes lesser known, for elements that seem to deviate from the known story. In the *Desseins de la Toison d'or*, Corneille even goes to far as to cite a source within a source to legitimize the play's ending: Denis Milesien, cited in Natale Conti's early seventeenth-century *Mythologie*.[10] Corneille authorizes his plot by relying on Conti, who is citing Milesien, who in turn suggests that Medea herself stole the Fleece and brought it to Jason as he waited on the *Argo*. Corneille thus declares how appropriately illustrious the Jason and Medea story is, befitting the occasion of Louis's XIV's marriage: "It était même absolument impossible d'en choisir une plus illustre matière."[11] (It was impossible to have picked a more illustrious theme.) In this record of the performance, directed at enlarging even further a public that could experience it via print, the multiple layers of temporality, signification, and reference are part of the subject's noble charge.

Beyond the question of how they nimbly mobilize the reverberations of mythological and historical characters, plays afford us another dimension that is useful for considering the specificities of premodern temporality, both in the ways Koselleck explored and in ways that challenge his vision of this period. Koselleck used the Altdorfer painting to show how a set of seeming anachronisms was not one at all. Well beyond the Horatian simile of *ut picture poesis*, the *poèmes dramatiques* (dramatic poetry) of theater afford us quite literally greater dimensionality in time and in space than a painting. The play can contain a much richer allegory of temporality than a play, in part because of its ability to make bare the joins between the primary action and everything else that it depends on, thus creating a context in time for that action. As a machine play, *La Conquête* adds even another dimension to the dramatic poem's action: its *machines*, its special effects that expanded what an audience could hope to experience. Beyond the oratorical skills of the actors, audiences saw the ropes, pulleys, tracks, harnesses, holes in the stage and scaffolding overhead which facilitated multiple scene changes; the movements of clouds and rainbows, as well as the flights of gods and dragons.

This is where the existence of this particular rare document, the *Desseins*, can change our vision of the experience of this performance. As archival particularity, the *Desseins* is a precious paratextual document not only because it frames the material of the play within a context intelligible to its first audience but also because its framing is that of performance. It is an account of the play's performance at the marquis de Sourdéac's château in Normandy and probably printed just weeks prior to the Paris premiere on 18 February 1661, so as to generate interest in the performance.[12] The goal of the *Desseins* seemed to secure in advance the audience's awe at the scenic technology. An advertising strategy that confirmed the play's multisensorial appeal, its account of the play included the plot as well as details about the spectacle's embellishment: its music and song and technological innovations of its machinery. The *Desseins* was prepared for printing at the same time as the first printing of the play, and sections of the *Desseins* describing the embellishments would be incorporated into the printed text of the play itself. In contrast to the play's "script," its lines of poetry which normally would stand in for the whole of the play, the *Desseins* can be considered a kind of ekphrastic exercise, whether prospective or retrospective, an account of the experience of being amazed by the *action* of the play.

Action is crucial to *La Conquête*, in ways that go well beyond its conceptual role in all classical drama. Each flight and scene change, usually interpreted as ancillary to the dramatic poetry, represents a specific temporal dimension within the play. *La Conquête de la Toison d'or* integrates the actions of these special effects not only into the spectacle but also into its narrative, changing the terms of what and how we know what will happen, indeed into what the concept of theater is, how it might represent a world we cannot predict. They allow the dramatics of *La Conquête* quite literally to fly us into a future, a future that is (contra Koselleck) truly premodern and yet truly unknowable. As we shall see, it is the conflictual violence that these machines allow that becomes the disruptive force allowing for this futurity.

## *From Flat Futurity to Uncertain Action:* La Conquête's *Prologue and Scenic Transformation*

The play's prologue appears to act merely as a performed dedication to the royal marriage, invoking fairly standard allegorical elements. It addresses the end of the Thirty Years' War with an encomium to the king that celebrates marriage as the usher of peace. Against an opening backdrop of "un pays ruiné par les guerres, et terminé dans son enfoncement par une ville, qui n'est pas mieux traitée" (a land ruined by wars, and in the background [of the stage setting] a city which has fared no better), Victory stands, lamenting. Despite the renown she brings to France, she is always accompanied by war, and so makes France long for peace. Peace, imprisoned in the palace of Mars, knows herself that only the will of "Le blond, et pompeux Hyménée" can "briser mes fers"[13] (The blond and majestic Hymen [marriage] . . . [can] . . . break my chains). With the arrival of L'Hyménée, holding in his right hand a shield decorated with the portrait of the Infanta Marie-Thérèse marriage is not just an instrument of peace but also its courier. The décor shifts—the first of the spectacle's six scene changes—and the play, set in ancient Colchis on the eve of Jason's famous struggle for the Fleece, begins.

Corneille asserts elsewhere that a prologue is merely an encomium and has little to do with the play that it accompanies. This kind of remark might be precisely what has prompted critics' attention to the differences between the prologue and the play that follows. But the two parts of the play also share a thematics that characterizes both the subject of the play and its structure, both its narrative fabric and its performance technology. If the first, that of marriage, seems obvious, it is enhanced by the second, that of magic: the magic of amorous passion and of passion's performative efficacy, and the magic of theater itself.

Through these two motifs, it is possible to consider many of the work's formal and thematic aspects to see in the play an inverted demonstration of the prologue. Thematically, if the prologue stages the role of marriage in creating peace for a land ravaged by war, the account of the Golden Fleece's theft, as it is told in this version, is the story of how the passion that is behind this marriage wreaks havoc on a land—that of Colchis. Marriage between Jason and Médée, sealed by their theft of the Fleece, thus will rob that kingdom of its abundance, stripping it of the magic—Médée's own spells—that made those "climats sauvages" (savage climes) inhabitable.

Furthermore, it is possible to read the play's conquest narrative as a kind of "undoing" of the positive action of the prologue—the reenchantment of Europe is undone by the robbery and rape of Colchis. The settings of the prologue and main play are also located at each other's geopolitical limits. The prologue's allegorical Europa, devastated by war, is the center, whereas the setting for the play, Colchis (or Colchos, as it is spelled in this play) is the antipodal point to the Greek world, beyond the edge of civilization. The prosperity of the first depends on the undoing of the second.

Examined together as part of the same spectacle, the prologue and play reveal a series of fascinating temporal and symbolic tensions. If we take seriously their relationship, and the experience of watching one following on the other, we might ask: How do we get from a pastoral encomium of the war-torn present moment to the mythologically eternal present of the main play? A closer look at the suture between the two parts reveals the work's formal, thematic, and critical concern with the temporality of this story.

By "suture" I mean the very place where the prologue cedes way to the play itself. The moment is tremendous. Marie-Thérèse's portrait, carried aloft embedded on the shield of Hyménée, announces the scenic shift toward the first scene of the play—a scene that will bring on a new time, a new place, and a new calamity to come. The décor of the stage shifts as l'Hyménée says, "Et formez des jardins, tels qu'avec quatre mots,/ Le grand art de Médée en fit naître à Colchos."[14] (And form such gardens as did, with just four words/Medea's great art created in Colchis.) Theatrical illusion, associated with Medean magic, is charged with realizing the "nouveau miracles" of l'Hyménée and fulfilling the real needs of a France devastated and ruined by war: to change "la face de ces lieux" (the aspect of this place).

Effecting the scene change from prologue to scene 1, the décor change links the terms of the prologue to those of the play: Marriage brings peace, who in turn will bring a new nature to the land; such a new nature is realized through the enchantment of the theater. This display of theatrical magic—the transformation of the prior scene's "funestes images" into a new nature, "fontaines, fleurs, bocages" (dire scenes . . . fountains, flowers, clusters of trees) is the first of six primary scene changes made possible by the technological innovations of engineers in the systems of pulleys and counterweights that allowed for a speed and ease of transformation quite new to the French theater.

The power of Médée's "quatre mots" (four words) to make verdant the barren land of Colchis through her occult arts is the same as the rapid transformation of the theater: "Tout le théâtre se change en un jardin magnifique," records the *Desseins*, detailing the new landscape: three rows of cypress trees, statues, water features, "diverses fleurs en confusion" (The whole theater is transformed into a magnificent garden . . . a profusion of various flowers), as well as two other more distant gardens, visible in perspective.¹⁵ In the printed text, combining the text of the play along with the description of the scenic action, Hyménée's brandishing of Marie-Thérèse's portrait is an instrument of transformation—not unlike the magic wand wielded by sorceresses, or the Medusa on Athena's shield.

And its effect is as instantaneous as that of enchantment. The appearance of a new locale before an audience's eyes was effected by simultaneously rotating multiple multisided forms, or scenic wings that were attached to tracks embedded in the stage.¹⁶ One might imagine that the very spinning of these wings, together revealing a new backdrop but without the usual twelve to fifteen stage hands to move them—would have been a novel sight, capable of inspiring wonder.

Sources of wonder—magic, enchantment, and sorcery—have all long been associated with the theater and its power of illusion, of transformation, of seduction. So too, the nefarious effects of magic have contributed to the moral ambiguity of the theater as a social institution. The idea of enchantment is a guiding topos of Corneille's theater, starting with his 1634 *Illusion comique*. In that *comédie*, the structural manifestation of magic is the *mise en abyme*, accomplished easily in performance through the common practice of dividing the stage into compartments; in this version of enchantment the change is as a rapid as the drawing of a curtain to reveal the proper compartment, but it is not as total in its effects as that of the scene changes. The closer cousin to Médée in *La Conquête* is Shakespeare's Prospero, who also appears in a machine play. In *The Tempest*, he utters words borrowed from the Ovidian Medea, from Golding's 1567 translation of the *Metamorphoses*, book 7. Both magicians offers an ambiguous portrayal of the science of transformation, invoking questions of conquest as well as the deployment and mastery of occult knowledge. Further, each performs this transformation using stage technology, calling on the spectator as a certain kind of witness to the "magic" of performance as a kind of science. The technology of *The Tempest* was most spectacular in its opening scene of natural catastrophe and shipwreck, whereas *La Conquête*'s greatest show of enchantment comes at the end, in the battle scene over the Golden Fleece. As in *The Tempest*, theater's unavoidable drive to enchant, to beguile, and to conquer is a recurring constitutive question of *La Conquête*, and one of its novelties was the amount of stage spectacle: the six scene changes on the stage itself, with an additional two above the stage.

What is key to this novelty is emphasized in the text—this enchantment occurs in the space of "quatre mots." The temporality of this enchantment is not merely rapid; it is nearly instant. It shares the qualities of Descartes's *admiration*, the same as "surprise.[17]" There is no modulation: Just as one cannot come slowly into admiration, one cannot be a little enchanted. Such is the temporality of theatrical illusion, which the technology of scene changes represents. It is grounded in the connection between theater and magic through their shared work of illusion, and mobilized by the acknowledged importance of the science behind such transformation. The Italian theater inventors most closely associated with these innovations—Gaspare Vigarani and Giacomo Torelli—came to be known as "grands sorciers," as if kin to Médée, whom Corneille calls (in his "Examen" to *La Conquête*) a "savante magicienne" (a wise magician).[18] Corneille's Médée-magician does indeed deploy knowledge to make unexpected change: Unlike Alcandre in *L'illusion comique*, who is so often compared to the playwright himself, Médée is not only a conjurer of worlds, she is also what Amy Wygant called the "Medea-machine."[19] Like the machinists who create visual spectacles through the use of ropes, pulleys, and barrels, Médée's dominion over what we see is both ludic and darkly sovereign.

The join between the prologue and the play places under the sign of theater a Médée who can make real and immediate the "second nature" of marriage. Its new landscape, that of peace and abundance, flourishes from a land of devastation. Médée's magic shares the performative qualities of marriage, wherein a union is created with just a few words. Marriage thus echoes the temporal qualities of the allegory with which it concludes. If the allegory's static figures chart out, its persistent presence is challenged only in the last moments by Hyménée solving the problem of a country without a future. This join, then, also moves us from the flat futurity of the prologue to another temporal regime entirely. The rest of the play mobilizes the prologue's twin concerns of marriage and magic, but in so doing it also offers a challenge to the regime of temporality under which they operate in the prologue. This challenge comes in the form of another technical innovation, the flight, which will assume primacy through the course of the play. More immediately, however, and eventually also alongside that change in signs of technical innovation, the prologue's instantaneous performance of change, the certainty of the future will be challenged in the first scene of the play, for in this very first scene, the question of *what will happen* is at stake.

## Telling the Future: From Interpretation to Certainty

The very first scene of the play's first act has in common with the prologue conditions of the aftermath of war, though in contrast to the prologue, the play opens not just on a landscape of verdant abundance but of a kingdom successfully defended from an attack. Offering a standard scene of exposition that situates the specific action of the play within its known history, act 1, scene 1 also presents a very different Médée from that in the prologue. No longer a witch, no longer powerful nor in control of what is to come, the young princess Médée is a powerless bystander to the political events that have tied her own fate uncertainly to that of Colchis, her father's kingdom. She and her widowed sister Chalciope exchange concerns about their roles as daughters to King Aète. They recount how, at the moment when King Aète's brother seemed to be triumphant in his attack against Colchis, and Médée's intended husband, Styrus, had perished in the battle, Jason and his Argonauts arrived fortuitously and fought with their father. Now that the kingdom has been saved, what shall become of Médée and how the Greek strangers will be rewarded for their valor are unknown. The sentiments of disquiet that brew between the sisters concern how each will serve the kingdom best. At particular issue is the impact of Médée's love for the Greek Jason, and Jason's apparent love for her.

It is worth pausing here to remind ourselves that seventeenth-century political theater, or tragedy, was not about *what happened*. In a culture where dramas drew their material from recorded history and its "enveloppe," as Corneille called the embellishments of *fable*, poetry depends on such embellishments to account for its tension. The audience's attention is kept not because it doesn't know what will happen next. We know that Jason will acquire the Fleece, taking it and Médée with him to Greece. Theater of the seventeenth century creates for its public what Corneille calls "une agréable attente" (an enjoyable wait) or "suspension"—a kind of suspense, not through previously unknown acts that surprise the audience but through how characters and the audience react to what they don't want or do not expect.[20] *La Conquête* expresses these particular conditions aptly in its first lines, where what is at stake are Chalciope's feelings, her reaction to their father's triumph. As Médée observes, Chalciope's demeanor betrays a division within her:

Parmi ces grands sujets d'allégresse publique,
Vous portez sur le front un air mélancolique;
Votre humeur paraît sombre, et vous semblez, ma soeur,
Murmurer en secret contre notre bonheur.

(1.1.1–4)

Amid these great reasons for public happiness
You wear a melancholic air about you
Your mood seems somber and you appear, my sister,
To murmur secretly against our happiness.

Many dramas begin rather on a note of certainty about what is to come. The intensity of this certainty ironically underscores the true precariousness of the situation—consider Jason's surprise and joy at the beginning of *Médée* upon seeing his old friend Pollux, or similarly Oreste's confidence that "ma fortune va prendre une face nouvelle" (my fortune will take a new course) at finding Pylade (*Andromaque*, 1.1.2). *Rodogune*'s Laonice opens the play declaring, "Enfin ce jour pompeux, cet heureux jour nous luit," when Queen Rodogune finally will declare her heir, "cessant de plus tenir la couronne incertaine" (1.1.1, 8). (Finally, this majestic day, this happy day brightens us; ... when Rodogune will stop keeping the crown in uncertainty.)

Plays like *La Conquête* that begin with anxiety about the future, also expose characters' vulnerability as part of the drama's dilemma. Sabine opens *Horace* with fourteen lines of poetry describing her tenuous control over her feelings of dread. She does so in terms not unlike those describing Chalciope in *La Conquête*: They both are living that noble predicament which is an everyday effect of the monarch's two bodies: the distinction between one's own "secret troubles" and the shared condition of the kingdom, between the dismay of a *particulier* (an individual) and acknowledgment of a general "allegresse publique" (public contentment). On what grounds might there be a division between the two, and to what effect? And, more precisely, what are the particular stakes of watching a combat "avec des yeux de fille et de sujette" (with eyes [both] of daughter and subject)?

The basic stakes of the play appear in Médée's concerns about her sister's potential divided loyalties, but they are presented first in inverted form. Médée suspects her sister of the very division upon which she will later act, and for which she is famous. Chalciope's assertion that "celles de notre rang/Ne savent point trahir leur pays, ni leur sang" (1.1.11–12) (those of our rank/Know not how to betray neither their land nor their blood) becomes ironically prescient. This emotional misdirection—one sister accusing another of the very divided loyalties upon which she will later act—sets up the issue of the play: the inevitable consequences of a division between particular passions and political allegiances. But instead of the usual reassurances that can characterize such intimate scenes of doubt, in this first scene, the doubt is redirected—back toward Médée. Chalciope does this by invoking the recent past and by invoking the necessary future, and it is in within these invocations that the conflict of the play emerges.

Chalciope has no reason for personal dismay—her husband Phryxus has been long dead—but she knows that Médée does. So Chalciope reinscribes the battle—the struggle between king Aète and his brother Persès, resolved by the coincidental arrival and bravery of Jason and his Argonauts—within its proper hermeneutic device, the oracular message delivered by her dead husband's ghost to Aète. Corneille is borrowing from the account of Phryxus's warning from Valerius Flaccus's *Argonautica*, in which the dead son-in-law not only warns that "dolour and ruin of thy realm shall abound for thee what time the fleece is stolen from the sleep-drugged grove" (5.236–37), but also that Medea must be married: "Let her look for betrothal to any suitor, suffer her not to abide in her father's kingdom."[21] In *La Conquête*, Chalciope's version of the ghostly prophecy is muddled within the recent conflict and the moment when Jason saved their kingdom: "Que Perses triomphait, que Styrus était mort,/Styrus que pour Epoux vous envoyait le Sort" (1.1.23–24). (That Perses would triumph, that Styrus would die/Styrus, whom Destiny sent you as Husband.) By immediately warning her sister not to fall in love with their father's savior, Chalciope underscores the poor interpretation of the message. Chalciope assumes that the meaning of the message conforms to that which she knows to have happened, that its promise has already been realized. In fact, its fulfillment is the subject of the play, and again, Chalciope's words are both wrong and prescient, since it is precisely Jason who will fulfill the promise of both aspects of Phryxus's message: the downfall of Colchis and the marriage of Médée.

Accounts of dreams, oracles, and prophecies in theater are forms of narration that operate along a continuum of ambiguity and precision regarding their meaning. Their interpretation suggests the security characters feel in seeing messages of the future as guides for action and measures of behavior. In the fifth act, as the Fleece has been stolen, a divine declaration offers Aète some justice after the loss of his kingdom and the wrongs of his daughter. The denouement is presented through the limpid and conclusive forecast by the gods of, first, Médée's own just deserts through a marriage undone by Jason's infidelity, and, second, Aète's dynastic security reestablished through Médée's founding of the Medes dynasty. The gods' promise is really a declaration: It functions on the same plane of history as the present. This kind of prediction orders events and create intelligibility, both within the play and without, in the space of performance. It also serves as context for the audience, anchoring drama within the known history from which it is derived.

The dream evoked in this first scene, like many oracles, is not a divine promise but a message to be interpreted, and would appear at the murky end of the spectrum of interpretable events. Like an oracle, a dream is always right but never understood until the moment of its actualization, when it comes into the present. Chalciope actualizes this ambiguity, seeing in recent events a partial fulfillment of the dream, when she speaks of the death of Styrus, Médée's intended. Chalciope's interpretation of the dream message is inflected by the events of the recent past: Styrus must have been the foreigner whom Médée was to marry. In assuming that its meaning conforms to what she knows has just happened, she also elides the conjunctive aspect of the dream that makes a warning: Médée's foreign marriage will entail the downfall of the kingdom.

The bearer of an erroneous interpretation of what is to come, Chalciope exemplifies the problem of an oracular relationship to the future. Yet her character finishes this same scene mobilizing an altogether different grammar of the future, one that will eventually obtain. Thus it serves as another prospective message—not oracular, not dreamlike, but prophetic.

In their debate about the duty of daughters to obey their fathers, Chalciope eventually extracts the truth of Médée's own feelings regarding the Argonaut Jason. Certain that Jason is in love with her and will ask for her hand, Médée confesses her own love for him. Yet Médée finishes her confession with a wooden echo of her sister's earlier declaration of loyalty to their father's sovereignty. She asserts, "Je suis prête à l'aimer, si le Roi le commande." Chalciope rebuts:

> Quittez ce faux devoir dont l'ombre vous amuse,
> Vous irez plus avant si le Roy le refuse,
> Et quoique votre erreur vous fasse présumer,
> Vous obéirez mal, s'il vous défend d'aimer.
> Je sais . . .
>
> (1.1.82, 85–89)

MÉDÉE.
   I am ready to love him, if the King commands it.
CHALCIOPE.
   Quit this false duty whose protection amuses you
   You will push further if the King refuses it
   And even though you erroneously presume,
   You will resist obeying, if he prohibits it.
   I know . . .

Chalciope's declaration works even beyond the level of the prediction or the calculation; it operates through a true grammar of the future. As the play will explore, what she says will indeed be realized in the acts to come: the lightness of Médée's sense of duty, the error suggesting that Jason will ask for her hand, the king's refusal of the eventual marriage offer, and Médée's ultimate rebellion against her father.

This first scene of the play offers a traditional expository scene framing the central tension of the play—how Jason and Médée's passion for each other will be realized, and at what price. It exposes the conclusion of the play as a reversal: the witch, who in the prologue ensured the prosperity of France, also creates the bounty of Aète's kingdom and safeguards its sovereignty by protecting the Golden Fleece. She will, however, ultimately unmake his rule and remove the Fleece. This reversal pits passion against duty, in a way unlike Corneille's other plays that take up this well-visited tension, by mobilizing the specter of filial infidelity. And it concludes by framing this inevitable reversal by juxtaposing two ways in which it is realized: two ways of considering the future. The first, on the order of oracles and dreams, is one that interprets what is to come based on the link between events of the past and anticipations of the future. The second, indicated by a grammar of the future that resembles the clarity of prophecy but without its divine authority, signals paradoxically the unknowability of the future: Such things will come to pass, but under what conditions and precisely when we cannot say.

Again, Chalciope's declarations are not surprising: They are indeed what will happen in the play. They are what has already happened, in a sense—in the literary tradition, they have occurred in Ovid, in Valerius Flaccus, Apollonius of Rhodes—in nearly every account of the Argonauts' voyage. In this way again, classical theater that relies on the stories of history and fable also mobilizes the past as a matter of the present. What is particularly remarkable about the double understanding of knowing the certainty of the future—Chalciope's error-riddled invocation of the dream as well as her certainty about Médée's passions and the events that will occur as a result—is its divorce between passion and actions. That is, if seventeenth-century plays are not propelled by the uncertainty of action but by the surprise of reactions, by the ways characters (and the audience) attend to being moved, the following scenes create such suspense, and even surprise, by making the outcome of Médée's passion uncertain.

Given the subject of the play, this divorce between passion and action, which manifests in an uncertainty about how Médée will feel, becomes an uncertainty about what she will *do*. In the poetic and performative space of a machine play especially—one in which Médée's first appearance is as an impassive creator of new landscapes—it is Médée's deeds that are really in question. The ambiguity of what Médée feels sets into motion the uncertainty of what she will do, and the play marks this problem of passion as suspense by the metaphors and actions of technology, where—as we shall see—*suspense* becomes literal *suspension*.

## Dramatic Suspense, Technological Suspension

Aristotelian poetics eschewed the uncertainty of concepts like suspense, but premodern dramaturges explored the temporal and rhetorical dimensions of "attente" (waiting) as a mechanism for engaging the spectator. Joseph Harris has traced how, in dramatic poetry, suspense becomes an increasingly important part of the complex constitution of spectatorial pleasure as theorized by Corneille's contemporaries.[22] What is at stake in this kind of pleasure, however, remained up for debate. Terence Cave has suggested that suspense, as we consider it today, first emerged in novelistic composition, an advent closely linked to the demise of the allegorical tradition but nevertheless with roots in rhetorical conventions of earlier centuries. Suspense in rhetoric was achieved by deferral through digression; *l'Astrée* would be the best example of such a technique.[23] Much like dramatic plots, novels did not excite their readers for the unexpected twists of plot; one knew the lovers would find each other. Rather, the commitment was to discover how they would be temporarily separated. Many premodern dramaturges and theorists argued that audiences ought to be confined to an intellectual state of uncertainty about how a play would turn out. Whether this uncertainty was best achieved by providing all the elements of the story needed to focus attention on the knots of its unfolding, or whether spectators should be confined to a state of ignorance on the level of what would actually transpire, so as to generate surprise more easily, was a matter of discussion. Either way, suspense as a part of theatrical pleasure has an epistemological component.

For Corneille, suspense occurs when spectators find themselves unsure about how an action will find its conclusion. Writing about the same time as *La Conquête*, Corneille argues that the unity of action can be achieved, "mais elle ne peut le devenir que par plusieurs autres imparfaites, qui lui servent d'acheminements et tiennent cet auditeur dans une agréable suspension" (but it can become so [unified] only by other less perfect actions, which serve as a conveyance, and keep the listener in a pleasant suspension). In his "Discours de la tragédie," Corneille directly distinguishes between such knowledge-based suspense and pathos. Using the example of a surprise revelation, just before death, of parenthood between characters, Corneille asserts that dramaturges "pourront produire par-là quelque agréable suspension dans l'esprit de l'auditeur, mais il ne faut pas qu'ils se promettent de lui tirer beaucoup de larmes"[24] (could, by that, produce some pleasant suspension in the listener's mind, but they should not be confident about causing too many tears to flow). There is a limit to the pathos of suspense, and audiences must find their commitment to the spectacle elsewhere within it. Instead, what should be sought is a suspension common to characters and spectators. Corneille underscores this with a real-time notion of *attente* when he underscores the importance of the time between acts as a moment of expectation for what will happen next.[25] Thus Katherine Ibbett identifies the perfect realization of Corneillian suspense in *Rodogune*, when Cléopâtre moves to break her silence, "pour ne tenir plus en suspens vos esprits" (so as to no longer keep in suspense your minds), referring by "vos esprits" both to her sons and to the audience. As Ibbett suggests, for Corneille "it is not just the spectators who are described by this language, but also the characters on stage whose confused suspension in some way figures our own."[26]

The idealized notion of action and tension which affects *acteurs* and audience alike also shapes *La Conquête*. A key scene uses a confusion of passions and actions to create a shared suspense. The crucial scene is in act 1, where the ground is set for Jason's legendary travails: his fighting of the bulls, soldiers, and dragons in order to gain the Fleece. Before he is given these tasks, a confusion of Corneille's own invention occurs, mirroring the confusion between passions and actions that inaugurated the play.

At stake here are the rules of hospitality, which King Aète happily wishes to follow, in order to offer Jason recompense for having saved his kingdom. Ready to give away his Médée, he receives an altogether different request, one that strikes at the heart of his sovereignty:

JASON.
   Seigneur, j'ose vous dire après cette promesse
   Que vous voyez la fleur des Princes de la Grèce
   Qui vous demandent tous d'une commune voix
   Un trésor qui jadis fut celuy de ses Rois
   La Toison d'Or, Seigneur, que Phryxus vostre gendre
   Phryxus nostre parent . . .
AÈTE.
   Ah, que viens-je d'entendre!
MÉDÉE.                              Ah, perfide!
JASON.
   À ce mot vous paraissez surpris!

(1.3.477–83)

JASON.

> Sire, I dare to ask, after this promise,
> That you see the greatest Princes of Greece
> Who ask you all, in once voice
> A treasure that was once that of its own Kings
> The Golden Fleece, Sire, that Phryxus your son-in-law
> Phryxus our relative . . .

AÈTE.

> Ah what have I just heard?

MÉDÉE.  Oh perfidious one!

JASON.

> You seem surprised!

Jason's reply feels superfluous, even cynical or ironic, unless we understand it as a kind of internal stage direction so common to this period's dramatic poetry, where the verses themselves tell the actors—and readers—what the onstage characters are meant to express. In this case, it might be needed: Aète and Médée's astonishment echoes the reaction of a spectator who knows that Jason is meant to want Médée in addition to the Fleece. In an instant, everything has changed. Jason's request for the Fleece and not for Médée is a surprise both on the stage and the parterre, not because spectators are ignorant of his reason for being at Colchis, but because it defers the union of passion and action that colors the known history of Jason and Medea's love and flight together. Instead, in eliciting Médée's rage against Jason, action will oppose passions. Jason will fight the enchantments but not with Médée's love. As Médée declares, the "affreux périls"—the enchanted adversaries he will need to conquer—are "legers" compared to her anger, and she stages her own anger-fueled powers as his final obstacle. Jason himself acknowledges as much in a following conversation with his Argonauts, when he laments the assaultive effect of his request and suggests that he might have gained the same through the patience of love. In the debate among the Greeks, what emerges is a dichotomy for which the *La Conquête* is generally held in derision: between action (getting the Fleece) and passion (Médée and Jason's joint passion). Jason's heroic request for the Fleece is pitted against the slower time of passion, and it is this passion that will come to dominate the next few acts.

The Argonauts' conundrum is solved in the next scene. Poetically, the solution is a "miracle," which the gods will perform for the Argonauts, by conquering Médée's *fureur* with conjured *Amour*:

JUNON.
> Tous vos bras et toutes vos armes
> Ne peuvent rien contre les charmes
> Que Médée en fureur verse sur la Toison;
> L'Amour seul aujourd'hui peut faire ce miracle . . .

PALLAS.
> Pour vous secourir en ces lieux,
> Junon change de forme et va descendre en Terre;
> Et pour vous protéger Pallas remonte aux Cieux.
>
> (1.6.621–33)

JUNON.
> All your strength and all your arms
> Can do nothing against the spell
> Which Médée furious has put on the Fleece;
> Only Love can make this miracle. . . .

PALLAS.
> To help you in this situation
> Junon will change form and come to Earth
> And to protect you Pallas goes back to the Heavens.

The accompanying spectacle shows the miracle with the first off-ground effect of the play. Iris appears on a rainbow, Junon and Pallas each in a chariot above the Argonauts' heads. Junon's plans then follow for the conquest of the Fleece, which can only occur with the help of Amour's charms. This plan is articulated through a topology of space and place that both opposes and links "Terre" and "Cieux" (Earth and Heavens), a linkage expressed visually through the transit between the two. As Pallas declares the promise of the gods to deliver the Fleece with Médée's love, the stage directions offer the visual indiction:

> Mais quoi qu'il puisse faire, assurez-vous qu'enfin
> l'Amour fera votre destin,
> Et vous donnera tout, s'il vous donne Médée
> *Ici tout d'un temps Iris disparaît, Pallas remonte au Ciel, et Junon descend en Terre, en traversant toutes deux le Théâtre, et faisant croiser leurs chars.*
>
> (1.6.639–41)

> Whatever happens, rest assured that ultimately
> Love will guide your destiny
> And will give you everything, when it gives you Médée

> *Here at the very same time, Iris disappears, Pallas goes back up to the Heavens, and Junon comes down to Earth, both crossing the theater, with their chariots crossing.*

At the moment when Jason will arm himself to combat "ce dragon, ces Taureaux, ces Gendarmes" (590) (this dragon, these bulls, these soldiers), the gods' deployment of Amour to help him will take place through a new kind of magic: not through the kind of scene-change enchantment by which Médée's own powers were invoked. Instead, it is materialized through suspension, a lifting up and expansion of the territory of nature and spectacle. Here, for the first time in the main action of the play, one of the major innovations of *La Conquête* is seen: Characters fly. This occurs at the very moment when the poetry sees a resolution to the suspense, when we are offered direction as to the way the play will resolve itself. Thus with one form of suspense resolved, another, physical version takes its place: the suspension of characters in the air. Replacing the uncertainty of the play's unfolding with a visual version of astonishment, the play redirects the narrative question toward the technological, exchanging the uncertainty of outcome for the suspension of flight.

It might not seem historically accurate to call flight a "major innovation" of this play, since by 1660 suspension and flight were established parts of machine plays. As early as the sixteenth century, machinery that could make angels and gods fly was used in ballets and passion plays. In his famous treatise on theater machinery first published in 1637, Nicolà Sabbatini follows several chapters on the deployment of clouds with instructions on "come si possa far calare dal'Cielo una Persona senza Nuvola, la quale venuta sopra il Palco possa subito caminare, e ballare" (how to, without using a cloud, make a person descend from the sky who also, as soon as landing on the floor, can walk and dance about).[27] Corneille's own *Andromède*, presented in Paris a decade before *La Conquête*, used flying gods in its spectacle. And before that, the 1634 *Médée* ended with the departure of Médée in a carriage drawn by dragons assisted by machinery. Lully's 1675 *Thésée* would harken back to the single machine of *Médée* by again featuring her aloft, dragon-borne. By the last quarter of the seventeenth century, in the machinery of the operas, flying characters would be a feature of *Phaeton*, whose theme of flight's dangers would be the culminating moment of such aerial feats. Specific to *La Conquête* is how the machinery, grounded solidly in the spectacular, designed to delight the audience through its technical prowess, also informs the unfolding of the events of the play, expanding the regime of temporality.

One way of reading *La Conquête's* flights is as part of its language of tragedy. For Christian Delmas it is through their flights that machine plays can be seen as extensions of "la vraie dimension" of tragedy, the "au-delà du réel demeuré trop souvent implicite dans la tragédie unie" (Tragedy's true dimensions, . . . the "beyond" the here and now that remains often only implied in regular tragedy).[28] Through flight, Corneille's machine plays share common symbolic territory with his tragedies and even actualize that which goes unseen if not unsaid, as flight "visualize l'élan héroïque des vertus humaines jusqu'à l'apothéose finale: le vol de l'homme suffit par lui-même à emplir l'espace de la terre au ciel"[29] (embodies the heroic surge of human virtues up until the final apotheosis: human flight is enough to fill the space between earth and heaven). Flights and scene changes are symbolically different from each other—for if flights are in a space above the stage, offering what Delmas might call a materialized dimensionality, scene changes stay largely terrestrial.[30] Furthermore, the instantaneity of scene changes marks a kind of nature-changing enchantment. In contrast, flights, wondrous as they may be, are spectacular precisely because they *take time*, their loftiness is witnessed.

Although scene changes extend the space of the stage, they don't have an easily discernible analogue within tragic spatiality. It might even be said that the multiplicity of spaces allowed by scene changes can destabilize and even fracture the focus of the work. Indeed, the spectacle of scene changes offers discontinuity, and does so instantly. One test of this distinction in *La Conquête* is one of its more bizarre features, the Venus-out-of-shell appearance of Hypsipyle, which Wagner considers unique in all of French theater since it is accompanied by a kind of immediate ekphrasis in the text: Absyrte describes in detail her arrival on—or rather in—a "grande Conque de Nacre" (a huge mother-of-pearl shell), which glides onto the stage, seemingly from the river Phasus in the background. We can imagine this shell on the tracks or runners used for scene changes. This machine is fascinating because it uses the technology and spatiality of the scene change but with the temporality of flight. Bringing Hypsipyle, Jason's lost lover and therefore Médée's rival, from the depths of the water, this machine announces her as in anticipatory opposition to Médée, who will come to dominate, unanchored, the skies above in the last scene.

Another significant scene change in *La Conquête* offers a productive contrast with the specific spatial and temporal qualities of the flights in the play. In most readings of *La Conquête de la Toison d'or* integrating the special effects into their analysis of the dramatic poetry, scene changes are read as producing and reflecting royal power by generating a kind of *éblouissement*, or bedazzlement. Accordingly, the *Dessein* for the setting for act 3, Aète's palace, notes that "nos Théâtres n'ont encore rien fait paraître de si brillant" (Our theaters have never before shown anything so brilliant).[31] Similarly, the setting for act 4, the "désert de Médée" consists largely of boulders: "Ces Rochers sont d'une pierre blanche & luisante" (These boulders are of a white, shining stone). For Marie-France Wagner, the use of gold in the palace and the play of light off the rocks are integral to the symbolics of power in this multimedia performance, and its drive to "reflect back" the king's power, allowing the sun—symbol of divine power—to eclipse the Fleece—symbol of earthly power.[32] In this way, scene changes appear to advance the symbolics of theater as a nature-changing enchantment whose aesthetics are associated with the totalizing nature of monarchical power.

The instantaneous time of enchanted theatricality can be seen as the time of such monarchical aesthetics. When the scene changes reach their acme, in act 3, the transformation that occurs alters both this aesthetic and its temporality. At first, it appears that Médée is a kind of dark imitator of such aesthetics and power, as through her magic arts performed among the glittering rocks of her "désert," Médée changes the gilt palace of her father into a "palais d'horreur," so as to frighten her rival Hypsipyle. The *Desseins* describes the scene as it would be experienced by an audience, complete with perspectival details:

> ... où tout ce qu'il y a d'épouvantable en la nature y sert de Termes. L'éléphant, le rhinocéros, le lion, l'once, les tigres, les léopards, les panthères, les dragons, les serpents, tous avec leurs antipathies à leurs pieds, y lancent des regards menaçants. Une grotte obscure borne la vue, au travers de laquelle l'oeil ne laisse pas de découvrir un éloignement merveilleux que fait la perspective. Quatre monstres ailés et quatre rampants enferment Hypsipyle, et semblent prêts à la dévorer.[33]

> ... where all that is frightening in nature appears as statues. The Elephant, the Rhinoceros, the Lion, the Snow Leopard, as well as Tigers, Leopards, Panthers, Dragons, Snakes, all with their antipathies at their feet, all giving threatening looks about. A dark grotto blocks the view, through which the eye nevertheless can discern a marvelous distant scene which creates perspective. Four winged monsters and four creepers enclose Hypsipyle, seemingly ready to devour her.

The scene change, at once a veritable product of magic and a spectacular theatrical effect, expands both what the magic of theater can do and the range of effects that Médée can impose by her terrestrial arts. As such it seems also to work as a counterpoint to the founding transformation of the prologue; Médée unmakes the verdant, peaceful world at will and so positions herself as a rival to an ever-powerful sovereign, appropriating his symbolics and his effects. Médée seems to play the ever-sovereign goddess.

Yet in the next scene, the motivation behind this transformation is revealed. Médée's ire is contrived and the *palais d'horreur* is revealed to have been premeditated as a ruse affording Médée's brother Absyrte the possibility of ingratiating himself to his love Hypsipyle by rescuing her. Neither signs of the wonders of enchantment nor signs of the unpredictability of the invisible, but rather a sign of strategy, the changes in the world wrought by "quatre mots" (or four pulleys and a barrel) are here premeditated tools of persuasion and seduction. In this way, the pinnacle of scene-change enchantment is revealed to be ultimately a contrivance.

The technology of suspension and flight in *La Conquête* rivals and eventually exceeds that of the scene changes, as the *Desseins* takes great pains to describe. In contrast with the changes in décor, associated with a form of *éblouissement* and so with the effects of enchantment and magic, suspension and flight seem to suggest another temporality. Emphasizing neither instantaneity nor a new, better nature, the technology of flight allows for a traversing, a visible trajectory from one point within the stage area to another. With them, and the machines they carry through the air, we attend to the magic as it moves across the stage. It is these movements that the *Desseins* emphasizes in its descriptions of the flights and machines. It shows that they follow a particular architecture of the spectacular, reaching ever more innovative heights with every act, as the *Dasseins* describes with great fervor the flight of Amour at the end of act 4:

> [l'Amour] s'élance aussitôt en l'air, qu'il traverse, non pas d'un costé du Theatre à l'autre, mais d'un bout à l'autre. Les curieux qui voudrant bien considerer ce vol, le trouvent assez extraordinaire, et je ne me souviens point d'en avoir vu de cette maniere.[34]

> Amour leaps into the air, which he crosses not from one side of the Theater to the other, but from one end to the other [toward the Spectators]. Those who are curious about this flight will find it quite extraordinary, and I do not remember ever having seen any others of this kind.

While the technology of spectacle was first associated with Médée's ability to create new terrestrial natures instantly, what comes to dominate the play is something quite different in its effect, spatiality, and temporality:

Figure 19. Jacques Le Pautre, "La Conqueste de la Toison d'or par les argonauts." 1682. Courtesy Metropolitan Museum of Art.

completely aerial machinery. So much so that even scene changes—the opening of new spaces and the revelation of new natures—begin to occur in the air. In the last two acts, the gods' palaces are revealed in the "ciel," first that of Vénus and then those of the sun and of Jupiter.

It is fitting that the play's last act culminates in the terrific fight, and flight, scene between Médée, upon her winged dragon and the Argonauts, who fight her from either side. A print by Jean Lepautre, often associated with festivities celebrating the birth of Louis XIV's grandson in 1682, might in fact be associated with the 1683 production at the Théâtre Royal, and it offers one proximate vision of the spectacle. Stage effects here are at their pinnacle of sophistication and innovation, befitting a scene that also held great narrative surprises for its audience. Abby Zanger considers that it is precisely through the stage technology that the play can neutralize the aspects of the Medea myth that were potentially difficult. It uses the flights to contain a "finely developed program for manipulating explosive symbols, like Medea, and making them function in the service of the state."

## Flying toward Futurity

In this reading, Médée and the Fleece in her hands, swinging back and forth together, are "two sides of the same enigmatic image,"[35] which allows a woman to be a dynamic agent in her own right. Médée fights against the Argonauts, inciting them to treat her like a warrior and to attempt strikes at her: "Donnez où vous pourrez, ce vain respect m'outrage, . . . Je vais voler moi-même au-devant de vos coups" (5.5.2088–90). (Strike a blow wherever you can, this empty respect outrages me. I will fly myself in front of your blows.) As Argonauts leave the fight and the stage to take refuge aboard the *Argo*, she disdains them: "Et malgré leur ardeur pour un exploit si beau,/Leur effroi les renferme au fond de leur vaisseau" (5.5.2095–96). (And despite their ardor for such a beautiful deed/Their fear shuts them up at the bottom of their vessel.) Médée maneuvers herself in front of the timid Argonauts' blows, contrasting her own midair bravery with their terrestrial timidity, which sends them scurrying as far down as possible—even into the hold of their ship.

For spectators too, this scene was a revelation: They literally had never seen anything of this kind before. The flights used to stage this scene were the first of their kind in France. What is so astonishing, urges the narrator of the *Desseins*, is how the combat occurs, with all its back-and-forth, entirely in the air:

> L'Art des Machines n'a rien encore fait voir à la France de plus beau, ni de plus ingenieux que ce combat. . . . Jusqu'à ici nous n'avons point vu de vols sur nos théâtres, qui n'aient été tout à fait de bas en haut, ou de haut en bas, comme ceux d'Andromède; mais de descendre des nues au milieu de l'air, et se relever aussitôt sans prendre terre, joignant ainsi les deux mouvements, et se retourner à la vue des spectateurs, pour recommencer dix fois la même descente, avec la même facilité que la première; je ne puis m'empêcher de dire qu'on n'a rien encore vu de si surprenant, ni qui soit exécuté avec tant de justesse.[36]

> The Art of Machinery (*special stage effects*) has never before produced in France anything so beautiful, nor so ingenious as this fight. . . . Up until now we have never seen flights in our theaters that were not completely from above to below, or from below to above, as those in *Andromède*. But to descend from the clouds to the middle of the air, and then to go back up without touching ground—thus combining the two movements—and then to return to the Spectators' view, only to repeat the same descent 10 times each with the same ease as the first: I can't help but say that never has anything so surprising, nor done so well, ever been seen before.

Here, suspension creates surprise: Audiences are astonished by the ability of the characters to move about in the air, suspended above the ground even as they parry.

Additionally, the surprise of physical suspension also creates suspense in the sense of suspended understanding, for it is a moment of singular ambiguity as to both action and passion. Médée's flying itself is the embodiment of suspense: Is she flying for Aète, as the play seems to indicate? Shouldn't she be flying for Jason, as legend has it? Abby Zanger calls this motion a kind of *fort-da*, and in a very compelling way it is indeed a practice of the record of absence and loss.[37] Whom will she love, her father or her love? The question in which whose name she flies, whether the father—his history, his dynasty—or the presumptive son-in-law—his future, the kingdom to which his return of the Fleece will entitle him—lends credence to such psychoanalytic readings of Médée's traces through the air.

Médée's flight additionally offers another kind of narrative suspense, in the temporally modern sense: What will be its issue? Will she leave or won't she? Will flying become flight? What is she defending, Colchis or her dominion of the Fleece and the magical powers of sovereignty it guarantees? What Médée says next is quite ambiguous, and it is possible that her gestures are equally difficult to predict:

> Ne laissons pas ainsi la victoire imparfaite:
> Par le milieu des airs, courons à leur défaite;
> Et nous-mêmes portons à leur témérité
> Jusque dans ce vaisseau ce qu'elle a mérité.
> *Médée s'élève encore plus haut sur le Dragon.*
>
> (5.5.2095–99)

> Let us not leave victory imperfect
> In the middle of these airs let us run to their defeat;
> And let us ourselves bring to their audacity
> right into this vessel, that which it deserves.
> *Médée upon her Dragon flies higher.*

Of what victory does Médée speak, of whose audacity, and what does it deserve? Her words here point to a desire to chase the Argonauts to their defeated retreat aboard the *Argo*, as if the victory in question belonged to the Colchians. When what seem to be Médée's parries against the Argonauts turn instead in favor of her own theft of the Fleece and these words must be interpreted in the opposite manner, the shift happens like a pivot, with no narrative preparation and as if instantaneously. Aète discerns the meaning of her words through her movement, this flight "even higher" on her dragon:

AÈTE.
    Que fais-tu ? La toison ainsi que toi s'envole!
    Ah ! Perfide, est-ce ainsi que tu me tiens parole,
    Toi qui me promettois, même aux yeux de Jason,
    Qu'on t'ôteroit le jour avant que la toison?
MÉDÉE, *en s'envolant.*
    Encor tout de nouveau je vous en fais promesse,
    Et vais vous la garder au milieu de la Grèce.
    Du pays et du sang l'amour rompt les liens,
    Et les dieux de Jason sont plus forts que les miens.

(5.5.2100–11)

AÈTE.
    What are you doing? The Fleece with you flies away
    Ah! Traitor, is this how you keep your word
    You who promised me before Jason's eyes,
    That you would lose your life before [losing] the fleece?
MÉDÉE, *flying away:*
    Once again I promise you so,
    And will guard it for you in the middle of Greece
    To country and blood love breaks my ties
    Jason's gods are stronger than mine.

It is only as Médée disappears that we understand how we have reached the realization of the play's central action. Nothing of it—besides Chalciope's certainty, and besides our knowledge of the legend—has led up to this moment. The play unites aerial *suspens* with both the suspense of ambiguity and the uncertainty of a narrative outcome to create its climax, wherein the flying technologies literally and figuratively perform their unpredictability.

Médée's disappearance, however, is not the end of the play. The aftermath, or denouement, works in both spectacular and poetic terms in order to safeguard a particular discourse of futurity. Aète seeks justice from the gods, who reveal themselves in the last aerial spectacle of the play, a static but opulent *mise en abyme* machine displaying first the palace of the sun, and then, above that, the throne of Jupiter. From on high, the gods will assure Aète. Dispossessed of the Fleece that guaranteed him his kingdom, he will lose his sovereignty. But the future will return this loss, Jupiter asserts. First, Médée will suffer from Jason's infidelity, and second, Aète's dynasty will be reestablished through Médée's descendants:

> Des arrêts du Destin l'ordre est invariable,
> . . . . . . . . . . . . . . .
> Mais la même légèreté
> Qui donne Jason à Médée
> Servira de supplice à l'infidélité
> . . . . . . . . . . . . . . .
> Car enfin de votre perfide
> Doit sortir un Médus qui vous doit rétablir ;
> À rentrer dans Colchos il sera votre guide
> Et mille grands exploits qui doivent l'ennoblir,
> Feront de tous vos maux les assurés remèdes,
> Et donneront naissance à l'empire des Mèdes.
> 
> (5.6.2194–2215)

> Destiny's decisions are unchangeable orders
> . . . . . . . . . . . . . . .
> But the same imprudence
> That gives Jason to Médée
> Will serve as supplicant to infidelity
> . . . . . . . . . . . . . . .
> For ultimately from your perfidy
> Will emerge Medus who will reestablish your line;
> He will be your guide returning you to Colchos
> And many great deeds will ennoble him,
> So becoming remedies to your great pains,
> And bringing forth the empire of the Medes.

These ends, delivered in fairly ambiguous language, placate Aète, who accepts this prophecy delivered from the mouths of the gods directly. Whereas the prophetic ending secures the future, however, Médée's flight nevertheless undoes the security established by the gods' promises to Aète. For what is not mentioned precisely is what kind of destruction she will wreak later in her travels: the murder of Pelias, the destruction of Corinth, the end of Jason's line, the murder of Agée's son.

If we accept this play for its marriage plot, then the lapsus becomes understandable; it focuses on the transmission of the warrant—the Fleece, back to its rightful owners, the Greeks—and the question of descendants, the Medes. Only the soon-to-be foreign bridge, Médée, will suffer from

Jason's infidelities. This reading also depends on a rapid elision, however: that of the war itself for which the theft of the Fleece is a symbol, and Médée's own agency as fighter in this battle.

Médée's own portability, her ability to steal the Fleece herself and deliver it to a passive Jason ensconced on the *Argo*, becomes at once a metaphor for the transmission of knowledge through war and conquest, and for the necessary omissions of war stories in history. So, the words of the gods—prophetic in their accuracy yet oracular (that is, misleadingly silent) in their elision of Médée's habit of regicide, are left undermined, by the lacunae upon which they depend.

In its final spectacle of suspension, suspense, and then flight, *La Conquête de la Toison d'or* takes a form of futurity uncommon to its mid-seventeenth-century context, a futurity of uncertainty and ambiguity, one in which a Médée has left the stage but will return. We just don't know when, or how, or at whose expense. In the space of this uncertainty is slotted the violence of her individual crimes, but also those of sovereign warfare, territorial conquest, and extramoral political contestation that seems, at any moment in history, inescapable.

CHAPTER 5

# Medea Overlived: The Future of Catastrophe

Neoclassical French tragedy has come to define the aesthetics, culture, and antimodernity of seventeenth-century France. By antimodernity, I mean first its alterity in establishing what we consider the social order today. As a figure of alterity to our "modernity," the "neoclassical" encapsulates the "before" of the ancien regime: It is an aesthetic and philosophical meditation on divine and Christian monarchy; it can be measured formally by the rigor of its technique; it is ossified in aesthetic values that uphold a long-gone culture, one which we have overcome. Its theater expresses such alterity perfectly: It is assessed based on poetic values of rigor and complexity, and not in the seeming humanity of its physical or psychological impersonations. There is a baseline of aesthetic purity that couples neatly with the well-worn story—not entirely mythological—about early modern French literature's unwavering complicity with its political order that sees the absolute values of a theater without passions as the summa of an absolutism without exceptions.

There is also the complicity of this portrait of the premodern with the modernist narrative. Today, we have moved beyond the values it debated; our theater has progressed to adopt more sophisticated notions of the individual and of techniques of performance. Neoclassical theater is the aesthetic regime we have overcome. Since modernity is in part defined by its having moved beyond whatever we have left behind, neoclassical tragedy is read as the history of ours which we know well because we have severed all relation to it.

If, however, we follow Fredric Jameson's four maxims of modernity and, with particular attention to the second, that "modernity is not a concept but rather a narrative category," we must also disrupt the narrative category of any modernity, including the premodern or early modern.[1] Early modernity cannot be an embryonic version of modernity, nor a precursor, nor the other side of a conceptual bridge. If "premodernity" is a narrative category as well, and we must disrupt that category's power to define modernity, we must also examine the mechanisms by which we can see it as its own narrative category.

There might be one play that thoroughly unsettles this comfort of easy periodization in myriad ways, and of which it is nearly impossible to have a singular reading: Racine's *Athalie* (1691). It certainly disrupts readings of neoclassical tragedy, which—to use the periodization that, since Fumaroli, has become structural to the genre—ends in 1677 with *Phèdre*.[2] As I explore in the Introduction, in this framework tragedy dies with Phèdre, and Racine retires from the stage, having realized tragedy's purest form: an art seemingly devoid of any violence. When literary scholars explain Racine's return to playwrighting, over twenty years later, they identify biographical reasons: Racine's increasing religious convictions or his canny political sense, which compels him to collaborate with Mme de Maintenon, the patron of his two final works, *Esther* and *Athalie*.

Taking place in the Temple of Jerusalem at Judah, the play recounts the drama of 2 Kings 11: the drama of the remaining descendant of the house of David named Joas. Having survived the massacre of his family as a baby, Joas is now being raised secretly and under the name Éliacin, within the temple by Joad, its High Priest. Joad is hiding Éliacin/Joas from Queen Athalie, Joas's grandmother, who ordered the massacre to eliminate all other claimants to the throne and is now a worshipper of Baal. Joad is determined to overcome Athalie and reinstate both Joas and the true religion in Judah. Racine's version focuses less on the youth Joas, or his protector Joad, than on Athalie: a Jew turned pagan, a murderous mother, a mourning daughter, a tolerant ruler. Her undoing occurs in a spectacular scene where the machined set design creates a double moment of revelation: The stage moves to reveal at once an inner scene of the young king now recognized and seated upon the throne, and his defenders lying in wait to attack Athalie.

Including *Athalie* in a longer story about the persistence of violence in tragedy troubles the historical frame that defines the occlusion of violence and therefore the terms of tragic art. In doing so, it also compels us to consider how this tradition positions the ruptures that violence performs as signs of its persistence. Both in the history of its performance and the unfolding of its drama, *Athalie* brings to the fore questions of what it means to be "last": Racine's last play, a people's last leader, the last moment of an era. Both in its performance history and within the play itself, *Athalie* is an inquiry into the problem of persistence.[3] Featuring an early meditation on the notion of catastrophe, *Athalie*'s reinterpretation of biblical prophecy in an early modern theatrical context suggests that what is at stake in our rehearsal of violence in tragedy is not just our interpretation of the past, but our relationship to the future.

This is a play whose performance history perversely resists any precise date, even though its 1691 composition and first production at Mme de Maintenon's school for impoverished aristocratic young women are well documented, as is its subsequent performance history. This is true of both the ensuing prohibition against its production and its reappearance in the eighteenth century. But because of its discontinuous performance history, its legendary role in the biography of Jean Racine, and its peculiar status in the eighteenth century, *Athalie* cleaves open our view of the neoclassical in many different ways: from the perspective of performance history, from that of literary history, and for the ways in which it seems to stage a certain idea about time itself. *Athalie* thus demands a peculiar reading of our place in time and our relationship to a temporality we cannot even pretend to control.

To effect such a reading, we need to disrupt the literary history of *Athalie*, which is already strangely split. *Athalie* is Racine's last tragedy, and it is understood as a pendant to his penultimate work, *Esther*. Both these plays were written for Louis XIV's last wife Mme de Maintenon, who wished to have the pupils at Saint-Cyr hone the rhetorical and other skills afforded by dramatic texts, without subjecting them to the dangers of profane theater. Jean Racine came out of his self-imposed retreat from dramaturgy to write these two plays, which were received with highly mixed reviews. Then Racine published the plays, with a privilege prohibiting their performance. Racine died, and the plays were allegedly forgotten, Louis XIV died, and Madame de Maintenon retired to Saint-Cyr and died too. The play was performed again before the young Louis XV during the regency and thereafter. Throughout the eighteenth century the play met with great acclaim as dramatic poetry, from, among others, Voltaire, Marmontel, and Diderot.

## Escaping the Bookends:
### Theater before and after the Rise of French Tragedy

Perhaps it is this peculiar reception history that has led scholars today to proclaim *Athalie* as "rather more a tragedy of the eighteenth than the seventeenth century."[4] This is in part due to the circumstances that bind us to traditional periodization: Written in the 1690s, and as Racine's last play, it marks the end of a century and of an era. To compound this terminal feeling, the prohibition against playing it generally was respected. It is as if it were abandoned by the seventeenth century and consequently seized with great affection by the eighteenth century. Might this imposition also have something to do with the ways literary history has shaped what a tragedy should be, what a seventeenth-century tragedy should be, and how this version of "classicism" ultimately was retired, rendered obsolete, by certain aesthetic and political revolutions? For this version of tragedy, shaped most forcefully by the undercurrents of nineteenth-century conceptions of freedom, heroism, and of the past that reverberated into the twentieth century, we can return to consider the Medean bookends of French tragedy as Marc Fumaroli had suggested, in particular the closing bookend, Racine's *Phèdre*—his first, or other, last tragedy.

In the first bookend, Corneille's *Médée*, the dramatization of regicide, infanticide, dynastic implosion, witchcraft, onstage burning, a justified revenge plot, and especially its concluding promise of suicide exemplify all that the next forty-five years of dramaturgy would purport to evacuate from the tragic stage. Neoclassical tragedy's closing bookend, 1677's *Phèdre*, so thoroughly banishes violence, passion, and action from the stage that its only most visible physical gesture is its eponymous character sinking to her knees. Together *Médée* and *Phèdre* figure allegorically the trajectory of classical theater and its writers over the course of the century. For Fumaroli, Médée, conjurer of words and the ruses made of such words, is the playwright, whereas *Phèdre* is an allegory of tragedy itself. Phèdre's fate is tragedy's fate; her suicidal last gasp is that of tragedy's own end. The mention of Medea in Phèdre's death soliloquy is also the unmasking of tragedy's secret past; within the abdication to Christian morality that *Phèdre* represents, Phèdre's dying gesture is also a revelation of the pagan, passionate, criminal poisons of desire. Phèdre's potion is the poison of passion, ever present in tragedy despite moralists' work to eliminate it. In her final demise after this famous tirade, she has killed off tragedy. In Fumaroli's essay, which reflects so many beliefs about classical tragedy that we still teach, tragedy ends when its evacuation of violence, passion, and action has turned on itself. Phèdre is a figure approaching a kind of Jansenist nihilism.

Did tragedy die with Phèdre and *Phèdre*? What to make of *Esther* and *Athalie*, Racine's two other tragedies written after over a decade-long hiatus during which Racine accepted a charge as royal historiographer? This question has been addressed as a generic one (are the biblical dramas really tragedies?), as a question of performance (does it matter that they were not open to the same public as other plays?), and as a matter of conscience (are they not renewed negotiations of Racine's Port-Royal education?). Or do *Athalie* and *Esther* mark such a radical departure from what preceded them that they are proposing an equally radical return of the tragic? If so, we might ask ourselves, is *Athalie* an encore, or the beginning of something new? A reprise? A renewal? A remnant? And what then comes after such a return?

Delving into the play offers fodder for these questions. *Athalie* presents a complex discourse on the nature of time, our attachments to the past and history, and the relationship between interpretation and time. But the drama also turns such questions into problems by staging them alongside a violent poetic rhetoric and scenes of conflict that are of central importance to the drama. The result is a meditation about time that occurs in the present, but which deeply troubles the integrity of that present, for *Athalie* is subject to an archaism that seems nevertheless prescient, a haunting of the past that is also about the inevitability—and illegibility—of the future, a play that asks us to accept the inevitability of catastrophe but not its finality, a play, finally, that asks us whether we wish to survive it.

## *Revivals, Remainders,* Rejetons

*Athalie*, from the moment of its eighteenth-century revival, was freighted with more significance than its writer could have ever intended. Racine's youngest son, Louis—himself an orphan at age six—recounts one of the first moments of this revival in the hagiographically styled memoirs he wrote of his father. The performance was held in the young Louis XV's apartments at the Tuileries in late March 1716, only six months after Louis XIV's death and just weeks after the very first general performances of the play since a moratorium on its staging a quarter-century earlier. The small audience of courtiers was moved to great tenderness and feeling as they watched the story of the young orphan Joas, hidden for his whole childhood in the temple, as he was revealed and ultimately crowned king of Judah, to reinstate the House of David. This triumph, of a "cher rejeton d'une vaillante race," (4.5.1457) (dear scion of a valiant race), repeatedly anticipated throughout the play, occurs in defiance of the monstrous apostate Athalie, queen of Jerusalem and former Jew, converted worshipper of Baal, whose execution concludes the tragedy.

This landmark performance before the royal audience occurred twenty-five years after the play's first bare-bones rehearsals and performances at Saint-Cyr and subsequent publication by Racine, and also nearly twenty years after the playwright's own death. The evening's performance in the king's apartments was a kind of encore after the Théâtre-Français performances at the beginning of the month, which themselves were the result of the regent's overturning of Racine's original 1691 interdiction against any public performances.

What we would call a "revival" was almost so in a literal sense, since the 1716 reprise resuscitated a play that had suffered near-extinction toward the end of Racine's life. As Louis Racine records, "Le succès fut étonnant, et les premières représentations faites à la cour donnaient un nouveau prix à cette Pièce"[5] (Its success was astounding, and the first performances at Court gave a new value to this play). Perhaps this renewal of a long-abandoned drama, a welcome haunting of the past, helped elicit from the small assembly those old Aristotelian values of terror and pity. The audience was so moved not just by the fact of the play's revival, nor the story itself, but rather by the analogical resonances between the play's depiction of the survival of a dynasty and the presence of the young Louis XV, who was about the same age as Joas:

> Parce que le Roi étant à peu près de l'âge de Joas, on ne pouvait sans s'attendrir sur lui, entendre quelques vers, comme ceux-ci:
>
> *Voilà donc votre Roi, votre unique espérance.*
> *J'ai pris soin jusqu'ici de vous le conserver ...*
> *Du fidèle David c'est le précieux reste ...*
> *Songez qu'en cet enfant tout Israël réside ...* [6]

> As the King was about the same age as Joas, it was impossible not to feel tenderness toward him when hearing certain verses such as these:
>
> *Here is your King, your only hope.*
> *I have taken care until now to keep him for you ...*
> *From Faithful David he is the precious remainder ...*
> *Consider that it is within this child that all of Israel lives.*

The legend of Louis XIV's living too long, and his son and grandson living not long enough, underscores the preciousness of Louis XV's survival, allowing for an experience of the tragedy *Athalie* in which Joas prefigures Louis XV, each a young and last direct heir to a dynasty, each a "précieux reste."

However anachronistic it might be, Racine's reading of scripture in *Athalie* imposes and invites such a typological reading, where in the Christian hermeneutical tradition, Old Testament stories are interpreted as types or foreshadowing of a corresponding element, or antitype, in the New Testament account of the Christian mystery. *Athalie*'s typological freight centers around Joas, who—like Esther, the subject of Racine's other religious play—is a Christ figure: a child who will save a people.

Typological readings allow for a kind of retrospective hope and a confirmation of unity and continuity in the divine plan, as they consider different historical moments under what Koselleck would call a "common historical plane."[7] In the context of early modern Christian hermeneutics and Gallican dynastic fragility, the survival of the reigning house is at once a miracle and a prefigured, guaranteed state. Racine was able to marry the Christianity of the story with the Aristotelian, pagan-based structure and values of classical tragedy through his deployment of a certain violent sublime, as Sylvaine Guyot has argued, that always finds its limits in the human body.[8] For Georges Forestier, the sublime revelation of the king encapsulates Racine's whole oeuvre: "Racine's modifications to the biblical story largely share the goal of transforming an expected denouement into a *sublime* denouement, in which Athalie's demise is the result of the unveiling of what was hidden: the unveiling of the hidden king. The theatrical device thus joins with the providential significance of the entire work."[9] The work of revelation in *Athalie*, however, contains within it a peculiar temporality that cannot be encapsulated alone by the notion of the sublime, the typological temporality of the Christian tradition of hermeneutics, or the mythological time of classical tragedy; the *survival* of the house of David, of the Jews, is something to be at once celebrated and feared: Survival is at once destiny and catastrophe.

## La Survie

*Survie*: survivorship—outliving, but also afterlife, a life continued into the hereafter and finally, perhaps *overliving*, or living too long. For Emily Wilson, overliving dominates literature from antiquity through the premodern period, reflecting a general temporality of the self characterized by the shadow of what she calls "an unending life in the body." Working against the long-standing tradition that sees tragedy as preoccupied singularly with death, Wilson suggests that anxieties about life's ceaseless repetition play within literature, producing "the disintegration of dramatic characters and frustrating audience expectations about dramatic and narrative structure."[10] In texts informed by a Christian tradition heavily imbued with Stoicism, Wilson explores how the discourse of tragic living suggests that all humans will find life too long.

Whereas Wilson's concept of overliving indicates the pain of a body-soul relationship that has gone on too long, we can also understand the notion of overliving with regard to a greater temporal complex of forces that implicate our lives' relationship to those of others. In this regard, the tension of the tragic scene as a confrontation between two scales of experience becomes important: between the finite dimensions of human living and the vast but discernible temporal dimensions of our world whose end is in sight. What is really interesting about the example of tragic drama in this landscape is the way in which it builds in another temporal dimension to the problem of life on a human scale—which is suggested by the convention of *in medias res*, of beginning the action after something has already happened, and confirmed by the playing out of actions and reactions that lead up to something and beyond it. Tragic personae live in and among great events: Andromaque remembering the devastation of the Trojan War and Suréna after his own military victories, to name two. They operate in a temporality of living supplementally, of experiencing survival as both a gift and a condemnation. Tragic literature receives and works from the burden of this paradox. Basic components of tragic narrative such as accounts of the past that serve to inform the audience of historical context convey this burden. Such hypotyposes as Andromaque's "Songe, songe Céphise" (Remember, remember Céphise), attempt to make an interlocutor relive such events of the past, while engaging in a kind of vivid, and even devastating overliving for the teller herself. Recalling the past in tragedy often calls into question the advisability of having survived it.

*Athalie* casts both of its most potent characters as survivors. Joas is the only survivor of the house of David after Queen Athalie's massacre, and the queen is the only survivor of her own family's decimation. Each embodies another facet of surviving: Joas is the personification of the truth of *survie* as the typological guarantor of Christ; he is also the exemplar of Christian compassion. As an object of spectacle for an audience, he elicits our *pitié*; this was true for the play's first audiences as well as for those in the next century—and perhaps beyond.

In contrast, Athalie's *survie*, we might say, resides more in horror than in pity or compassion. Whereas we might imagine that Athalie experiences her own life as too long—the vivid nightmares from which she suffers point to this possibility, as does the account of the real fate of her family, each and every one of them killed in the massacre. Rather more acutely, the audience might have wished her to have already died, since the play recounts the massacre of the house of David that she leads to become queen. It is Josabet, the head priest's wife who saved Joas, who recounts the events:

> De Princes égorgés la chambre était remplie.
> Un poignard à la main l'implacable Athalie
> Au carnage animait ses barbares Soldats,
> Et poursuivait le cours de ses assassinats.
> Joas laissé pour mort, frappa soudain ma vue.
>
> (1.2.243–47)

> The princes lay there, slaughtered savagely;
> Goading her barbarian henchmen to butchery,
> The implacable Athalie, knife in hand,
> Pursued her murderous project.
> Then I suddenly spied Joas, left for dead.[11]

Athalie's own "implacable" self here is nestled between the corpses of the "princes égorgés" that fill the room and the assassination program that she directs; that she does so by "animating" her soldiers adds a word of irony to her endeavors. More generally, however, Athalie's living is defined by excess in myriad ways: This description of her own bloody acts of murder seems over the top, while her own mother's horrific death, described earlier in the play (her mother Jézabel was defenestrated and left on the ground to be dismembered and eaten by dogs), serves as catalyst to, if not a justification of, her carnage. Her own relating of her dreams contributes to these excessive demonstrations, which are also proof, in all their excess, that she also has lived *beyond* others. That is, she has not just lived longer than maybe she should have, or longer than others; she has lived in relative excess to others' mortal suffering: Her life has required the excess of their pain and death.

These vivid accounts show how horror affords simultaneous presentations of different forms of *survie*. The complexity of this thematic is made clearer by a poetic chain of causality in *Athalie* that almost implies a kind of division of labor: One person overlives while another survives. For example, Athalie's own overliving is followed by Joas's survival, rescued from under the bloody breast of his nurse's body. This survival is rendered fleshly in the sense that Joas survives by being protected by his nurse's body, the baby pressed under her.

The most stunning of those excessive demonstrations of Athalie's over-living is the dreamed embrace with her mother, where the dream form allows a hypotypotic moment of something not just impossible to stage but genuinely impossible to witness: the sleeping visions of another:

> Ma mère Jézabel devant moi s'est montrée,
> Comme au jour de sa mort pompeusement parée.
> Ses malheurs n'avaient point abattu sa fierté.
> Même elle avait encor cet éclat emprunté,
> Dont elle eut soin de peindre et d'orner son visage,
> Pour réparer des ans l'irréparable outrage.
> Tremble, m'a-t-elle dit, fille digne de moi.
> Le cruel Dieu des Juifs l'emporte aussi sur toi.
> Je te plains de tomber dans ses mains redoutables,
> Ma fille. En achevant ces mots épouvantables,
> Son Ombre vers mon lit a paru se baisser.
> Et moi, je lui tendais les mains pour l'embrasser,
> Mais je n'ai plus trouvé qu'un horrible mélange
> D'os et de chairs meurtris et traînés dans la fange,
> Des lambeaux pleins de sang, et des membres affreux
> Que des chiens dévorants se disputaient entre eux.
>
> (2.5.491–506)

> My mother Jezebel appeared to me,
> Dressed as on her death day, splendidly.
> Her sorrows had not felled her pride.
> She even had that spark borrowed
> From having painted and decorated her face,
> To repair the outrageous damage of years' decay.
> "Tremble," she said to me, "my worthy daughter,
> The Jews' cruel God has marked you too,
> I fear that you might fall into his fearsome grasp,
> My daughter." And finishing these frightful words,
> Her shadow seemed to lean toward my bed,
> And me, I reached out my arms to embrace her
> But found only a horrible mess
> Of bones and putrid flesh dragged through the mud
> Shreds of blood-soaked skin and horrible limbs,
> Over which devouring dogs fought each other.

Here, the link between overliving and survival is made through the maternal connection, or rather its failure. The ghost of Jézabel comes to Athalie in a dream—the nightmare as a kind of perfect example of how to overlive—to warn her daughter and plead for Athalie's survival. Athalie's stretched-out arms—*survival trying to touch overliving*—delving into the morass of tissue and gore is *prosopopoeia* taken to the extreme: A living woman channels the dreamed voice of a dead mass of flesh. Athalie's overliving becomes conflated with the excesses of the play. Devastation punctuates the "before"; it threatens the "during"; and it characterizes predictions of the future—this in a drama that was to be without passions, in the name of its young performers' moral purity, but instead is replete with horrific description.

Athalie's dream is therefore an exceptional moment in the play, and as such it is tempting to relegate this rupture in tone and taste to a dream that is recounted: we are steps away from this action as fact. Athalie's dream, however, is also an affirmation of Derrida's notion of "la survivance," that is, the "gestural, verbal, written, or other trace" which ensures "the survival in which the opposition of the living and the dead loses and must lose all pertinence."[12] Here, Athalie's dream is a kind of archive, through which she brings to us a living but dead Jézabel, a nearly literally touchable ghost. Her description points out the tenuous relationship between the present and the past, made most poignant by the maternal thread, poetically revealed to be continually ruptured: Athalie's mother Jézabel dies, abandoning her, only to return as a dreamed zombie. Athalie herself will feel something critics have often called a "maternal" feeling for the child Éliacin/Joas, whom she will eventually want to kill. We see this problem poetically underscored in the vehemence of her tirade: from "Ma Mère" to the "Ma Fille," it is punctuated by an overdetermined, Medean *M* that marks not only *mère* but also the *mains* and the *mélange* and *membres meutris*. With "Ma Fille" as poetic *rejet*, that is, in a position of enjambment at the start of the new line, Athalie is poetically isolated. Missing a mother and never having had a *fille*, she has no legacy to pass on. This empty transmission further is figured when Jézabel leans forward and Athalie offers her hands for an embrace: The impossibility of these two generations touching is first because of the double material realities of their conditions: a dream first, but also—more importantly—a dismembered corpse. This very impossibility, however, also allows for the eruption of an absent past made present: That is, through the record of violence, Jézabel's violent death (which is Athalie's legacy) emerges again, but in a strangely or ambivalently material form. This account of violence's continual role in history, evacuating even the maternal from its power to symbolize regeneration, ratchets up the most important tension of the play: Who will survive? And what will they survive? What is the end of this play?

To know the "end" of a play might be either a question of plot or one of moral utility. How does the play end? How does it conclude? Or, what is the aim of the play? That is: What does the totality of the drama, once apprehended, mean to convey? Either way, this is a not question we normally need ask of classical tragedy, for the conclusions to their histories are already known, as are the possibilities for edification. Even in a tragedy such as *Athalie*, modeled not on any then-known antique sources but on an Old Testament story that was less familiar to first audiences, the text itself presages the bloody end repeatedly, and mobilizes a chorus that reminds us of the stakes at play. *Athalie* wants us to know its end.

Even so, we are hard-pressed to imagine a way out of the temple, as it were. How will we get out, and at what price? In this space, in this play, a massacre will certainly occur, and it will be one much like the one that brought Athalie to power. But can one imagine a massacre on stage, in 1691, at a girls' school, in front of a king? What then, precisely, will be performed? What, dramaturgically, is to be survived?

## *Living Catastrophe*

In the vocabulary of classical drama, we'd say that surviving characters of a drama outlive the *catastrophe*, the play's final moments. This definition—a neutral term associated with the resolution in structured, Aristotelian drama—is the predominant one until the eighteenth century. *Catastrophe*'s first usages among ancient writers are quite close to its etymology: "sudden turn," "conclusion," "upheaval," or "resolution" appear in both historical and dramaturgical texts. *Catastrophe* quickly became associated with theater terminology nearly exclusively, where it remained neutral or even positive, as in Scaliger's 1561 *Poetics*, one of the more prominent European commentaries on Aristotle's newly rediscovered treatise. For Scaliger, *catastrophe* is "the conversion of the troubled affair into an unexpected tranquility."[13] At least as late as the 1690s, it is synonymous with *dénouement*, as d'Aubignac insists, or it is distinguished as the "essence" of the dénouement, its "nature."[14]

We note that three words crucial to the dramaturgical transmission of violence—tragedy, horror, and catastrophe—today belong to the lexicon of historical thinking. This vocabulary generally accounts for that which is not survivable. Throughout the sixteenth and seventeenth centuries, however, *catastrophe* remained a theatrical term first. When reapplied to events of history, as in military campaigns, astronomical or geological events, it signaled the resolution of a series of events. As late as the 1680s, cosmographer Thomas Burnet offered a theory of the end of the world aligning biblical evidence with evidence from natural philosophy, especially geology. Describing the end of the world, which, he held, came about through volcanic eruption, collisions of meteors, and fire everywhere, he suggested that "the next catastrophe is the CONFLAGRATION, to which a new face of Nature will accordingly succeed, . . . and so it is call'd the *Restitution* of things, or *Regeneration* of the World."[15] Yet even in this dismal view of great happenings in the universe, "catastrophe" is rather a significant change with lasting consequences, not unlike the early modern notion of "revolution," a concept that in the early modern period was informed by astronomy's vision of cyclical, regular rotations of natural bodies as events.

*Athalie* too has its catastrophe, its great sudden turn that converts trouble into a form of tranquility. Its catastrophe is what Voltaire, Jean-François de La Harpe, and others loved about the play: a spectacular scene. The inner sanctum of the temple is revealed when the young king Joas is crowned, his supporters armed and ready to fight. Voltaire says, "I'll begin by saying of *Athalie* that is there where catastrophe is most admirably put into action," by which he means the last scene.[16] By the 1750s, however, writings on the earthquakes of Lisbon and other natural disasters suggest the emergence of a new meaning to the word *catastrophe* and a new arena for its use: natural disasters that were unforeseen.[17]

Over the course of one hundred years, then, dramatic catastrophe goes from being synonymous with a turn that ends a play, the scenic space's final straw as it were, and comes to designate an unanticipated and usually natural disaster of unforeseeable devastation. It goes from a structural aesthetic element denoting a conclusion, to a full-blown cataclysm with specific temporal dimensions and—crucially—a feature of unpredictability. Catastrophe, by the eighteenth century, is the measure of what escapes human knowledge and understanding on a grand scale.

How did we get from dramaturgical denouement, or even more precisely and technically, the coda to a denouement, to an unforeseeable cataclysm of societal scale? Over the course of the decades of *Athalie*'s creation, retirement, and revival the word *catastrophe* takes on a very different set of valences. It is in the late seventeenth century that natural philosophers begin to modify the term so that "catastrophe" became anchored in geological discourse. Those whom today we would call geological scientists began to use the word *catastrophe* to talk about what Olaf Briese calls a "positive apocalyptic transformation" in the earth.[18] As a theory of geological formation, *catastrophe* becomes highly ambiguous morally and temporally: It is both positive and foreboding, both inaugural and final.

*Catastrophe* passes through another movement in the late seventeenth and early eighteenth centuries when it comes to denote a personal, individual, or local "boulversement" or disruption, again not always bad.[19] This is also a shift from something that is predictable to something that is without origin in the past. In the trajectory of *catastrophe*'s shifting semantic landscape, there is at once a qualitative change (technical resolution and confirmation of events), a scalar shift (from theater to the world, through the individual and the local), and a temporal change (from the predictable to the unpredictable).

*Athalie* is a privileged scene for the conflation of these concepts of catastrophe, with the question of *survie* implicated in each and concentrated in their conflation, where *survie* means both living beyond and living excessively, and catastrophe means both resolution *and* devastation. The interplay between *survie* and catastrophe informs the play's aesthetics, the interpretations it demands, and the reception and literary histories it has inspired.

The play's resolution stages a collision between these two ideas of catastrophe, in the multilayered denouement it uses. One might consider the revelation, to Athalie, of the inner temple, with Joas crowned and protected by the Levites, to be the scene of denouement. Beginning with a willed misunderstanding, in which Joad has promised Athalie the "treasures" of the temple as well as the child Éliacin, the temple's curtains draw back, and we will live the conflation of these, in the person of Joas.

> JOAD.
>     Sur-le-champ tu seras satisfaite:
>     Je te les vais montrer l'un et l'autre à la fois.
>     *(Le rideau se tire.)*
>     Paraissez, cher Enfant, digne sang de nos rois.
>     Connais-tu l'héritier du plus saint des monarques,
>     Reine ? De ton poignard connais du moins ces marques.
>     Voilà ton Roi, ton Fils, le Fils d'Ochosias.
>     Peuples, et vous, Abner, reconnaissez Joas.
> ABNER.
> Ciel!
>     ATHALIE, à JOAD.
>         Perfide!
>
>                                        (5.5.1717–23)

JOAD.
> You shall see them right away.
> I'll show you both at once: look over there.
> —Appear, dear child, worthy blood of our king's.
> *(The curtain is drawn.)*
> You recognize the saintly David's seed?
> Observe the scars that mark your murderous deed!
> Here's your true king, your son, the son of Ochoasias!
> People, and you too, Abner, recognize Joas!

ABNER.
> Heavens!

ATHALIE, to JOAD.
> > Villain!

Joad's exhortation to all to "recognize" Joas can be read as an internal stage direction, useful for those reading the play but seemingly redundant for a performance. As a political performance, however, it offers this collision between an acknowledgment of sovereignty of one that is also a fatal defeat of another. What ensues is the battle between the Levites, hidden in the inner temple, who envelope Athalie. They lead the queen off, out of the sacred space her presence is defiling, her fate certain, as Joad orders: "De leur sang par sa mort faire cesser les cris. / Si quelque audacieux embrasse sa querelle, / Qu'à la fureur du glaive on le livre avec elle" (5.6.1791–96). (With her death let their cries be stopped. / And if any brazen souls take up her side, / Let the fury of the blade deliver them with her.) What follows, then, would be termed the *catastrophe*, in the dramaturgical, seventeenth- and eighteenth-century sense. That is, Athalie's death is the *catastrophe*, insofar as it is the logical consequence of the crisis.

To what extent, however, does this promise of an execution really clean up the play's remaining questions or tensions? The play does not really warrant Athalie's execution as a necessary outcome to Joas's revelation and coronation. Athalie's death is neither sacrifice nor expiation. Instead, the interpretative structures of the play suggest that these characters are defined less by their oppositionality than by the interplay of their types operating in concert with each other, to be read not for their conflict but for the way they mutually constitute, inform, and guarantee each other through their affects. So why is Athalie's death the *catastrophe*—what does it do, and to whom?

As others have noted, Athalie is not simply a foil against which the forces of right fight; rather she is a complex, multivalent character. Far from instrumentalizing her, then, the tragedy puts Athalie at the center of the drama: not just as present tyrant but also as a figure with its own particular history, fears, and determination. For Derval Conroy, there are three different Athalies: monster, sovereign, and woman.[20] Close attention to this multiplicity of characters suggests that Athalie's shifts are intimately linked to the clashes between pagan and biblical temporalities that define her history. The monstrosity whose aberrant behavior is the subject of Josabet and others' accounts occurs during the religious battle which Athalie will win. The work of sovereign shows itself most acutely in her scene with Éliacin, the hidden Joas.

As sovereign, she is the voice of moderation, religious tolerance, of truth-telling in the play. Athalie does not deny her past, but as sovereign she lives in the present. As she says,

> Je ne veux point ici rappeler le passé,
> Ni vous rendre raison du sang que j'ai versé.
> Ce que j'ai fait, Abner, j'ai cru le devoir faire.
> . . . . . . . . . . . . . . .
> Par moi Jérusalem goûte un calme profond.
> Le Jourdain ne voit plus l'Arabe vagabond
> Ni l'altier Philistin, par d'éternels ravages,
> Comme au temps de vos Rois, désoler ses rivages;
> Le Syrien me traite et de Reine et de Soeur.
>
> (2.5.465–77)

> I do not want now to recall the past,
> Nor to explain the blood I have spilled.
> What I've done, Abner, I've believed necessary.
> . . . . . . . . . . . . . . .
> And because of me Jerusalem tastes tranquility.
> Marauding Arabs no longer trouble the Jordan
> Nor the do the haughty Philistines and their unending raids,
> as they did during the time of your kings;
> The Syrian King sees me as a sister and a queen.

The entire region knows peace, even the feared Jéhu, "me laisse en ces lieux souveraine maîtresse" (2.5.483) (leaves me to be the sovereign mistress of these lands). Later, when she invites Joas, hidden under the name of the orphan Éliacin, to live with her, she affirms the liberty of Éliacin/Joas to pray to his god. Athalie as sovereign, then, is quite the opposite of her monstrous self. This is the scene that captivated many eighteenth-century theater critics and writers, and horrified others. The asymmetry displayed in the meeting of these two survivors, the contrast between the older woman and the child, the tyrant and the innocent, made Athalie's tenderness toward Éliacin/Joas particularly striking. In the context of eighteenth-century debates about religious tolerance, Athalie's invitation that he come live with her and be free to worship as he chose was arresting. How could an architect of massacre be an advocate for religious tolerance?

Underneath her politics, and following her monstrous behavior, Athalie the ruler reveals another facet of her self uniting the first two. Although it might be considered gendered, closer attention suggests that it is more than gendered: It is *vulnerable*, it is *sensible*. Athalie's sensitivity first shows itself in her impulse to recount the dream of her mother that has affected her so deeply as to have interrupted her current state of contentment:

> Mais un trouble importun vient depuis quelques jours,
> De mes prospérités interrompre le cours.
> Un songe (Me devrais-je inquiéter d'un songe?)
> Entretient dans mon coeur un chagrin qui le ronge.
> Je l'évite partout, partout il me poursuit.
>
> (2.5.485–89)

> But for the past few days, something troubling has come
> To interrupt the regular course of my happiness.
> A dream (should I even worry about a dream?)
> has introduced an affliction that gnaws at my heart.
> I flee it everywhere; everywhere it follows me.

What affects Athalie is the "chagrin" of a vivid dream where she is a *child*, who feels horror at her mother. But what moves her to action in the present moment, what leads her to the temple at that very moment, is the second part of the dream, which can be read as an answer to the first:

> Dans ce désordre à mes yeux se présente
> Un jeune Enfant couvert d'une robe éclatante,
> Tels qu'on voit des Hébreux les Prêtres revêtus.
> Sa vue a ranimé mes esprits abattus.
> Mais lorsque revenant de mon trouble funeste,
> J'admirais sa douceur, son air noble et modeste,
> J'ai senti tout à coup un homicide acier.
> Que le traître en mon sein a plongé tout entier.
> De tant d'objets divers le bizarre assemblage

Peut-être du hasard vous paraît un ouvrage.
Moi-même quelque temps honteuse de ma peur
Je l'ai pris pour l'effet d'une sombre vapeur.
Mais de ce souvenir mon âme possédée
A deux fois en dormant revu la même idée.
Deux fois mes tristes yeux se sont vu retracer
Ce même enfant toujours tout prêt à me percer.

(2.5.507–22)

Amid this disorder came before my eyes
A young child in a glittering gown
Such as what the Hebrew priests wear.
The sight revived my dampened spirits
Just as I was recovering from my mournful state
Admiring his sweetness, his noble and modest air,
All of a sudden I felt a murderous blade
Which that traitor had plunged deep into my breast.
Perhaps this mess of so many diverse elements
Seems to you a product of chance
Even I, at first ashamed of my fright,
Took it as the effect of a dark vapor.
But this memory has possessed my soul,
Having seen two times while sleeping the same idea,
Two times my sad eyes have retraced
This same child, every ready to run me through.

Her "instinct" having pushed her to "le temple des Juifs" with gifts to "to appease their God," she arrives and encounters the unknown child. Her first reaction is to register the resemblance between the innocent yet homicidal child of her dreams and the young man before her: "Ô ciel! plus j'examine, et plus je le regarde . . . / C'est lui! D'horreur encore tous mes sens sont saisis" (2.7.620–21) (Oh heavens! The more I examine him, the more I look . . . / It is him! Horror again seizes all my senses). As she interviews him, however, she is seized by another feeling, more particular, less familiar it would seem, and so harder to name:

Quel prodige nouveau me trouble, et m'embarrasse?
La douceur de sa voix, son enfance, sa grâce,
Font insensiblement à mon inimitié
Succéder . . . Je serais sensible à la pitié?

(2.7.651–54)

> What new wonder comes to trouble me?
> The sweetness of his voice, his youth, his grace,
> Heartlessly compelled my hatred
> To cede to . . . have I been seized by pity?

Barely able to identify the feeling, she cannot explain this order of sentiments. She can't even understand where it comes from within her: It must have conquered her from without. So she is compelled to pity as if by conquest. Athalie here as in her dream attests to an internal experience brought on by an external force, another party. In her experience of the world, both dreaming and living, she performs the very thing that spectators and readers are meant to do: She feels horror and pity—compassion. Athalie does what an ideal audience should do, and in so doing, she shows us how to experience the messianic Joas and the prophetic horrors that contextualize his emergence from the temple. Athalie thus functions as Éliacin/Joas's first spectator. She is an ideal one, letting herself be disposed to feel according to his performance. Within this release of herself, her giving of herself over to his performance, she necessarily releases herself from her own temporality: Past and recurring dreams operate on one plane with the present moment.

## *Palimpsestic History*

Racine gives us a telling model for this mode of signification in the architecture of the play itself, in particular around his use of the temple. The preface to *Athalie* opens with a detailed description of the temple. By way of justifying this choice, something of a curious setting for a tragedy, he offers the details of the locale to those less schooled in Old Testament stories. Racine concentrates on three details of note: the family relationships that create sacred roles around the temple, the architecture of the temple itself, and the temple's historic location. This last detail shapes the significance of the temple for the tragedy, as its history provides a model for the layered yet porous temporalities that inform *Athalie*.

As Racine avers, tradition dictated clearly that the temple stood on the mountain where Abraham prepared to sacrifice his son. The sacred geography of place is also a typological one. That is, a contemporary structure, the temple, stands literally upon a more ancient altar, and symbolically instantiates the relationship cemented earlier between God and the family of Abraham on the mountain. In these layers of literal sediment, history wends back and forth in time to justify the messianic interpretation of

*Athalie* that Racine proposes, and makes the sacred space of the temple the most fitting locale for his drama:

> Comme les rois de Juda étaient de la Maison de David, et qu'ils avaient dans leur partage la Ville et le Temple de Jérusalem, tout ce qu'il y avait de prêtres et de Lévites se retirèrent auprès d'eux, et leur demeurèrent toujours attachés. Car, depuis que le Temple de Solomon fut bâti, il n'était plus permis de sacrifier ailleurs.... Ainsi le culte légitime ne subsistait plus que dans Juda.... Les Prêtres étaient de la Famille d'Aaron, et il n'y avait que ceux de cette Famille, lesquels pussent exercer la Sacrificature. Les Lévites leur étaient subordonnés, et avaient soin, entre autres choses du chant, de la préparation des victimes, et de la garde du temple.... Tout l'édifice s'appelait en général le Lieu saint. Mais on appelait plus particulièrement de ce nom cette partie du Temple intérieur où étaient le Chandelier d'or, l'Autel des parfums et les Tables des pains de proposition. Et cette partie était encore distinguée du Saint des Saints, où était l'Arche.... C'était une Tradition assez constante que la Montagne sur laquelle le Temple fut bâti était la même Montagne, où Abraham avait autrefois offert en sacrifice son fils Isaac.[21]

> Since the Kings of Judah were from the house of David, and they were given the city and temple of Jerusalem, all the priests and Levites moved there, and remained forever connected to that area. For since the construction of Solomon's temple, it was no longer permitted to make sacrifices anywhere else.... Thus the true worship practices survived only in Judah.... The priests were from the family of Aaron, and only those from this family could perform sacrifices. The Levites were subordinate to them, and cared for—among other things—the chanting, the preparation of victims, and the guarding of the temple. The whole building was generally referred to as the holy space, but this was also the name given more specifically to the part of the interior temple where the golden candelabrum, the altar of incense, and the Shewbread table. This area was distinct from the Holy of Holies, where the Ark was.... Tradition maintained that the mountain on which the temple was built was the same mountain where Abraham had once offered his son Isaac in sacrifice.

Racine here signals how a typological reading operates not only backward and forward in time, but also physically, geologically uncovering and thereby deciphering the palimpsests of layered meaning that we inhabit. So operates Athalie. Athalie's *survie*, both her survival and her overliving, is such a self. Like the temple, its history and its significance, she is constructed out of layered meanings. Massacring monster, suffering daughter, childless woman, and tolerant sovereign: These are not just facets of the same person this is one person in history, whose meaning is created through the folding back and folding over of the layers of that history.

Arguably, if Joas might be said, just like Athalie, to have overlived, his character is also multilayered. Just as his survival of the massacre was guaranteed by the protective layer of his nurse's body, so too the name Élician operates as a shield, in the physical sanctuary of the temple. Unlike Athalie, of course, Joas is the one who will survive this tragedy to guarantee the house of David; though this significance remains to be realized in the future.

In this same future, he will also, as the priest Joad proclaims, ultimately return that house to near ruination. Joad's proclamation takes the form of a rueful warning, a lesson imparted too late to the young king, who can no longer be taught. Joad's tirade begins by acknowledging the newly changed relationship they have, since Joas is no longer even nominally his son:

> Ô mon fils, de ce nom j'ose encor vous nommer,
> . . . . . . . . . . . . . . .
> Hélas! vous ignorez le charme empoisonneur.
> De l'absolu pouvoir vous ignorez l'ivresse,
> Et des lâches Flatteurs la voix enchanteresse.
> Bientôt ils vous diront que les plus saintes Lois,
> Maîtresses du vil peuple, obéissent aux Rois,
> Qu'un roi n'a d'autre frein que sa volonté même,
> Qu'il doit immoler tout à sa grandeur suprême,
> Qu'aux larmes, au travail le Peuple est condamné,
> Et d'un sceptre de fer veut être gouverné,
> Que s'il n'est opprimé, tôt ou tard il opprime.
> Ainsi de piège en piège, et d'abîme en abîme,
> Corrompant de vos moeurs l'aimable pureté,
> Ils vous feront enfin haïr la Vérité,
> Vous peindront la vertu sous une affreuse image.
>
> (4.4.1394–1481)

> Oh my son—if I dare still call you that,
> . . . . . . . . . . . . . . .
> Alas! You are unaware of the poisonous charms,
> the intoxication of absolute power,
> and the enchanting voice of cowardly flatterers.

> Soon they will tell you that the holiest laws
> while masters of the vile people, must obey kings,
> That a king has no other bridle but his own will,
> That he must sacrifice everyone to his own supreme grandeur,
> That the people is condemned to tears and to work
> And that it is with an iron scepter that he must govern.
> Thus from trap to trap, from abyss to abyss,
> Corrupting the lovely purity of your ways,
> They will make you hate the truth,
> Painting of virtue a hideous image.

Joad's hesitation at the final filial rupture seems sentimental: Joas is soon to be no longer his son, for not only will the disguise be lifted and his true filiation be known, but the boy will become a king. This last lesson of Joad expresses not just a sentiment of loss but a lesson not yet taught, and perhaps unteachable. Having been locked in the temple, Joas is ignorant of the treacherous politics of kingship; so ignorant that he does not even know that he is unaware. In this moment, Joad marks the distance between the innocent state of the present and the knowledgeable, corrupt state of what is yet to come. The character of Joas personifies here the concept of potential, since his power will accrue only in the future, when he denies his people and turns wicked. If Athalie's death guarantees the apotheosis of Joas, it guarantees future carnage and the deferral of the messiah.

What then does Athalie mean? What does she stand for? Typologically, she is at once a kind of perverse Marian figure, an adoptive mother who does not know her chosen offspring is the Savior, and she is a sacrifice without whose demise the scion of the house of David could not emerge. But Athalie is also a measure of good rule, a rare instance of a Queen of Israel, and a peaceful one at that. Her demise ushers in the end of a period of prosperity for Israel and foreshadows a future time of abused power and the subjugation of its people. Athalie's demise is thus the play's *catastrophe* in that it adeptly finishes the work of the tragedy, but only insofar as her end functions also as an invitation to the more modern form of *catastrophe*: the real carnage of Joas's future barbaric actions. Her death resolves nothing; it only leaves open future cycles.

In this way we would do well to reconsider the position of *Athalie* the tragedy and the ways critics have imposed on it a literary history of which it is at least partially innocent. Georges Forestier has summarized this history aptly:

Revenir sur ce mythe critique, c'est revenir sur l'idée selon laquelle le théâtre profane de Racine, commencé par une *Thébaïde* adapté d'Euripide, aboutit à une *Phèdre* inspirée d'Euripide, et selon laquelle, plus largement, tout son parcours dramatique aboutit à *Athalie*, là où le vrai Dieu et sa Providence ont remplacé les faux dieux païens et leur obscur destin, substituts poétiques placés là comme en attente.[22]

To question this critical myth is to reconsider the idea that Racine's secular theater begins with a *Thébaïde* adapted from Euripides and ends with a *Phèdre*, also inspired by Euripides, and that his entire dramaturgical career culminates in *Athalie*, where the real God and His Providence have replaced those earlier false pagan gods and their obscure fortunes, poetic stand-ins parked there as if in waiting (for the real ones).

If we return to the scene Louis Racine imagined for us in his memoirs of his father, the typological casting of Louis XV would suggest that we read him as a survivor of a particular denouement, the denouement of the longest reign in French history. But what is the corresponding *catastrophe*? Would it be the regency, which was—politically and economically—a catastrophe? And what would this catastrophe stand for typologically? What future catastrophe? Would it be the catastrophic and definitive downfall of Louis XV's own house and kingdom, fifteen years after his death?

Without resorting to such exaggeration, it is nevertheless important to point out that Racine's 1691 play creates the terms, in its characters, for such accretion, and in its deployments of certain dramatic terms of feeling and change like horror, pity, and *catastrophe*, for a simple denouement to signal an enormous cataclysm. A play that sets up this kind of paradigm creates a sliding frame of reference, where history works both palimpsestically and providentially.

That is, finally, the nature of catastrophe: It is not the terrible, unanticipated event that we barely survive, but the logical resolution of something we knew would happen (and one that allows great hardship to occur), but that also accrues meaning through our subjective relationship to its history. Working temporally both backward and forward, figured as layers of meaning that must be uncovered even as they are already known, *Athalie* the tragedy dramatizes the relation between overliving and catastrophe, placing us forever on the move toward both renewed living *and* bloody destruction.

Today, we might see this as a relatively new problem; political theorists continually rediscover concepts and applications of biopolitics in contemporary life, well beyond what Foucault's initial philosophical gambit admitted. And social thinkers have identified the failures of "modernity" with the high price of living in what Ulrich Beck called already in the 1980s a "risk society," one structured around the negotiation, management, and therefore perpetuation of dangers that it created itself.²³ Philosopher Frédéric Neyrat has a different word for the same quality. He says, "Comparé au terme de risque, celui de catastrophe dramatise l'extension et l'intensité des bouleversements, le degré d'interruption possible du cours normal des événements; alors que, semble-t-il, paradoxalement, rien ne change, et rien ne s'interrompt vraiment."²⁴ (Compared to the term "risk," "catastrophe" underscores the extension and intensity of the turmoil, the degree of interruption that can occur during the normal course of events; even as it appears that, paradoxically nothing is changing, and nothing is interrupted.) Catastrophe proposes the integration of the "loss of a stable ground," to use Nigel Clark's term, as constitutive of contemporary life.²⁵ We might be reminded of a note that Walter Benjamin made around the time he wrote his theses *On the Concept of History*, when he sensed Europe was on a course of devastation that could not be reversed: "Catastrophe is progress; progress is catastrophe. Catastrophe [should be seen] as a continuum of history." For the victims of history, the march forward in time through history is a march over its losses; history in this sense is a story of catastrophe for the oppressed. For this reason, Benjamin would also muse, "The concept of progress must be grounded in the idea of catastrophe. That things continue as before: that is the catastrophe."²⁶ Catastrophe feels contemporary, in its banality. Or is it the temporality that we have ascribed to catastrophe that makes it feel ours and ours alone? Is it the never-changing reality of cataclysm and cruel oppression that is the catastrophe? Or rather is it the temporality of surprise, of forced unanticipation, of tragedy without origin, that creates the sense of modern devastation?

Perhaps it was, at a moment when we began to abandon the multiple temporality of a history lived simultaneously then, now, and in the faraway future, that the usual course of events became the seed for catastrophe. That is, the future as the repository of the unknown became our ever-repeated, unavoidable destiny, which we accepted even as we disavowed any knowledge or relation to it. At what price do we cleave ourselves from a future known by the past, if all too well ignored by the present, to be a promised disaster?

The violence in *Athalie* seems to have truly been the last word on seventeenth-century French tragedy, despite—or because of—its remarkable afterlife in the eighteenth century. It stands in particularly deep contrast to the first "last word" on the matter, Racine's *Phèdre*, where offstage violence erupts in the extended meditation on Hippolyte's death, and onstage violence is concentrated in the collapsing body of Phèdre. The physicality of both these deaths appears to mean two separate things to us. Whereas one is mangled spectacularly by his namesake horses, the other is destroyed from within by her own passions. Taken together, they seem to offer a contrast between the physically heroic and the passionately shameful. The tragedy *Phèdre* seeks to consider both of these violences as of a piece, but also weighs them differently: After all, it is over the heroic that we are given free reign, both compelled and permitted to construct ourselves while we apprehend the slight spectacle of shameful passion together, as a public. *Athalie* is a different matter, however; arguably it inverts our relation to violence. In contrast to *Phèdre*, its heroic spectacularity is visible onstage and in an extended manner, with the assault on the inner sanctum creating a fabulous *coup de théâtre*. The contrast with this potentially expiative violence is rather to be found on the periphery, well offstage: in Athalie's dream of her mother, in the prophecy that as ruler Joas will ruin his people, the next generation.

There is something terrible about violence that is organized to occupy the spaces of our dreams and our future. Is it worse, however, than ordering our relationship to violence's presence as if the future were completely unknown?

# Epilogue: The Cosmopolitics of Literature

My endeavor in this book has been to explore how reading violence as a persistent and necessary force in tragedy can help us read it differently. There has been a politics behind my interest in refusing this as a "book about Medea" or a "thematic" study of that character, and throughout this work I have gone so far as to try to avoid considering Medea as a character, or in any other way indexable to a person. Moreover, and in a perverse way even more challenging is that Medea is not exclusively indexed to women (this understanding was so important to me that for a long time I tried writing without using a gendered pronoun to describe Medea). That is, what is more important is not that Medea is a "woman" or that such a figure is like real people in our world but that the gestures shaping its myth and giving it its currency indicate how we decide when humans get to be humans based on their violence. Violence here is shown to have an epistemological structure that gives it meaning. There is a commonplace that violence is heroic if it occurs during wartime or in a moment of sacrifice. Medean violence is well outside of this realm, since it is retributive, passionate, and, perhaps most significantly, barbaric. By this I mean to signal that Medean violence is organized along a foreign epistemological order.

It is skilled; it is controlled; it follows rules; it is often contained or targeted. It is barbaric because its reasons are not part of our order. And it is for this reason that it has so much destructive power.[1] But we have also seen that this barbarian nature has a history: It is distinctly a "modern" invention to describe a "premodern" perdurance.

It has been a claim of this book that the premodern Medean principle of violence has a privileged role in seventeenth-century French tragedy, from Rotrou and Corneille (both 1634) to Racine (1691). Nita Krevens has explored how Medea is the only female consistently associated with the foundations of cities—as well as with the more familiar aura of destruction.[2] Is it significant that the myth's particular persistence in political tragedy occurred at the time that France was in the act of becoming a modern nation-state? It is as if the myth both ushers in the law as it founds the nation-state and yet indicates what can never be assimilated.

Another figure of the same nature is that of the cosmopolitan. Cosmopolitanism as a philosophical category has a varied and checkered history, and like Medea, it reappears occasionally. At the turn of the twenty-first century, cosmopolitanism made a reappearance. Public intellectuals, from Martha Nussbaum to Anthony Appiah, strove to determine the most ethical stance regarding the purported "clash of civilizations" of a post-9/11 world. To consider oneself a cosmopolitan is to judge one's behavior, to regulate one's basest impulses and passions, by always acting as a "person whose allegiance is to the worldwide community of human beings."[3] This has often been interpreted as a perhaps more global and yet personal, individual, version of the Golden Rule: Do unto yourself as you would have others do unto themselves.

The sticking point for this kind of a rule remains: Who is in that community of human beings of others whom we measure against ourselves? And who can adequately measure such allegiance? By what standards would such measures be evaluated—epistemological, territorial, political? A true cosmopolitan challenges not only what we mean by nation and citizen but also what we mean by "morality" and "body" and "knowledge." A true cosmopolitan, then, exists outside our moral and epistemological framework. In this sense, then, Medea is a true cosmopolitan. What makes her a cosmopolitan is precisely what makes her unassimilable in Greece: her conviction that the stuff of this world can do things others think it cannot—that is, her foreign knowledge, which we might call supernatural.

It is, then, not so much who can or cannot be admitted into the worldwide community but what those who would be admitted must lose or give up in order to be considered "citizens" of that community. What must they forget? Philosopher of science Isabelle Stengers uses the term "cosmopolitics" to speak of a politics of thinking about the cosmos that is also necessarily a politics of thinking about how science and knowledge order the world and exclude certain forms of belief.[4] A cosmopolitan would be, perhaps, one whose thinking, acting, and material being makes manifest this ordered world and the forms of belief it excludes. Bruno Latour has asserted that "the main weakness of legal and humanitarian forms of cosmopolitanism is to forget entirely the theory of science that has been surreptitiously used to assemble the cosmos in a peaceful manner but without due process."[5] For Latour and Stengers, it is politically urgent to reorganize our epistemological and ontological a priori framework to integrate the co-relational embeddedness of ourselves with things. In the smallest of allegorical manners, Medean violence seems to work as a continual cautionary tale. In a world that bases peace on belonging and on universal sympathy, what happens to the cruel, the criminal, the barbarian, the transient? Hiding from them, or refusing them entry into the world, does not work.

Turning to instances of our creative imagination in art and literature, where barbarians express their persistent being and commit themselves to altering the fabric of our society, provides insight into why a society that constantly banishes the violence of the epistemological other will not rest easy. Whether offering examples of violence exposed or violence covered up, these moments might also give us insight into how we can attend to violence without letting it overtake us, and how we can acknowledge the violence we can't help but create even as we disavow it.

Corneille refused the simple worry about violence onstage when he pointed out that Médée's wrongs are so blatant as to be tempting to no one, as he advocated for a value of theater that exposed the horrifying in order that the public could confront and reject it. It is unclear whether even that strategy has ever worked to mitigate violence or better the moral fiber of a public, but it remains a way we contend with the proliferation of cultural expressions of violence today. And I think that it is possible to locate and consider the work of Medean principles of violence well beyond the sphere in which I have located them. Doing so can tell us something about how we make violence circulate. I will close this book by tracking the circulation of Medean violence and its availability for analysis in contemporary art and culture. This closing gambit is to make a cosmopolitics of Medean violence available to us well beyond seventeenth-century French political drama.

## Soft Songs: Medea beyond Tragedy

A certain form of Medean violence appears to punctuate news reports of domestic dramas, and Leïla Slimani drew on these reports for her 2016 Prix Goncourt–winning novel *Chanson douce*, translated for the British market directly as *Lullaby* and for the American market as *The Perfect Nanny*. It begins: "Le bébé est mort. Il a suffit de quelques secondes. Le médecin a assuré qu'il n'avait pas souffert" (The baby is dead. It took only a few seconds. The doctors said he didn't suffer).[6] In contrast to dramatic versions of Medea that offer the slaying of her children as the climax of the plot, in Slimani's interpretation, it is in the opening paragraph describing what happened in the moments of the baby Adam's death, alongside his sister, Mila. The narrative unfolds from that description as a flashback. It tracks the events that led up to the siblings' deaths and to the attempted suicide of the nanny, Louise. As we read what comes before the children's death, we must sit with the asymmetry of our understanding: The reader works in the aftermath of such knowledge whereas the characters do not. The reading is complicated not just by a sense of dread, since we know it ends terribly, like all tragedies. The weight also comes from reading through the banality of what preceded the killings, the unremarkable and even petty struggles of a bourgeois family. The first part of the book gives a plodding account of Myriam Charfa and Paul Massé's family, Paul's success in music production, Myriam's sacrifice of her legal career for her children, her paralyzing and paralyzed grip on them, her seemingly difficult relationship with her daughter, her social anxiety, and her uneven relationship with Paul, as well as the money problems that life in Paris imposes on young families of the gentrifying class. All these inform the couple's quest for a nanny.

The quest itself is among the most significant "events" of the novel. Slimani's style, emphasizing action and internal thought over any direct access to characters' emotional life, leaves us amassing details on the conditions for the infanticide. These conditions are not psychological; they are social. And they are not just individual; they are about classes of people: the young culture class, the middle-aged service class, the class of undocumented immigrants, and so on. Carefully and dispassionately establishing the socioeconomic situation that brings the nanny Louise to the Massé family and integrates her into its fabric, Slimani chronicles not maternal love or sacrifice, but maternal outsourcing and all the tensions of contemporary urban life that this gesture includes. This includes complex racial and class-based tensions that Myriam experiences as a North African woman—she gets condescended to at a boutique nanny agency until the director realizes that she is a client not a job seeker. This complexity is passed on to the nanny herself: "Not too old, no veils and no smokers," Paul declares.[7] Myriam seems to agree, if for other reasons. Rejecting a Moroccan candidate with excellent credentials, "She fears that a tacit complicity and familiarity would grow between her and the nanny. That the woman would start speaking to her in Arabic . . . asking her all sorts of favors in the name of their shared language and religion" (18). Myriam does not fear being supplanted in her children's eyes, but she fears being pulled into a relationship brought on by common culture. Intimacy is feared more than replaceability.

The hiring of Louise, a middle-aged widow with a grown daughter and impeccable references, solves Myriam and Paul's problems as it increases the reader's anxiety: We now know who the murderer is. We will follow her as she becomes more and more imbricated in the Massé family; we will reflect on her own history of heartbreak and abuse, her money problems, and her increasingly bizarre dependence on the family. Her Medean alterity appears in her domestic prowess:

> The nanny is like those figures at the back of a theater stage who move the sets around in the darkness. Louise watches in the wings, discreet and powerful. She is the one who controls the transparent wires without which the magic cannot occur. She is Vishnu, the nurturing divinity, jealous and protective; the she-wolf at whose breast they drink, the infallible source of their family happiness. (53)

And like Medea, her violence has its history, though not in her own hand: Louise is the widow of a violent bully who leaves her traumatized and with financial debt. Violence here is networked in the sense that it traces social patterns of oppression that are also relational and familial—whether constituted by blood, marriage, or paid service.

It does not seem tenable to say simply, however, that *Chanson douce* is about a mother who kills her children. The narrative does go through the paces of how a thriller would stage the replacement of Myriam by Louise. For example, as Myriam embraces her work, Louise becomes "simultaneously invisible and indispensable. Myriam no longer calls to warn her that she's going to be late and Mila stops asking when Mama is coming home." The impetus behind the shift is complicated, however, since Louise has, in Myriam, an active partner in this transformation. She is even portrayed as the recipient of Myriam's conscious abdication: "Myriam lets herself be mothered. Every day she abandons more tasks to a grateful

Louise" (53). Louise not only supplants Myriam as a source of love and intimacy for the children but also, besting her in domestic tasks, extends that mothering to Myriam herself. In turn, Myriam thrives.

Even in her replacement of Myriam as a maternal figure, Louise is no more insidious, suspect, or culpable than other characters. Like Corneille, who wanted to adjust the weight of responsibility to implicate all characters, Slimani has written a network of responsibility. No one here is innocent of structural participation in a culture and economy that exploits the poor and keeps them from flourishing. Myriam's thoughts are conveyed more than anyone else's, but Slimani keeps the emotional interiority of all of her characters at bay. Even as her prose offers insight into all of them; we learn much about Paul and his relationship with Louise. Although Louise can be seen as a kind of parasite, who camps out surreptitiously in the Massé apartment while the family is on vacation without her, the family also invites her on vacation and asks her to join them for a dinner party. Through these pushes and pulls of intimacy, however, Louise remains "as nervous as a foreigner, an exile who doesn't understand the language being spoken around her" (59); integration into a family does not dissolve the boundaries of class or the scars of history.

At first glance, then, the connection between Myriam and Louise can seem to compose a story about two incommensurable facets of contemporary motherhood: one biological, ambivalent, and sane; the other cultural, committed, and homicidal. *Chanson douce* can be interpreted as a single portrait of motherhood divided, much as Medea in antiquity was portrayed as divided by her passion for both revenge and her children.

*Chanson douce* complicates this binary critique of parenting, however, and does so on several levels. First, it places the father Paul with the two women at the heart of the narrative, giving him his own relationships to Louise and to the children, and his own ambivalences about outsourced parenting. Paul is also a child: His own mother is the true rival to Myriam, a *soixante-huitarde* (France's version of the aging radical who flourished in the 1960s) convinced of her own rectitude and of the political flimsiness of the next generation, especially when it comes to parenting. It is perhaps rather not just motherhood but parenthood, in its concomitant functions as caregiver, economic engine, and fully realized and authoritative individual, which is at stake. And the text multiplies the examples of divided mothers: Louise is part of a class of nannies, who come from all over the world and have various immigration statuses, whereas Myriam too has echoes in the novel among other women of the gentrifying class, whose status as mothers creates discomfort for them, like Emma, "who has so many anxieties and to whom no one listens, [who] envies Myriam for being able to depend on this Sphinx-like nanny" (59).

Second, Slimani flips on its head Adriana Cavarero's feminist philosophy that elevates the mother to an ontologically primary status and which makes mothering care the first gesture of being. Slimani's novel reveals care to be social, and socially fragile. It must be said that for Cavarero, maternal care is also a choice—there is the possibility of "turning away." But to turn away from care, as we saw in *Horrorism*, is also a "denial of the human condition."[8] In its account of a "soft" turn away from motherhood, in Myriam and Paul's outsourcing of care to a nanny, alongside a "hard," homicidal denial of care in Louise's murder of the children, *Chanson douce* complicates our moralizing shock at the first pages of the book, even as it instills in us a narrative sense of inevitability alongside a social portrait of something that never should have happened.

The final chapter, which follows the police procedure of reconstituting the crime at its scene, is also a rehearsal of the crime after the fact: The police captain Nina Dorval knows what role she will play: "'I will play the nanny,' she said" (221). The narrative recapitulation of the crime is both Dorval's rehearsal for this police procedure and a reinhabiting of Louise by another woman. Networked through family configurations, marked by psychosis and therefore "unnatural" and unassimilable, the killings cannot be explained, rationalized, limited, or purged. They can only be repeated.

There is nothing universal, archaic, or timeless about *Chanson douce*. Even as the narrative frontloads the crime and so secures its inevitability, it manages arguably to put the burden not on the crime, but on the structures that created its conditions. In this way, it is a chronicle of a problem within its particular society. Slimani has spoken about its inspirations, the 2012 murder of Leo and Lucia Krim by Yoselyn Ortega, and she has cited as a source for the nanny's name Louise Woodward, who was convicted and then acquitted of murder of her infant charge Matthew Eappen in 1997. In the laying bare of domestic violence, even—or especially—in its most extreme form, as a social and economic program that implicates immigration, racism, gentrification, and generations of abuse, the novel also shows the pervasiveness of Medean violence and its cosmopolitical dimensions.

A key to these dimensions might be contained in a vignette in *Chanson douce*, which is so brief it is easy to miss, and yet so unresolved it bears scrutiny. Louise goes to Greece with the family. On the boat trip to their island destination, she sees a woman suntanning herself on an upper deck.

> She is wearing a bikini: a thong and a strip of material around her chest that barely hides her breasts. She has very dry platinum-blond hair, but what strikes Louise is her skin. It is purplish and covered with large brown stains. In places—inside her thighs, on her checks, just above her breasts—her skin is blistered and raw, as if she's been burned. She is immobile, like the corpse of a flayed torture victim, left out as a warning to the others. (64)

This spectacle acquires a public, as other passengers gather to stare and giggle. Louise too is transfixed; she "can't stop looking at the scrawny body, streaming with sweat. That woman consumed by the sun, like a piece of meat thrown on the embers" (64–65). No mother, this woman, no criminal, no agent of care given or refused. Her torture is self-inflicted, in the name of a sense of beauty perhaps. The sight nauseates Louise, and she remains sick for the rest of the journey. What does it mean to be totally unattached, a lone body which has laid itself out to bake? She has, like Medea with Creusa, burned herself, but the wounds are self-inflicted and seemingly desired. The woman who consumes herself in the vacation sun seems to be an isolated instance, an extreme moment in the narrative. Isolated perhaps, but inescapable. Literally in the same boat as Louise, Myriam, and Paul, she is a product of leisure and the tourist class, proof of the social circulation of violence among, for, by, and upon women, whether mothers or not.

*Chanson douce* refracts violence, spreading its history and its present impact. and thus proliferating it across multiple actors. Like seventeenth-century drama, it offers no resolution, as it anchors violence at least partly in the social. Its imbrication within contemporary questions of violence in society—from infanticide to harassment—suggests again that literature does nurture violence because violence underpins so much. This also suggests that we remain fascinated by and committed to the presence of unexpiable violence in our lives and art.

As many have opined before me, the notion of "tragedy" seems out of place today, or at best instrumentalized to offer an affective cover for a political or social issue that could be changed or avoided, but won't be. I'm less concerned about whether we should call either Slimani's novel a "tragedy" than about how its circulation and critical acclaim are indications of an interest in working with the potential for art to help us face the structures of violence ungirding our lives. The question then remains whether we can face a critique of this violence that we love to watch, read, and think about, even when such a critique calls into question, and even refuses to accept, how we might idealize a world without Medeas.

ACKNOWLEDGMENTS

The research for this book first took shape during a residency at the University of Minnesota's Institute for Advanced Study, and found archival footing during a short-term fellowship at the Folger Shakespeare Library. The University of Minnesota Libraries offered research support and physical space that provided much-needed continuity. UMN's Provost's Imagine Fund also provided crucial research support. Medea finally landed at Fordham University Press, and I thank especially Tom Lay, Eric Newman, and Teresa Jesionowski for the terrific work and energy they contributed. Katharine Cobey's *Boat with Four Figures*, featured on the cover of the book, became my figure for an alternative Medean *Argo*, and a symbol of the feminist project to which I hope this book contributes. I thank Katharine Cobey for an enlightening afternoon in Warren discussing Medea, boats, structure, and spinning. I also thank Sarah Hewitt for her assistance.

Portions of this book were presented by kind invitation at Miami University of Ohio, The Johns Hopkins University, Harvard University, the University of North Carolina–Chapel Hill, UC Berkeley, University of Iowa, University of Southern California, University of Kentucky, Macalester College, and the University of Pittsburgh. I thank colleagues and students at each institution for their hospitality and lively intellectual engagement.

The scholarly communities of SE17 and NASSFCL have enriched this research with their collegiality, candor, and generosity. In particular I thank Hélène Bilis, Jean-Vincent Blanchard, Laura Burch, Katherine Dauge-Roth, Gilles Declercq, Nina Ekstein, Perry Gethner, Sylvaine Guyot, Chloé Hogg, Jean Leclerc, Hélène Longino, Nick Paige, Roland Racevskis, Jennie Row, Hélène Visentin, Sarah Wellman, and Abby Zanger. Hall Bjørnstad, Ellen McClure, and Jeff Peters are HEJJ!, who read parts of this book at critical moments, and their advice has been invaluable, even when it took anonymous reviewers to make me heed it. At points along the way, some terribly distant, Wilda Anderson, Mark Buchan, Tom Conley, Steven Hinds, Elena Russo, and Kathleen Wine offered expertise and perspectives from well outside my field, and I am so grateful for their interventions.

At the University of Minnesota I have been lucky to work with students, colleagues, and friends who have enriched this project with their generosity, contagious curiosity, and spirit of intellectual exchange over the past fifteen years: Tom Augst, Francesca Bortoletti, Greta Bliss, Dan Brewer, Mária Brewer, Melanie Bowman, Tony Brown, Lydia Garver, David Hanzal, Maki Isaka, Sonja Arsham Kuftinec, Laura Loth, Jason McGrath, Michelle Miller, Susan Noakes, Anaïs Nony, Ioana Pribiag, Kathy Rider, Arun Saldanha, Simona Sawhney, Jani Scandura, Aleksander Sedzielarz, and Eileen Sivert. Christophe Wall-Romana and Bruno Chaouat especially have pushed, prodded, and shoved—often in the same direction. J. B. Shank and Michael Gaudio have been near-constant interlocutors since well before Medea ever visited our Arcadia-like research group TEMS, and have made Minnesota an intellectual home for me. Anna Rosensweig has helped me take the risks of which I am most proud. I thank Andrew Billing, Julie Crawford, Kathryn Gilje, Hilde Hoffmann, Rayna Kalas, Ethan Laubach, Sharon Oster, Allison Stedman, Valerie Tiberius, Margaret Wall-Romana, Margaret Werry, and Liza Yukins, who, at different yet seemingly always crucial times, have supported this work as writing partners, cooking companions, harpies, and very dear friends.

Rita Raley, Diane Berrett Brown, and Jenn Marshall each shaped this project from the beginning to the end, gave me reasons to write, and told me when to stop. For much patience and optimism, I am so grateful to Matthias Rothe, colleague, friend, and family; to my mother, sisters, brothers-in-law, and nieces; to consummate co-parent Michael Opperman; and to Lucie, who knew the difference between Medea and Medusa at a shockingly young age.

# NOTES

### INTRODUCTION: COMING AFTER VIOLENCE IN LITERATURE

1. Euripides, *Medea*, trans. James Norwood (Oxford: Oxford University Press, 1998), 32.
2. Stephen J. Pyne, *World Fire: The Culture of Fire on Earth* (New York: Henry Holt, 1995), esp. 14–19.
3. Stephen J. Pyne, "Forged in Fire: History, Land, and Anthropogenic Fire," in *Advances in Historical Ecology*, ed. William L. Balée (New York: Columbia University Press, 1998), 98.
4. Caroline Levine, *Forms: Whole, Rhythm, Hierarchy, Network* (Princeton, N.J.: Princeton University Press, 2014), 4–5. On the proliferation of the tragic beyond tragedy, see Vassilis Lambropoulos, *The Tragic Idea* (London: Duckworth Press, 2006).
5. The collection of essays edited by J. J. Clauss and S. I. Johnston remains an excellent analysis of the myth: *Medea: Essays on Medea in Myth, Literature, Philosophy and Art* (Princeton, N.J.: Princeton University Press, 1997). See Alain Moreau's dense, insightful appraisal of the myth's permutations in *Le Mythe de Jason et Médée: Le va-nu-pied et la sorcière* (Paris: Les Belles Lettres, 2014). See also Heike Bartel and Anne Simon, eds., *Unbinding Medea: Interdisciplinary Approaches to a Classical Myth from Antiquity to the 21st Century* (London: Legenda, 2010), and Aurélien Berra, ed., *Médée, versions et interpretations d'un mythe* (Besançon: Presses Universitaires de Franche-Comté, 2016).
6. Jean-Pierre Vernant and Pierre Vidal-Naquet, *Myth and Tragedy in Ancient Greece* (Cambridge, Mass.: Zone Books, 1988), 242.
7. Pierre de Villiers, *Entretien sur les tragédies de ce temps* (Paris: Etienne Michallet, 1675), 100; 5.
8. The genre's warrant to convey universalist truths about human nature emerged only in the nineteenth century through German idealism; see Joshua Billings, *Genealogy of the Tragic: Greek Tragedy and German Philosophy* (Princeton, N.J.: Princeton University Press, 2014). Thus the need to inquire of premodern tragedy its historical specificity, as Blair Hoxby has done in *What Was Tragedy? Theory and the Early Modern Canon* (Oxford:

Oxford University Press, 2015), or to investigate the changing nature of "action" in light of the emergence of eighteenth-century productivist political economy, as Richard Halpern has explored in *Eclipse of Action: Tragedy and Political Economy* (Chicago: University of Chicago Press, 2017). In the case of French tragedy, its role in these histories has been shaped by its status in French culture, especially education, what Christian Jouhaud has called the "monumentalization" of the seventeenth century or the transformation of the "grand siècle" into the "Grand-Siècle," an object transcending time. Christian Jouhaud, *Sauver le Grand-Siècle? Présence et transmission du passé* (Paris: Seuil, 2007).

9. Florence Dupont, *Aristote ou le vampire du théâtre occidental* (Paris: Aubier, 200), 7.

10. Marc Fumaroli, "De *Médée* à *Phèdre*: Naissance et mise à mort de la tragédie cornélienne," 1980, in *Héros et orateurs: Rhétorique et dramaturgie cornéliennes* (Geneva: Droz, 1996), 493–518.

11. Louis Marin, "Théâtralité et pouvoir, magie, machination, machine: *Médée* de Corneille," in *Le pouvoir de la raison d'état*, ed. Christian Lazzeri and Dominique Reynié (Paris: PUF, 1992), 231–59. Hélène Merlin builds on this argument in her reading of *Médée* in *Public et littérature en France au XVIIe siècle* (Paris: Les Belle Lettres, 1994), esp. 253–63.

12. Christian Biet insists on the notion of the specificity, and therefore multiplicities, of violence in late sixteenth- and early seventeenth-century political theater. "Discours et représentation: La violence au théâtre," *Litteratures Classiques* 73, no. 3 (2010): 415–29. Andrea Frisch traces how, in the long aftermath of the Wars of the Religion, historiography and tragedy were both informed by a strategic politics of "oubliance." Andrea Frisch, *Forgetting Differences: Tragedy, Historiography, and the French Wars of Religion* (Edinburgh: Edinburgh University Press, 2015), esp. 107.

13. Christopher Semk, *Playing the Martyr: Theater and Theology in Early Modern France* (Lewisburg, Penn.: Bucknell University Press, 2017), esp. xix.

14. Hippolyte-Jules Pilet de la Mesnardière, *La Poétique* (1639), ed. Marc Civardi (Paris: Champion, 2015).

15. François Hédelin d'Aubignac, *La pratique du théâtre*, ed. Hélène Baby (Paris: Champion Classiques Littératures, 2011), book 2, chap. 1, p. 114. For a fine discussion of *vraisemblance* and especially of Corneille's intervention, see Emma Gilby, *Sublime Worlds: Early Modern French Literature* (London: Legenda, 2006), 52–54.

16. Charles de Marguetel de Saint Denis de Saint-Évremond, "De la tragédie," 1672, in Projet "Haine du Théâtre," *Observatoire de la vie littéraire*, ed. Nina Hugot (Paris: Université Paris-Sorbonne, LABEX OBVIL, 2014); René Rapin, *Réflexions sur la poétique et sur les ouvrages des poètes anciens et modernes* (1684), ed. Pascale Thouverin (Paris: Champion Classiques, 2011).

For the English context, see Bruce R. Smith, *Ancient Scripts and Modern Experience on the English Stage, 1500–1700* (Princeton, N.J.: Princeton University Press, 2014), 27–32.

17. Horace was also among the first to make a distinction between what should be said and what should be shown on stage; Medea's murder of her children is the first act to be proscribed. Medea also appears first in his examples of the consistency of character: "Let Medea be fierce and untractable, Ino an object of pity, Ixion perfidious, Io wandering, Orestes in distress," 124.

18. On the politics of Ovid's exile poetry, the classic study remains Betty Nagle's *The Poetics of Exile: Program and Polemic in the "Tristia" and "Epistulae ex Ponto" of Ovid* (Brussels: Latomus, 1980). More recently, Garth Williams has taken up the question of poetic duplicity in *Banished Voices: Readings in Ovid's Exile Poetry* (Cambridge: Cambridge University Press, 1994).

19. d'Aubignac, *La pratique du théâtre*, book 2, chap. 1, p. 113.

20. Compassion is "at the center of theatrical emotion" for d'Aubignac; see Katherine Ibbett, *Compassion's Edge: Fellow-Feeling and Its Limits in Early Modern France* (Philadelphia: University of Pennsylvania Press, 2017), 83.

21. It is outside of the purview of this study to pursue some of the connections between the politics of authority motivating the Quarrel of the Ancients and Moderns, and the debates among dramaturges and moralists about onstage violence, but it seems that a reappraisal of the ways in which tragedy fundamentally challenged the Modern perspective on ancient aesthetics, theology, and sociability is warranted. See Larry Norman's fine reading of virtue and the celebration of the alterity of the ancients in *The Shock of the Ancient: Literature and History in Early Modern France* (Chicago: University of Chicago Press, 2011), for example, 130–34.

22. Lisa Freeman, *Antitheatricality and the Body Politic* (Philadelphia: University of Pennsylvania Press, 2017).

23. Samuel Chappuzeau, *Le théâtre françois* (Lyon: Mayer, 1674), book 1, chap. 23, pp. 55–56.

24. Henri-Jean Martin et al., "Typographie et littérature: La mise en texte du livre classique." In *La naissance du livre moderne: Mise en page et mise en texte du livre français* (Paris: Editions du Cercle de la Librairie, 2000), 417–30.

25. Véronique Lochert, *L'écriture du spectacle: Les didascalies dans le théâtre européen aux XVIe et XVIIe siècles* (Geneva: Droz, 2009), 118–20.

26. Pierre Laudun d'Aigaliers, *Horace*, in *Les poésies de Pierre de Laudun d'Aigaliers, contenans deux tragédies* (Paris: David Le Clerc, 1596), 66.

27. Martin et al., "Typographie," 425.

28. Sylvaine Guyot, *Racine et le corps tragique* (Paris: Presses Universitaires de France, 2014), esp. 90–93.

29. François de Salignac de La Mothe Fénelon, "Projet d'un traité sur la tragédie," *Oeuvres*, vol. II, ed. Jacques Le Brun, Bibliothèque de la Pléiade (Paris: Gallimard, 1993), 1171.

30. Christian Biet has insisted on the ambiguities of interpretations of catharsis in seventeenth-century dramatic discourse. See, for example and most recently, "French Tragedy during the Seventeenth Century: From Cruelty on a Scaffold to Poetic Distance on Stage," in *Politics and Aesthetics in European Baroque and Classicist Tragedy*, ed. Jan Bloemendal and Nigel Smith (Leiden: Brill, 2016), 305. For a more traditional overview of catharsis in the period, see Georges Forestier, *La tragédie française: Passions trageiques et règles classiques* (Paris: Armand Colin, 2010), 129–40. For the ambiguities of assessments of catharsis, see Ibbett, *Compassion's Edge*, 85–88.

31. Susanne Langer, *Feeling and Form: A Theory of Art* (New York: Charles Scribner's Sons, 1953), 351.

32. Emily Wilson, *Mocked with Death: Tragic Overliving from Sophocles to Milton* (Baltimore: Johns Hopkins University Press, 2004).

33. Pierre Corneille, "Discours de la tragédie," 1660, in *Oeuvres*, ed. Georges Couton, Bibliothèque de la Pléiade (Paris: Gallimard, 1980), 3:145.

34. Pierre Corneille, "[Épître] À Monsieur P. T. N. G.," 1639, in Pierre Corneille, *Oeuvres*, 1:535–36.

35. Alain Riffaud, "Les succès éditoriaux du théâtre français au XVIIe siècle," *Revue d'Histoire Littéraire de la France* 117, no. 4 (2017), 802–3.

36. There is evidence that Corneille oversaw the iconography in at least one of his other works: the *Imitation de Jesus-Christ* (1653). Abby Zanger, "On the threshold of print and performance: how prints mattered to bodies of/at work in Molière's published corpus," *Word & Image*, 17, no. 1–2 (2001), 25–26. See also Catherine Guillot, "Les éditions illustrées du théâtre de Corneille," in *Pratiques de Corneille*, ed. Myriam Dufour-Maître (Mont-Saint-Aignan, Publication des universités de Rouen et du Havre, 2012), 78.

37. Guillot contextualizes an earlier version of this image within Corneille's consideration of the historical foundations of his history plays' principal actions. "Les éditions illustrés," 81–82.

38. Pierre Laudun d'Aigaliers, *Horace*, 67.

39. Larry F. Norman, "Tragic Violence in Performance and Print Illustration: From Monléon's *Thyeste* to Corneille and Racine," *Biblio* 17, 161 (2005), 143–56.

40. Pierre Corneille, *Le théâtre de P. Corneille, reveu et corrigé et augmenté* (Suivant la copie imprimée à Paris: Amsterdam, A. Wolfgang, 1664).

41. This runs counter to a certain liberatory strain of Medea criticism, which seeks in her defiant emancipation a postmodern, even revolutionary, stance. See, for example, Amy Wygant, *Medea, Magic, and Modernity in France: Stages and Histories, 1553–1797* (Aldershot, Eng.: Ashgate, 2007).

Many versions of the Euripidean play explore its feminist and liberatory dimensions; see, for example, Kevin J. Wetmore Jr., *Black Medea. Adaptations for Modern Plays* (Amherst, N.Y.: Cambria Press, 2013) for a range of interpretations that reflect an African diaspora, emphasizing its American history.

42. Lorraine Daston, "The Morality of Natural Orders: The Power of Medea," part 1 of Tanner Lectures on Human Values (Cambridge, Mass.: Harvard University Press, 2002), 371–92. This tendency to archaize Medea has been traced as far back, however, as Roman iconography, which insists on the foreign, "oriental" dress of her and her father. Vassiliki Gaggadis-Robin, *Jason et Médée sur les sarcophages* (Rome: Ecole française de Rome, 1994), 63, 192.

43. Isabelle Stengers, *Souviens-toi que je suis Médée: Medea nunc sum* (Paris: Les Empêcheurs de Penser en Rond, 1993), 7.

44. For an interpretation of the political ontology of living "in the wake" as the Black experience of living after slavery, see Christina Sharpe, *In the Wake: On Blackness and Being* (Durham, N.C.: Duke University Press, 2016).

45. Michael Foucault, "Nietzsche, Genealogy, History," in *Language, Counter-Memory, Practice: Selected Essays and Interviews by Michel Foucault*, ed. Donald F. Bouchard (Ithaca, N.Y.: Cornell University Press, 1980), 144–45. Translation modified.

46. Judith Butler, *Antigone's Claim: Kinship between Life and Death* (New York: Columbia University Press, 2000); Bonnie Honig, *Antigone Interrupted* (Cambridge: Cambridge University Press, 2013).

47. Bruno Latour, *We Have Never Been Modern*, trans. Catherine Porter (Cambridge, Mass.: Harvard University Press, 1993), 42.

48. Didier Anzieu, *Le moi-peau* (Paris: Dunod, 1985).

49. Reinhart Koselleck, *Futures Past: On the Semantics of Historical Time*, trans. K. Tribe (Cambridge, Mass.: MIT Press, 2004).

MEDEA, A MANIFESTO

1. Marguerite Yourcenar, "Antigone ou le choix," in *Feux* (Paris: Grasset, 1936); Jean Anouilh, *Antigone*, in *Nouvelles pieces noires: Jézabel, Antigone, Roméo et Jeannette, Médée* (1944; Paris: Edition de la Table ronde, 1946); François Ost, *Antigone voilée* (2005; Brussels: De Boeck, 2010); Seamus Heaney, afterword to *The Burial at Thebes: Sophocles' "Antigone,"* by Sophocles (London: Faber & Faber, 2004), 75–76.

2. Jonathan Strauss, *Private Lives, Public Deaths: Antigone and the Invention of Individuality* (New York: Fordham University Press, 2013), 3. There is a lively debate among scholars about the relationship between tragedy and death, especially as it plays out in Antigone studies; Strauss discusses one facet of this in his reading of Bonnie Honig's and Helene Foley's arguments, *Private Lives*, 29–31.

3. Strauss, *Private Lives*, 7.

4. Judith Butler, *Antigone's Claim: Kinship between Life and Death* (New York: Columbia University Press, 2000), esp. 57–82.

5. Bonnie Honig, *Antigone Interrupted* (Cambridge: Cambridge University Press, 2013), 56.

6. Honig, *Antigone Interrupted*, 194.

7. Honig, *Antigone Interrupted*, 187.

8. Richard Halpern, "Theater and Democratic Thought: Arendt to Rancière," *Critical Inquiry* 37, no. 3 (2011): 545.

9. Anna Rosensweig, "Reaching *Antigone*: Relational Rights in Early Modern Drama," (presentation, University of Rochester, February 2016). See also Rosensweig, "'Toute la cité pleure': Mise en scène du peuple thébain dans *Antigone ou la Pieté* de Robert Garnier," *Cahiers Forell—Formes et Représentations en Linguistique et Littérature: La Foule au Théâtre* (April 2015).

10. Honig, *Antigone Interrupted*, 17, 20.

11. Jacques Rancière, "The Ethical Turn of Aesthetics and Politics," *Critical Horizons* 7, no. 1 (2006): 5.

12. Luce Irigaray, *Le temps de la différence* (Paris: Éditions Hachette, 1989), 84.

13. Nicole Loraux, *Tragic Ways of Killing a Woman*, trans. Anthony Forster (1985; Cambridge, Mass.: Harvard University Press, 1991), 10.

14. Anne Carson, *Antigonick* (2012; New York: New Directions, 2015).

15. Emile Benveniste, "'MED' et la notion de mesure," in *Le vocabulaire des institutions indo-européenes*, vol. 2: pouvoir, droit, religion (Paris: Éditions de Minuit, 1969), 129.

16. Pierre Chantraine, "μέδω," *Dictionnaire étymologique de la langue grecque: Histoire des mots*, vol. 3, Δ–Π (Paris: Klincksieck, 1968), 675.

17. Helene Foley asserts that Euripides' Medea, gendered feminine quite clearly, also is a means of exploring questions of heroism that go beyond the traditional Greek mold of heroism; this determination transcending beyond gender norms can be heard in her name. See Helene Foley, *Female Acts in Greek Tragedy* (Princeton, N.J.: Princeton University Press, 2001), esp. 266.

18. David Konstan, "Medea: A Hint of Divinity?" *Classical World* 101, no. 1 (2007): 93–94.

19. William Kerwin, *Beyond the Body: The Boundaries of Medicine and English Renaissance Drama* (Amherst: University of Massachusetts Press, 2005), 62–96.

20. For an overview of this iconographical trend and a quite different interpretation of its significance, see Amy Wygant, *Medea, Magic, and Modernity in France: Stages and Histories, 1553–1797* (Aldershot, Eng.: Ashgate, 2007), 35–43.

21. Jacques Derrida, "Plato's Pharmacy," in *Dissemination*, trans. Barbara Johnson (1981; Chicago: University of Chicago Press, 2004), 76.

22. Derrida, *Dissemination*, 133–34.

23. Vassiliki Gaggadis-Robin, *Jason et Médée sur les sarcophages* (Rome: Ecole française de Rome, 1994), 144–45.

24. Bruno Latour, *We Have Never Been Modern*, trans. Catherine Porter (Cambridge, Mass.: Harvard University Press, 1993), 13.

25. See Jean-Pierre Vernant's classic essay on fire, "Prometheus and the Technological Function," 1965, in *Myth and Thought among the Greeks* (London: Routledge & Kegan Paul, 1983), 237–47.

26. Adriana Cavarero, *Horrorism: Naming Contemporary Violence*, trans. William McCuaig (2007; New York: Columbia University Press, 2009), 29. Citations hereafter are included in the text parenthetically.

27. Medusa and Medea have another aspect in common in this schema: They are both excluded from the human. Medusa petrifies through her serpentine locks, a portrait of fatal hybridity that itself is toxic instantly. Medea's inhumanity is not inscribed in her body but rather in the temporality of her actions and in our inability to access her interiority.

28. Adriana Cavarero, *Inclinations: A Critique of Rectitude*, trans. Amanda Minervini and Adam Sitze (2014; Stanford, Calif.: Stanford University Press, 2016),105–6.

29. Bernard Stiegler, *What Makes Life Worth Living: On Pharmacology* (Cambridge: Polity Press, 2013), 25.

30. Marvin Carlson, *The Haunted Stage: The Theatre as Memory Machine* (Ann Arbor: University of Michigan Press, 2001). Amy Wygant has called this quality proper to Medea's "schizomythia," a mythical personality that is multiple and unconcerned with, even resistant to, the reconciliation of different aspects. Wygant, *Medea, Magic*, 48.

### 1. SURFACE SELVES: *MÉDÉE*, 1634

1. Hélène Merlin, *Public et littérature en France au XVIIe siècle* (Paris: Les Belles Lettres, 1994), 255; Chris Braider, *The Matter of Mind: Reason and Experience in the Age of Descartes* (Toronto: University of Toronto Press, 2012), 148–49; Hélène Bilis, *Passing Judgment: The Politics and Poetics of Sovereignty in French Tragedy from Hardy to Racine* (Toronto: University of Toronto Press, 2016), 105–10.

2. Pierre Corneille, "Épître," in *Oeuvres complètes*. Edited by Georges Couton. 3 vols. Bibliothèque de la Pléiade (Paris: Gallimard, 1980–87), 1:535.

3. Alain Riffaud, "Corneille et l'impression de ses livres: De l'indifférence à l'innovation," in *Pratiques de Corneille*, ed. Myriam Dufour-Maître (Mont-Saint-Aignan: Presses universitaires de Rouen et du Havre,

2012), 55–74, and in the same volume, Alain Viala, "Corneille premier auteur moderne," 29–40.

4. A quick survey of Corneille's prefatory texts such as dedications reveals that any such ambiguity is quickly resolved in his plays named after a character. For example, *Melite* is discussed initially with the same ambiguity of gender, but it is resolved with the mention of "représentations" (productions), clarifying the theatrical event as object. In the case of *Cinna*, Corneille refers to the "pièce" (play), while *Horace* is a "portrait," *Polyeucte* is "une pièce de théâtre" (a theater play), *Théodore* a "tragédie," and *Don Sanche* a "poème d'une espèce nouvelle" (a new kind of poem), Cf. Pierre Corneille, *Oeuvres*.

5. Corneille, "Épître," *Oeuvres*, 1:535.

6. *Dictionnaire de l'Académie française*, vol. 2 (Paris: Coignard, 1694).

7. Corneille, "Épître," *Oeuvres*, 1:536.

8. Similarly, Déborah Blocker calls its publication a provocation to Richelieu's men. *Instituer un "art": Politiques du théâtre dans la France du premier XVIIe siècle* (Paris: Honoré Champion, 2009), 435

9. Corneille, "Épître," *Oeuvres*, 1:535–36.

10. Michèle Longino, *Orientalism in French Classical Drama* (Cambridge: Cambridge University Press, 2002), 28–35.

11. Corneille, "Examen," in *Oeuvres*, 1:539.

12. Longino, *Orientalism*, 57.

13. Amy Wygant, *Medea, Magic, Magic, and Modernity in France: Stages and Histories, 1553–1797* (Aldershot, Eng.: Ashgate, 2007), 49–50. Seneca, *Medea*, in *Tragedies, Volume I: Hercules, Trojan Women, Medea, Phaedra*, ed. and trans. John G. Fitch, Loeb Classical Library 62 (Cambridge, Mass.: Harvard University Press, 2018), 328–29, 330–31, 394–495.

14. Corneille, "Examen," *Oeuvres*, 1:536.

15. *Dictionnaire de l'Académie française*, 1694.

16. Martha Nussbaum, *The Therapy of Desire: Theory and Practice in Hellenistic Ethics* (Princeton, N.J.: Princeton University Press, 2009), 449.

17. On this point see Bilis, *Passing Judgment*. For a reading of Medea as a model for Corneillian sovereignty, see 106–10.

18. Mitchell Greenberg has interpreted her position as one "beyond (or before) the Law," and so is a threat insofar as it refuses to cede to power. In this regard it may be considered "an anarchical stance which is inimical to any ideal of community based on privation." Mitchell Greenberg, *Corneille, Classicism, and the Ruses of Symmetry* (Cambridge: Cambridge University Press, 1986), 23.

19. Esther Bick, "The Experience of the Skin in Early Object-Relations," *International Journal of Psychoanalysis* 49 (1968): 484–86. Martin Schmidt gives an overview of the psychoanalytic exploration of the skin, though he

uses it as a metaphor for the protective function of the psyche. See also Martin Schmidt, "Psychic Skin: Psychotic Defences, Borderline Process and Delusions," *Journal of Analytical Psychology* 57 (2012): 21–39.

20. Juliet Fleming, *Graffiti and the Writing Arts of Early Modern England* (London: Reaktion Books, 2001), 83–84; Claudia Benthien, *Skin: On the Cultural Border between Self and the World*, trans. Thomas Dunlap (New York: Columbia University Press, 2002).

21. For Merleau-Ponty, this borderland does not distinguish between people but in fact constitutes the relation between subject and object, between the seer and the seen, where "visibility" is a form of touch: "The look . . . envelops, palpates, espouses visible things. As though it were in a relation of pre-established harmony with them, as though it knew them before knowing them" (*The Visible and the Invisible*, ed. Claude Lefort and trans. Alphonso Lingis [Evanston, Ill.: Northwestern University Press, 1968], 133). Site of connection and mutual constitution, it is also the locus of a confrontation between ourselves as active and as passive, as touching but tangible, of what Marc Richir called the "non-coincidence" or "impossible coincidence" defying the idea of any transcendent "I" (Marc Richir, *Fragments phénoménologiques sur le temps et l'espace* [Paris: Jérôme Millon, 2006], 313).

22. Didier Anzieu, *The Skin-Ego*, trans. Naomi Segal (London: Karnac Books, 2016), 19. Translation modified.

23. Anzieu, *Skin-Ego*, 38.

24. Like many psychoanalysts, Anzieu was interested in fairy tales and edited a book on them. Naomi Segal details how Anzieu's relation to the skin haunts his thoughts another way too; Anzieu's mother, Marie Pantaine, was the replacement child for an older sister who burned to death after she stood too close to the family hearth: The thin dress she was wearing—a veritable ceremonial garment donned especially for church—caught fire (Naomi Segal, *Consensuality: Didier Anzieu, Gender, and the Sense of Touch* [Amsterdam: Rodopi, 2009]). Pantaine was Jacques Lacan's patient (and eventual housekeeper) known as "Aimée" in the section of Lacan's thesis featuring her: Jacques Lacan, "Le cas Aimée ou la paranoia d'auto-punition," in *De la psychose paranoïaque dans ces rapports avec la personalité* (Paris: Le François, 1932). Pantaine's treatment by Lacan, and his lack of candor about this relation, spurred Anzieu to break off his own analysis with Lacan and eventually to develop his notion of the *skin-ego*. Naomi Segal calls this generational inheritance "'ghosting' (skin containing other skins)" ("The Other French Freud: Didier Anzieu—The Story of a Skin," *SAS-Space*, 2006, http://sas-space.sas.ac.uk/id/eprint/62, 2).

25. Ann Rosalind Jones and Peter Stallybrass, *Renaissance Clothing and the Materials of Memory* (Cambridge: Cambridge University Press, 2000), 210.

26. Seneca, *Medea*, in *Tragedies*, vol. 1, 369–71, 1.570–75. Translation modified.

27. Créuse's ekphrasis of her first encounter with the gown calls to mind another sunlit gown which inspires a lengthy ekphrasis in Apollonius of Rhodes's *Argonautica* (1.730–76), , given to Jason by Pallas Athena (1.721–24) which he wears first during his seduction of Hypsipyle, and second during his trials at Colchis (4.421–34). Apollonius Rhodius, *Argonautica*, ed. and trans. William H. Rice. Loeb Classical Library 1 (Cambridge, Mass.: Harvard University Press: 2009).

28. Jean Starobinski, *L'oeil vivant* (Paris: Gallimard, 1970), 72.

29. Wygant, *Medea, Magic*, 90.

## 2. THE MEDEAN PRESENCE: VIOLENCE UNMADE AND REMADE

1. Noa Steimatsky, *Italian Locations: Reinhabiting the Past in Postwar Cinema* (Minneapolis: University of Minnesota Press, 2008), 119.

2. On the notion of contamination, see Steimatsky, *Italian Locations*, esp. 125–26, 160.

3. André de Leyssac, Introduction to *Médée*, by Pierre Corneille (Geneva: Droz, 1978), 17–22.

4. Ovid, *Metamorphoses*, trans. Charles Martin (New York: W. W. Norton, 2004), 1.1–2.

5. Gotthold Ephraim Lessing, *Laocoön: An Essay on the Limits of Painting and Poetry*, ed. E. A. McCormick (1766; Baltimore: Johns Hopkins University Press, 1984).

6. W. J. T. Mitchell, *Picture Theory: Essays on Verbal and Visual Representation* (Chicago: University of Chicago Press, 1995), 178.

7. Mitchell, *Picture Theory*, 176.

8. Valentine Cunningham, "Why Ekphrasis?" *Classical Philology* 102, no. 1 (2007): 57.

9. Lessing, *Laocoön*, 20–21.

10. Kathryn Gutzwiller, "Seeing Thought: Timomachus' Medea and Ecphrastic Epigram," *American Journal of Philology* 125, no. 3 (2004): 363.

11. Quoted in Gutzwiller, "Seeing Thought," 377.

12. Bettina Bergmann, "The Pregnant Moment: Tragic Wives in the Roman Interior," in *Sexuality in Ancient Art*, ed. Natalie Kampen (Cambridge: Cambridge University Press, 1996), 199–218.

13. Richard Tarrant, "Ovid and Ancient Literary History," in *The Cambridge Companion to Ovid*, ed. Philip Hardie (Cambridge: Cambridge University Press, 2002), 29.

14. Steven Hinds, "Medea in Ovid: Scenes from the Life of an Intertextual Heroine," *Materiali e discussioni per l'analisi dei testi classici* 30 (1993): 46.

*Notes to pages 107–21*

15. Dan Curley, *Tragedy in Ovid: Theater, Metatheater, and the Transformation of a Genre* (Cambridge: Cambridge University Press, 2013), 4–5. One of the foundational works for thinking the creativity and visuality of Ovid is Joseph B. Solodow, *The World of Ovid's Metamorphoses* (Chapel Hill: University of North Carolina Press, 1988).

16. Timothy Bahti, "A Minor Form and Its Inversions: The Image, the Poem, the Book in Celan's "Unter ein Bild," *MLN* 110, no. 3 (1995): 565.

17. Marina Warner, *Fantastic Metamorphoses, Other Worlds* (Oxford: Oxford University Press, 2004), 2.

18. E. H. Gombrich, *Art and Illusion: A Study in the Psychology of Pictorial Representation* (1960; Princeton, N.J.: Princeton University Press, 1969).

19. François Rigolot, *Les métamorphoses de Montaigne* (Paris: PUF, 1988), 97–98.

20. Kathryn L. McKinley, *Reading the Ovidian Heroine: The "Metamorphoses" Commentaries 1100–1618* (Amsterdam: Brill, 2001), 18.

21. Carole Newlands, "The Metamorphosis of Medea," in *Medea: Essays on Medea in Myth, Literature, Philosophy, and Art*, ed. J. J. Clauss and S. I. Johnson (Princeton, N.J.: Princeton University Press, 1997), 178–208.

22. See Introduction.

23. Ovid, *Metamorphoses*, vol. 2, Loeb Classical Library, trans. Frank Justus Miller, ed. G. P. Goold (Cambridge, Mass.: Harvard University Press, 1916), 7.297–99. This translation is by Charles Martin, in Ovid, *Metamorphoses* (New York: W. W. Norton, 2005), 7.416–20, p. 235.

24. "If Ovid's brand of tragic theatricality assimilates the violence of the amphitheater, here it seems to reach in a new direction as both tragic and ritual performance merge in Medea's sorcerous bacchanal" (Curley, *Tragedy in Ovid*, 126–27).

25. Curley, *Tragedy in Ovid*, 129.

26. See Barbara Pavlock, *The Image of the Poet in Ovid's "Metamorphoses"* (Madison: University of Wisconsin Press, 2009), 50–59; Christine Binroth-Bank, *Medea in den Metamorphosen Ovids: Untersuchungen zur ovidischen Erzähl- und Darstellungsweise* (Frankfurt: Peter Lang, 1994), 140.

27. For a succinct understanding of how current scholarship positions this fragment, see Curley, *Tragedy in Ovid*, 42.

28. Helene Foley, *Female Acts in Greek Tragedy* (Princeton, N.J.: Princeton University Press, 2001), 243–71, esp. 256–57.

3. STAYING POWER: PERFORMING THE PRESENT MOMENT OF TRAGEDY

1. Jean Rotrou, *Hercule mourant*, in *Théâtre choisi*, vol. 2, ed. D. Moncond'huy, B. Louvat, and A. Riffaud (Paris: Société des textes français modernes, 1999). On Rotrou's use and adaptation of Seneca, see Moncond'huy,

introduction to *Hercule mourant*, 32. In the premodern period the attribution of *Hercules Oetaeus* to Seneca was unquestioned.

2. Robert James Nelson, *Immanence and Transcendence: The Theater of Jean Rotrou, 1609–1650* (Columbus: Ohio State University Press, 1969), 7.

3. Seneca, *Hercule furens*, trans. John G. Fitch (Ithaca, N.Y.: Cornell University Press, 1987), 1.1–278.

4. On this tradition, see M.-R. Jung, *Hercule dans la littérature française du XVIᵉ siècle: De l'Hercule courtois à l'Hercule baroque* (Geneva: Droz, 1966), and F. Bardon, *Le portrait mythologique à la cour de France sous Henri IV et Louis XIII* (Paris: Picard, 1975).

5. J. Trabant, *Der gallische Herkules: Über Sprache und Politik in Frankreich und Deutschland* (Tübingen: A. Francke Verlag, 2002); Sara Melzer, "'Voluntary Subjection:' France's Theory of Colonization/Culture in the Seventeenth Century," in *Structures of Feeling in Seventeenth-Century Cultural Expression*, ed. S. McClary (Toronto: University of Toronto Press, 2013), esp. 98–103.

6. Wallace Bacon, *The Art of Interpretation* (New York: Holt, Rinehart and Winston: 1979), esp. 40.

7. Jacques Derrida, *De la grammatologie* (Paris: Éditions de Minuit, 1967), 102–3.

8. Peggy Phelan, *Unmarked: The Politics of Performance* (New York: Routledge, 1993), 146.

9. Philip Auslander, *Liveness: Performance in a Mediatized Culture* (London: Routledge, 1999).

10. Jon Erickson, "Tension/Release and the Production of Time in Performance," in *Archaeologies of Presence*, ed. Gabriella Giannachi, Nick Kaye, and Michael Shanks (London.: Routledge, 2012), 89.

11. Gordon Coonfield and Heidi Rose, "What Is Called Presence," *Text and Performance Quarterly* 32, no. 3 (2012): 193, 201. This concept of "thisness" intersects with Bill Egginton's idea of a materiality of performance in Baroque theater; see *How the World Became a Stage: Presence, Theatricality and the Question of Modernity* (Albany: State University of New York Press, 2002).

12. Marvin Carlson, *The Haunted Stage: The Theatre as Memory Machine* (Ann Arbor: University of Michigan Press, 2001).

13. Stanley Cavell, *Disowning Knowledge in Seven Plays of Shakespeare* (1987; Cambridge: Cambridge University Press, 2003), 93.

14. *Hercules Oetaeus*, l.823–25. In Riley translation adapted from Kathleen Riley, *The Reception and Performance of Euripides' "Herakles": Reasoning Madness* (Oxford: Oxford University Press, 2008), 109.

15. Laurent Mahelot, *Mémoire pour la décoration des pièces qui se représentent par les Comédiens du Roi*, ed. Pierre Pasquier (Paris: Champion, 2005), 101–3.

16. M. Vuillermoz suggests that the designer's numbers of props even exceed that demanded by the text itself. See Marc Vuillermoz, *Le système des objets dans le théâtre français des années 1625–1650 : Corneille, Mairet, Rotrou, Scudéry* (Geneva: Droz, 2000), 32–33. The gap between textual performances and those onstage is also well documented; Hélène Visentin shows that theaters used machines and other props to augment spectacles. "Le 'Dessein' de la pièce à machines, un cas particulier d'inscription du texte spectaculaire," *Texte* 33/34 (2003): 139–65.

17. Eugène Green, *La parole baroque* (Paris: Desclée de Brouwer, 2001),

18. A. J. Boyle, *Tragic Seneca: An Essay in the Theatrical Tradition* (1997; New York: Routledge, 2013), 186.

19. Hans Ulrich Gumbrecht, *Production of Presence: What Meaning Cannot Convey* (Stanford, Calif.: Stanford University Press, 2003), xiv.

20. Gumbrecht, *Production of Presence*, 2.

21. Aristotle, Longinus, Demetrius, *Aristotle: Poetics; Longinus: On the Sublime; Demetrius: On Style*, trans. Stephen Halliwell, W. Hamilton Fyfe, Doreen C. Innes, and W. Rhys Roberts; rev. Donald A. Russell, Loeb Classical Library 199 (Cambridge, Mass.: Harvard University Press, 1995).

22. Paul de Man, *The Rhetoric of Romanticism* (New York: Columbia University Press, 1984), 5.

23. Jennifer L. Roberts, "The Power of Patience: Teaching Students the Value of Deceleration and Immersive Attention," *Harvard Magazine*, November/December 2013; http://harvardmagazine.com/2013/11/the-power-of-patience; T. J. Clark, *The Sight of Death: An Experiment in Art Writing* (New Haven, Conn.: Yale University Press, 2008).

24. Michael Chaney, "The Concatenate Poetics of Slavery and the Articulate Material of Dave the Potter," *African American Review* 44, no. 4 (2011): 608.

## 4. FLYING TOWARD FUTURITY: SPECTACULARITY AND SUSPENSION

1. The literature on this question is vast. For an argument about the cyclical nature of history, see Alicia Marchant, "A Landscape of Ruins: Decay and Emotion in Late Medieval and Early Modern Antiquarian Narratives," in *Gender and Emotions in Medieval and Early Modern Europe: Destroying Order, Structuring Disorder*, ed. Carolyn Broomhill (New York: Routledge, 2016), 109–25, esp. 120–23. For an examination of the recurring structure of time in architectural histories, see Caroline van Eck, *Classical Rhetoric and the Visual Arts in Early Modern Europe* (Cambridge: Cambridge University Press, 2007), 171–75. For the "polytemporality" of Renaissance objects, see Jonathan Gil Harris, *Untimely Matter in the Time of Shakespeare* (Philadelphia: University of Pennsylvania Press, 2009).

2. See John Powell, *Music and Theatre in France, 1600–1680* (Oxford: Oxford University Press, 2000), 31, for a précis of this history. The propagandist aspects of the play are felt mostly, it seems, through a disjointed composition that yields an imperfect array of allegorical references, mobilizing stage technology for superficial éclat.

3. On machine plays, see Hélène Visentin, "Le théâtre à machines: Succès majeur pour un genre mineur," *Littératures Classiques* 51 (2004): 205–22. On the relation between machine plays and opera, see Powell, *Music and Theatre*, esp. 226–29.

4. Despite the problem of the shifting ground of historiography in his model, see François Hartog, *Regimes of Historicity: Presentism and Experiences of Time*, trans. Saskia Brown (New York: Columbia University Press, 2015).

5. Reinhart Koselleck, *Futures Past: On the Semantics of Historical Time* (1979), trans. and intro. Keith Tribe (1979; New York: Columbia University Press, 2004).

6. Koselleck, *Futures Past*, 10.

7. Koselleck, *Futures Past*, 10.

8. Angus Fletcher, *Allegory: The Theory of a Symbolic Mode* (1964; Princeton, N.J.: Princeton University Press, 2006), 2.

9. Angus Fletcher, "Allegory without Ideas," *boundary 2* 33, no. 1 (2006): 78.

10. Natale Conti, *Mythologiae*, trans. John Mulryan and Steven Brown, 2 vols. (Tempe: Arizona Center for Medieval and Renaissance Studies, 2006), vol. 2, book 6, chap 8.

11. Pierre Corneille, *La Conquête de la Toison d'or*, ed. Marie-France Wagner (Paris: Honoré Champion, 1998), 211.

12. Hélène Visentin, "Le 'Dessein' de la pièce à machines, un cas particulier d'inscription du texte spectaculaire," *Texte* 33/34 (2003): 144–45.

13. Corneille, *La Conquête*, 211.

14. Corneille, *La Conquête*, 211.

15. Corneille, *La Conquête*, 211.

16. Frank Mohler, "The Survival of the Mechanized Flat Wing Scene Change: The Court Theatres of Gripsholm, Cesky, Krumlov and Drottningholm." *Theatre Design & Technology* 35, no. 1 (1999): 46–56. The standard work on seventeenth-century stage technology remains Per Bjurström, *Giacomo Torelli and Baroque Stage Design* (Stockholm: Almqvist & Wiksell, 1961). See also *Giacaomo Torelli: L'invenzione scenica nell'Europa barocca* (Fano: Fondazione Cassa di risparmio di Fano, 2005)

17. There is a rich body of scholarship on the idea of surprise, in particular with regard to the epistemology of wonder and specifically Descartes. See most recently Christopher R. Miller, *Surprise. The Poetics of the Unexpected from Milton to Austen* (Ithaca, N.Y.: Cornell University Press, 2015), esp. 19–22.

18. This epithet, originally given to Torelli, has been applied to Vigarelli over the course of the last two centuries. It might represent the accretion of wonder imputed retrospectively to an incredulous, superstitious seventeenth-century public by eighteenth-century commenters, since the earliest mention of it that I have found is from Louis-Abel de Fontenay's *Dictionnaire des artistes*: "Torelli showed such singular effects and changes, that the public started calling him *the Great Witch*; they were convinced that what he made happen on a daily basis was unnatural." Louis-Abel de Fontenay, *Dictionnaire des artistes* (Paris: Chez Vincent, 1776), 641. Corneille, *La Conquête*, 211.

19. Amy Wygant, "Pierre Corneille's Medea-Machine," *Romanic Review* 85, no. 4 (1994): 535–50.

20. Corneille, *Discours de la tragédie*, in *Oeuvres*, ed. Georges Couton. 3 vols. Bibliothèque de la Pléiade (Paris: Gallimard, 1980–87), 3:154.

21. Phryxus says: "O thou who didst suffer me, a fugitive from my native land in search of a home, to settle in these abodes, and soon offering thy daughter invited me to be thy son-in-law, dolour and ruin of thy realm shall abound for thee what time the fleece is stolen from the sleep-drugged grove. Moreover, Medea, who now is consecrated to Diana of the underworld and leads the holy dance—let her look for betrothal to any suitor, suffer her not to abide in her father's kingdom." Valerius Flaccus, *Argonautica*, trans. J. H. Mozley, Loeb Classical Library 286 (Cambridge, Mass.: Harvard University Press, 1934), 5.233–40.

22. Joseph Harris, *Inventing the Spectator: Subjectivity and the Theatrical Experience in Early Modern France* (Oxford: Oxford University Press, 2014), 110.

23. Terence Cave, "Towards a Pre-history of Suspense," in *Recognitions: A Study in Poetics* (Oxford: Clarendon Press, 1988), 158–67.

24. Corneille, "Discours de la tragédie," in *Oeuvres*, 3:158–59.

25. Corneille, "Discours des trois unités," in *Oeuvres*, 3:175.

26. Katherine Ibbett, *The Style of the State in French Theater, 1630–1660: Neoclassicism and Government* (Farnham: Ashgate, 2009), 117.

27. Nicolà Sabbatini, *Pratica di fabricar scene e machine ne' teatri* [Manual for Constructing Theatrical Scenes and Machines] (Ravenna, 1638), 154–55.

28. "Mythological machine plays, use the technologies of spectacle to realize concretely the 'beyond' [cet au-delà] that has remained too often only implied in regular tragedies, even those with a mythological subject." In Christian Delmas, *Mythologie et mythe dans le théâtre français (1660–1676)* (Geneva: Droz, 1985), 7.

29. Delmas, *Mythologie et mythe*, 34. As Delmas also asserts, "A total theater, the machine play reveals a vision of the world in which the hero is inscribed in relation to the heavens, but nevertheless always within a monarchical frame" (62).

30. "Like a perpendicular line going from the Heavens to Hell," Jean Claveret, *Le ravissement de Proserpine* (Paris: Antoine de Sommaville, 1639), qtd. in Delmas, *Mythologie*, 34.
31. Corneille, *La Conquête*, 211.
32. Marie-France Wagner, introduction to Corneille, *La Conquête*, 220–25.
33. Corneille, *Desseins*, 18.
34. Corneille, *Desseins*, 21–22.
35. Abby Zanger, *Scenes from the Marriage of Louis XIV: Nuptial Fictions and the Making of Absolutist Power* (Stanford, Calif.: Stanford University Press, 1997), 112, 122.
36. Corneille, *Desseins*, 23–24.
37. Zanger, *Scenes from the Marriage of Louis XIV*, 126–27.

### 5. MEDEA OVERLIVED: THE FUTURE OF CATASTROPHE

1. Fredric Jameson, *A Singular Modernity: Essay on the Ontology of the Present* (London: Verso, 2013), 40.
2. Marc Fumaroli, "De *Médée à Phèdre*: Naissance et mise à mort de la tragédie cornélienne," 1980, in *Héros et orateurs: Rhétorique et dramaturgie cornéliennes* (Geneva: Droz, 1996), 493–518.
3. For a stunning reading of *Athalie* as a play about a different form of persistence, that of Jews in Racine's time, see Susan Maslan, "Melancholy Racine: Benjamin's 'Trauerspiel' and Literary Jews," *Yale French Studies*, no. 124 (2013): 64–78.
4. Renaud Bret-Vitoz, *L'espace et la scène: Dramaturgie de la tragédie française, 1691–1759* (Oxford: Voltaire Foundation/SVEC, 2008).
5. Louis Racine, *Mémoires sur la vie de Jean Racine* (Paris: Marc-Michel Bousquet, 1747), 239.
6. Racine, *Mémoires*, 206.
7. Reinhart Koselleck, *Futures Past: On the Semantics of Historical Time*, trans. K. Tribe (1979; New York: Columbia University Press, 2004), 10.
8. Sylvaine Guyot, *Racine et le corps tragique* (Paris: PUF, 2014), esp. 148–49 and, for *Athalie*, 222–23.
9. Georges Forestier, *La tragédie française: Passions tragiques et règles classiques* (2003; Paris: Armand Colin, 2010), 170–71.
10. Emily Wilson, *Mocked with Death. Tragic Overliving from Sophocles to Milton.* (Baltimore: Johns Hopkins University Press, 2004), 18–20.
11. Translation liberally adapted from Geoffrey Alan Argent, *Athaliah: The Complete Plays of Jean Racine* (University Park: Pennsylvania State University Press, 2010), 4:47.
12. Jacques Derrida, *The Beast and the Sovereign*, trans. by Geoffrey Bennington (Chicago: University of Chicago Press, 2011), 2:130.

13. Julius César Scaliger, *Poetices libri septem* (Lyon: Apud Antonium Vincentium, 1561), 1.9: "Catastrophe [est], conversio negotii exagitati in tranquillitatem non expectatam."

14. François Hédelin d'Aubignac, *La pratique du théâtre*, ed. Hélène Baby (Paris: Champion Classiques Littératures, 2011), 2.9.203.

15. Thomas Burnet, *The Theory of the Earth: Containing an Account of the Original of the Earth, and of All the General Changes which it hath already undergone, or is to undergo, Till the Consummation of all Things* (London: Printed by R. Norton, for Walter Kettilby, 1684), 326.

16. Morvan de Bellegarde, *Lettres curieuses* (1702), 332–33, cited in Jacques Schérer, *La dramaturgie classique en France*, ed. G. Forestier (1959; Paris: Armand Colin, 2014), 126. See also Pierre Édouard Lemontey, *Histoire de la régence et de la minorité de Louis XV, jusqu'au ministère du cardinal de Fleury* (Paris: Paulin, 1832), 1:182.

17. By Marmontel in the 1780s, catastrophe is the "achèvement" of whatever needs to be resolved for the play to end. This leads Schérer to offer the following definition: "Le dénouement d'une pièce de théâtre comprend l'élimination du dernier obstacle ou la dernière péripétie et les événements qui peuvent en résulter; ces événements sont parfois désignés par le terme de catastrophe." (The denouement of a play includes either the elimination of the last obstacle or the very last event of the drama, and its results. These events often called the catastrophe.) Schérer, *La dramaturgie classique*, 128.

18. Olaf Briese, "Genommen auß den Comoedien: Katastrophenbegriffe der neuzeitlichen Geologie," in *Wissenschaftsgeschichte als Begriffsgeschichte: Terminologische Umbrüche im Entstehungsprozess der modernen Wissenschaften*, ed. Michael Eggers and Matthias Rothe (Heidelberg: Bielefeld, 2009), 33. Briese quotes the 1684 translation of Thomas Burnet's *Telluris Theoria Sacra*, or *Sacred Theory of the Earth*: "From the Creation to this Age hath undergone but one Catastrophe, and Nature hath had two different faces; The next Catastrophe is the CONFLAGRATION, to wich a new face of Nature will accordingly succeed, *New Havens* and a *New Earth, Paradise* renew'd."

19. Montesquieu's *Lettres persanes* (1721) and Prévost's *Manon Lescaut* (1731) each provides an example of a nonnegative catastrophe, a disruption in the usual course of events, but one that does not shift what the future holds.

20. Derval Conroy, "Gender, Power and Authority in *Alexandre le Grand* and *Athalie*," in *Racine: The Power and the Pleasure*, ed. Edric Caldicott and Derval Conroy (Dublin: University College Dublin Press, 2001), 67–74.

21. Racine, "Préface," *Athalie*, 1009–10.

22. Georges Forestier, Introduction to Racine, *Oeuvres complètes*, xvi.

23. Ulrich Beck, *Risk Society: Towards a New Modernity* (1986; London: Sage, 1992).

24. Frédéric Neyrat, *Biopolitique des catastrophes* (Paris: Editions MF, 2008), 12.

25. Nigel Clark, *Inhuman Nature: Sociable Life on a Dynamic Planet* (London: Sage, 2011), 18, 163.

26. Walter Benjamin, *Arcades Project*, trans. Howard Eiland and Kevin McLaughlin (Cambridge, Mass.: Belknap Press of Harvard University Press, 1999), N9a,1, 474.

EPILOGUE: THE COSMOPOLITICS OF LITERATURE

1. I therefore refuse categorically the metaphor of the "Medea hypothesis," Peter Ward's anti-Gaian suggestion that life on earth is ultimately inhospitable, even self-consuming. *The Medea Hypothesis: Is Life on Earth Ultimately Self-Destructive?* (Princeton, N.J.: Princeton University Press, 2009). Whether this is an apt model for considering the dynamics of life is one question; whether Medean violence is "naturally" and irreducibly self-destructive is a facile misperception of the myth's complexity, especially with regard to its temporal dynamics.

2. Nita Krevens, "Medea as Foundation-Heroine," in *Medea: Essays on Medea in Myth, Literature, Philosophy, and Art*, ed. J. J. Clauss and S. I. Johnson (Princeton, N.J.: Princeton University Press, 1997),71–82.

3. Martha Nussbaum, "Patriotism and Cosmopolitanism, in *For Love of Country: Debating the Limits of Patriotism* (Boston: Beacon Press, 1996), 4.

4. Isabelle Stengers, *Cosmopolitics I*, trans. Robert Bononno (Minneapolis: University of Minnesota Press, 2010).

5. Bruno Latour, "Whose Cosmos, Which Cosmopolitics? Comments on the Peace Terms of Ulrich Beck," *Common Knowledge* 10, no. 3 (2004): 454.

6. Leïla Slimani, *Chanson douce* (Paris: Gallimard 2016), 13; *The Perfect Nanny*, trans. Sam Taylor (New York: Penguin, 2018), 1.

7. Slimani, *Perfect Nanny*, 5. Citations hereafter are included in the text parenthetically.

8. Adriana Cavarero, *Horrorism: Naming Contemporary Violence*, trans. William McCuaig (New York: Columbia University Press, 2009), 109. See also the Manifesto.

# BIBLIOGRAPHY

### PREMODERN SOURCES

Apollonius Rhodius. *Argonautica*. Edited and Translated by William H. Rice. Loeb Classical Library 1. Cambridge, MA: Harvard University Press, 2009.

Aristotle, Longinus, Demetrius. *Aristotle: Poetics. Longinus: On the Sublime. Demetrius: On Style*. Translated by Stephen Halliwell, W. Hamilton Fyfe, Doreen C. Innes, W. Rhys Roberts. Revised by Donald A. Russell. Loeb Classical Library 199. Cambridge, MA: Harvard University Press, 1995.

d'Aubignac, François Hédelin. *La pratique du théâtre*. Edited by Hélène Baby. Paris: Champion Classiques Littératures, 2011.

Chappuzeau, Samuel. *Le théâtre françois*. Lyon: Mayer, 1674.

Claveret, Jean. *Le ravissement de Proserpine*, tragédie. Paris: Antoine de Sommaville, 1639.

Conti, Natale. *Natale Conti's Mythologiae*. Translated and annotated by John Mulryan and Steven Brown. Tempe: Arizona Center for Medieval and Renaissance Studieseetee, 2006.

Corneille, Pierre. *Desseins de la Toison d'or, tragédie*. Paris: Augustin Courbé et Guillaume de Luyne, 1661.

———. *La Conquête de la Toison d'or*. Edited and introduced by Marie-France Wagner. Paris: Honoré Champion, 1998.

———. *Le théâtre de P. Corneille, reveu et corrigé et augmenté*, Suivant la copie imprimée à Paris. Amsterdam: A. Wolfgang, 1664.

———. *Médée*. Paris: François Targa, 1639.

———. *Oeuvres complètes*. Edited by Georges Couton. 3 vols. Bibliothèque de la Pléiade. Paris: Gallimard, 1980–87.

*Dictionnaire de l'Académie française*. 2 vols. Paris: Coignard, 1694.

Euripides. *Medea*. Translated by James Norwood. Oxford: Oxford University Press, 1998.

Fénelon, François de Salignac de La Mothe. *Oeuvres*. Edited by Jacques Le Brun. Bibliothèque de la Pléiade. Paris: Gallimard, 1993.

Fontenay, Louis-Abel de Bonafous, abbé de. *Dictionnaire des artistes*. 2 vols. Paris: Vincent, 1776.

Horace. (Q. Horatius Flaccus). *The Art of Poetry: To the Pisos*. Edited by C. Smart and Theodore Alois Buckley. New York. Harper & Brothers,1863. http://data.perseus.org/citations/urn:cts:latinLit:phi0893.phi006.perseus-eng1:1-43.

Laudun d'Aigaliers, Pierre. *Horace*. In *Les poésies de Pierre de Laudun d'Aigaliers, contenans deux tragédies*, 36–81. Paris: David Le Clerc, 1596.

Lessing, Gotthold Ephraim. *Laocoön: An Essay on the Limits of Painting and Poetry*. Edited by E. A. McCormick. Baltimore: Johns Hopkins University Press, 1984.

Mahelot, Laurent. *Mémoire pour la décoration des pièces qui se représentent par les Comédiens du Roi*. Edited and introduction by Pierre Pasquier. Sources Classiques 58. Paris: Champion, 2005.

Mesnardière, Hippolyte-Jules Pilet de la. *La poétique*. Edited by Marc Civardi. Paris: Champion, 2015.

Ovid. *Metamorphoses*. Translated by Charles Martin. New York: W. W. Norton, 2004.

———. *Metamorphoses*. Vol. 2. Translated by Frank Justus Miller. Edited by G. P. Goold. Loeb Classical Library. Cambridge, Mass.: Harvard University Press, 1916.

Racine, Jean. *The Complete Plays of Jean Racine*. Vol. 4, *Athaliah*. Translated by Geoffrey Alan Argent. University Park: Pennsylvania State Press, 2010.

———. *Oeuvres*. Edited by Georges Forestier. Bibliothèque de la Pléiade. Paris: Gallimard,1999.

Racine, Louis. *Mémoires sur la vie de Jean Racine*. Paris: Marc-Michel Bousquet, 1747.

Rapin, René. *Réflexions sur la poétique et sur les ouvrages des poètes anciens et modernes*. 1684. Edited by Pascale Thouverin. Paris: Champion Classiques, 2011.

Rotrou, Jean. *Hercule mourant*. In *Théâtre choisi*, vol. 2. Edited by D. Moncond'huy, B. Louvat, and A. Riffaud. Paris: Société des textes français modernes, 1999.

Sabbatini, Nicolà. *Pratica di fabricar scene e machine ne' teatri*. Ravenna: Pietro de' Paoli and Gio. Battista Giovannelli stampatori camerali, 1638.

Saint-Évremond, Charles de Marguetel de Saint Denis. "De la tragédie." 1672. In Projet "Haine du Théâtre," *Observatoire de la vie littéraire*. Edited by Nina Hugot. Paris: Université Paris-Sorbonne, LABEX OBVIL, 2014. http://obvil.paris-sorbonne.fr/corpus/haine-theatre/saint-evremond_de-la-tragedie_1692/.

Scaliger, Jules César. *Poetices libri septem*. Lyon: Apud Antonium Vincentium, 1561.

Seneca, *Hercule furens*. Translated by John G. Fitch. Ithaca, N.Y.: Cornell University Press, 1987.

———. *Medea*. Translated by A. J. Boyle. Oxford: Oxford University Press, 2014.
———. *Tragedies*. 2 vols. Edited and translated by John G. Fitch. Loeb Classical Library 62. Cambridge, Mass.: Harvard University Press, 2018.
Valerius Flaccus. *Argonautica*. Translated by J. H. Mozley. Loeb Classical Library 286. Cambridge, Mass.: Harvard University Press, 1934.
Villiers, Pierre de. *Entretien sur les tragédies de ce temps*. Paris: Etienne Michallet, 1675.

MODERN SOURCES

Anouilh, Jean. *Antigone*. 1944. In *Nouvelles pieces noires: Jézabel, Antigone, Roméo et Jeannette, Médée*. Paris: Edition de la Table ronde, 1946.
Anzieu, Didier. *Le moi-peau*. Paris: Dunod, 1995.
———. *The Skin-Ego*. Translated by Naomi Segal. London: Karnac Books, 2016.
Auslander, Philip. *Liveness: Performance in a Mediatized Culture*. London: Routledge, 1999.
Bacon, Wallace. *The Art of Interpretation*. New York: Holt, Rinehart and Winston, 1979.
Bahti, Timothy. "A Minor Form and Its Inversions: The Image, the Poem, the Book in Celan's 'Unter ein Bild.'" *MLN* 110, no. 3 (1995): 565–78.
Bardon, Françoise. *Le Portrait mythologique à la cour de France sous Henri IV et Louis XIII: Mythologie et politique*. Paris: Picard, 1975.
Bartel, Heike, and Anne Simon, eds. *Unbinding Medea. Interdisciplinary Approaches to a Classical Myth from Antiquity to the 21st Century*. London: Legenda, 2010.
Beck, Ulrich. *Risk Society: Towards a New Modernity*. 1986. London: Sage, 1992.
Benjamin, Walter. *Arcades Project*. Translated by Howard Eiland and Kevin McLaughlin. Cambridge, Mass.: Belknap Press of Harvard University Press, 1999.
Benthien, Claudia. *Skin: On the Cultural Border between Self and the World*. Translated by Thomas Dunlap. New York: Columbia University Press, 2002.
Benveniste, Emile. "'MED' et la notion de mesure." In *Le vocabulaire des institutions indo-européenes*, vol. 2 : *Pouvoir, droit, religion*, 123–32. Paris: Éditions de Minuit, 1969.
Bergmann, Bettina. "The Pregnant Moment: Tragic Wives in the Roman Interior." In *Sexuality in Ancient Art*, edited by Natalie Kampen, 199–218. Cambridge: Cambridge University Press, 1996.
Berra, Aurélien, ed. *Médée, versions et interpretations d'un mythe*. Besançon: Presses Universitaires de Franche-Comté, 2016.

Bick, Esther. "The Experience of the Skin in Early Object-Relations." *International Journal of Psychoanalysis* 49 (1968): 484–86.
Biet, Christian. "Discours et représentation: La violence au théâtre." *Litteratures Classiques* 73, no. 3 (2010): 415–29.
———. "French Tragedy during the Seventeenth Century: From Cruelty on a Scaffold to Poetic Distance on Stage." In *Politics and Aesthetics in European Baroque and Classicist Tragedy*, edited by Jan Bloemendal and Nigel Smith, 294–316. Leiden: Brill, 2016.
Biet, Christian, and Marie-Madeleine Fragonard. "Représentation, hyper-représentation et performance des violences politiques et religieuses (mi-XVIe/ mi-XVIIe siècle)." *Littératures classiques* 73, no. 3 (2010): 5–15.
Bilis, Hélène. *Passing Judgment: The Politics and Poetics of Sovereignty in French Tragedy from Hardy to Racine*. Toronto: University of Toronto Press, 2016.
Billings, Joshua. *Genealogy of the Tragic: Greek Tragedy and German Philosophy*. Princeton, N.J.: Princeton University Press, 2014.
Binroth-Bank, Christine. *Medea in den Metamorphosen Ovids: Untersuchungen zur ovidischen Erzähl- und Darstellungsweise*. Frankfurt: Peter Lang, 1994.
Bjurström, Per. *Giacomo Torelli and Baroque Stage Design*. Stockholm: Almqvist & Wiksell, 1961.
Blocker, Déborah. *Instituer un "art": Politiques du théâtre dans la France du premier XVIIe siècle*. Paris: Honoré Champion, 2009.
Boyle, A. J. *Tragic Seneca: An Essay in the Theatrical Tradition*. 1997. New York: Routledge, 2013.
Braider, Christopher. *The Matter of Mind: Reason and Experience in the Age of Descartes*. Toronto: University of Toronto Press, 2012.
Bret-Vitoz, Renaud. *L'espace et la scène: Dramaturgie de la tragédie française, 1691–1759*. Oxford: Voltaire Foundation/SVEC, 2008.
Briese, Olaf. "Genommen auß den Comoedien Katastrophenbegriffe der neuzeitlichen Geologie." In *Wissenschaftsgeschichte als Begriffsgeschichte: Terminologische Umbrüche im Entstehungsprozess der modernen Wissenschaften*, edited by Michael Eggers and Matthias Rothe, 23–50. Heidelberg: Bielefeld, 2009.
Butler, Judith. *Antigone's Claim: Kinship between Life and Death*. New York: Columbia University Press, 2000.
Carlson, Marvin. *The Haunted Stage: The Theatre as Memory Machine*. Ann Arbor: University of Michigan Press, 2001.
Carson, Anne. *Antigonick*. New York: New Directions, 2015.
Cavarero, Adriana. *Horrorism: Naming Contemporary Violence*. Translated by William McCuaig. New York: Columbia University Press, 2009.
———. *Inclinations: A Critique of Rectitude*. 2014. Translated by Amanda Minervini and Adam Sitze. Stanford, Calif.: Stanford University Press, 2016.

Cave, Terence. *Recognitions: A Study in Poetics*. Oxford: Clarendon Press, 1988.
Cavell, Stanley. *Disowning Knowledge in Seven Plays of Shakespeare*. 1987. Cambridge: Cambridge University Press, 2003.
Chaney, Michael A. "The Concatenate Poetics of Slavery and the Articulate Material of Dave the Potter." *African American Review* 44, no. 4 (2011): 607–18.
Chantraine, Pierre. *Dictionnaire étymologique de la langue grecque: Histoire des mots*. Volume 3 (Δ–Π). Paris: Klincksieck, 1968.
Civardi, Marc. *La querelle du Cid (1637–1638): Édition critique intégrale*. Paris: Champion, 2004.
Clark, Nigel. *Inhuman Nature: Sociable Life on a Dynamic Planet*. London: Sage, 2011.
Clark, T. J. *The Sight of Death: An Experiment in Art Writing*. New Haven, Conn.: Yale University Press, 2008.
Clauss, J. J., and S. I. Johnston, eds. *Medea: Essays on Medea in Myth, Literature, Philosophy and Art*. Princeton, N.J.: Princeton University Press, 1997.
Conroy, Derval. "Gender, Power and Authority in *Alexandre le Grand* and *Athalie*." In *Racine: The Power and the Pleasure*, ed. Edric Caldicott and Derval Conroy, 55–74. Dublin: University College Dublin Press, 2001.
Coonfield, Gordon, and Heidi Rose. "What Is Called Presence." *Text and Performance Quarterly* 32, no. 3 (2012): 192–208.
Cunningham, Valentine. "Why Ekphrasis?" *Classical Philology* 102, no. 1 (2007): 57–71.
Curley, Dan. *Tragedy in Ovid: Theater, Metatheater, and the Transformation of a Genre*. Cambridge: Cambridge University Press, 2013.
Daston, Lorraine. "The Morality of Natural Orders: The Power of Medea." Tanner Lectures on Human Values, part 1. Cambridge, Mass.: Harvard University Press, 2002.
Delmas, Christian. *Mythologie et mythe dans le théâtre français (1660–1676)*. Geneva: Droz, 1985.
de Man, Paul. *The Rhetoric of Romanticism*. New York: Columbia University Press, 1984.
Derrida, Jacques. *The Beast and the Sovereign*. Vol. 2. Translated by Geoffrey Bennington. Chicago: University of Chicago Press, 2011.
———. *De la grammatologie*. Paris: Éditions de Minuit, 1967.
———. "Plato's Pharmacy." In *Dissemination*, translated by Barbara Johnson, 63–171. Chicago: University of Chicago Press, 2004.
Dupont, Florence. *Aristote ou le vampire du théâtre occidental*. Paris: Aubier, 2007.
Egginton, William. *How the World Became a Stage: Presence, Theatricality and the Question of Modernity*. Albany: State University of New York Press, 2002.

Erickson, Jon. "Tension/Release and the Production of Time in Performance." In *Archaeologies of Presence*, edited by Gabriella Giannachi, Nick Kaye, and Michael Shanks, 82–99. London: Routledge, 2012.
Fleming, Juliet. *Graffiti and the Writing Arts of Early Modern England*. London: Reaktion Books, 2001.
Fletcher, Angus. *Allegory: The Theory of a Symbolic Mode*. 1964. Princeton, N.J.: Princeton University Press, 2006.
———. "Allegory without Ideas." *boundary 2* 33, no. 1 (2006): 77–98.
Foley, Helene. *Female Acts in Greek Tragedy*. Princeton, N.J.: Princeton University Press, 2001.
Forestier, Georges. *La tragédie française: Passions tragiques et règles classiques*. 2003. Paris: Armand Colin, 2010.
Foucault, Michel. "Nietzsche, Genealogy, History." In *Language, Counter-Memory, Practice: Selected Essays and Interviews by Michel Foucault*, edited by Donald F. Bouchard, 139–64. Ithaca, N.Y.: Cornell University Press, 1980.
Freeman, Lisa. *Antitheatricality and the Body Politic*. Philadelphia: University of Pennsylvania Press, 2017.
Frisch, Andrea. *Forgetting Differences: Tragedy, Historiography, and the French Wars of Religion*. Edinburgh: Edinburgh University Press, 2015.
Fumaroli, Marc. "De *Médée* à *Phèdre*: Naissance et mise à mort de la tragédie 'cornélienne.'" 1980. In *Héros et orateurs: Rhétorique et dramaturgie cornéliennes*, 493–518. Geneva: Droz, 1990.
Gaggadis-Robin, Vassiliki. *Jason et Médée sur les sarcophages*. Rome: Ecole française de Rome, 1994.
Gilby, Emma. *Sublime Worlds: Early Modern French Literature*. London: Legenda, 2006.
Green, Eugène. *La parole baroque*. Paris: Desclée de Brouwer, 2001.
Greenberg, Mitchell. *Corneille, Classicism, and the Ruses of Symmetry*. Cambridge: Cambridge University Press, 1986.
Gombrich, E. H. *Art and Illusion: A Study in the Psychology of Pictorial Representation*. Princeton, N.J.: Princeton University Press, 1969.
Guillot, Catherine. "Les éditions illustrées du théâtre de Corneille." In *Pratiques de Corneille*, edited by Myriam Dufour-Maître, 75–92. Mont-Saint-Aignan, France: Publication des universités de Rouen et du Havre, 2012.
———. "Richelieu et le théâtre." *Transversalités* 117, no. 1 (2011): 87–102.
Gumbrecht, Hans Ulrich. *Production of Presence: What Meaning Cannot Convey*. Stanford, Calif.: Stanford University Press, 2003.
Gutzwiller, Kathryn. "Seeing Thought: Timomachus' Medea and Ecphrastic Epigram." *American Journal of Philology* 125, no. 3 (2004): 339–86.
Guyot, Sylvaine. *Racine et le corps tragique*. Paris: Presses Universitaires de France, 2014.

Halpern, Richard. *Eclipse of Action: Tragedy and Political Economy*. Chicago: University of Chicago Press, 2017.

———. "Theater and Democratic Thought: Arendt to Rancière." *Critical Inquiry* 37, no. 3 (2011): 545–72.

Harris, Jonathan Gil. *Untimely Matter in the Time of Shakespeare*. Philadelphia: University of Pennsylvania Press, 2009.

Harris, Joseph. *Inventing the Spectator: Subjectivity and the Theatrical Experience in Early Modern France*. Oxford: Oxford University Press, 2014.

Hartog, François. *Regimes of Historicity: Presentism and Experiences of Time*. Translated by Saskia Brown. New York: Columbia University Press, 2015.

Hinds, Steven. "Medea in Ovid: Scenes from the Life of an Intertextual Heroine." *Materiali e discussioni per l'analisi dei testi classici* 30 (1993): 9–47.

Heaney, Seamus. Afterword to *The Burial at Thebes: Sophocles' "Antigone,"* by Sophocles, 75–79. London: Faber & Faber, 2004.

Honig, Bonnie. *Antigone Interrupted*. Cambridge: Cambridge University Press, 2013.

———. "Antigone's Laments, Creon's Grief: Mourning, Membership, and the Politics of Exception." *Political Theory* 37, no. 1 (2009): 5–43.

Hoxby, Blair. *What Was Tragedy? Theory and the Early Modern Canon*. Oxford: Oxford University Press, 2015.

Ibbett, Katherine. *Compassion's Edge: Fellow-Feeling and Its Limits in Early Modern France*. Philadelphia: University of Pennsylvania Press, 2017.

———. *The Style of the State in French Theater, 1630–1660: Neoclassicism and Government*. Farnham: Ashgate, 2009.

Irigaray, Luce. *Le temps de la différence*. Paris: Éditions Hachette, 1989.

Jameson, Fredric. *A Singular Modernity: Essay on the Ontology of the Present*. London: Verso, 2013.

Jones, Ann Rosalind, and Peter Stallybrass. *Renaissance Clothing and the Materials of Memory*. Cambridge: Cambridge University Press, 2000.

Jouhaud, Christian. *Sauver le Grand-Siècle? Présence et transmission du passé*. Paris: Seuil, 2007.

Jung, M.-R. *Hercule dans la littérature française du XVI$^e$ siècle: De l'Hercule courtois à l'Hercule baroque*. Geneva: Droz, 1966.

Kerwin, William. *Beyond the Body: The Boundaries of Medicine and English Renaissance Drama*. Amherst: University of Massachusetts Press, 2005.

Konstan, David. "Medea: A Hint of Divinity?" *Classical World* 101, no. 1 (2007): 93–94.

Koselleck, Reinhart. *Futures Past: On the Semantics of Historical Time*. 1979. Translated by K. Tribe. New York: Columbia University Press, 2004.

Krevans, Nita. "Medea as Foundation-Heroine." In *Medea: Essays on Medea in Myth, Literature, Philosophy, and Art*, edited by J. J. Clauss and S. I. Johnson, 71–82. Princeton, N.J.: Princeton University Press, 1997.

Lacan, Jacques. *De la psychose paranoïaque dans ces rapports avec la personalité.* Paris: Le François, 1932.
Lambropoulos, Vassilis. *The Tragic Idea.* London: Duckworth Press, 2006.
Langer, Susanne. *Feeling and Form: A Theory of Art.* New York: Charles Scribner's Sons, 1953.
Latour, Bruno. *We Have Never Been Modern.* Translated by Catherine Porter. Cambridge, Mass.: Harvard University Press, 1993.
———. "Whose Cosmos, Which Cosmopolitics? Comments on the Peace Terms of Ulrich Beck." *Common Knowledge* 10, no. 3 (2004): 450–62.
Lemontey, Pierre Édouard. *Histoire de la régence et de la minorité de Louis XV, jusqu'au ministère du cardinal de Fleury.* Paris: Paulin, 1832.
Levine, Caroline. *Forms: Whole, Rhythm, Hierarchy, Network.* Princeton, N.J.: Princeton University Press, 2015.
Leyssac, André de. Introduction to *Médée*, by Pierre Corneille, 7–44. Geneva: Droz, 1978.
Lochert, Véronique. *L'écriture du spectacle: Les didascalies dans le théâtre européen aux XVIe et XVIIe siècles.* Geneva: Droz, 2009.
Longino, Michèle. *Orientalism in French Classical Drama.* Cambridge: Cambridge University Press, 2002.
Loraux, Nicole. *Tragic Ways of Killing a Woman.* Translated by Anthony Forster. Cambridge, Mass.: Harvard University Press, 1991.
Marchant, Alicia. "A Landscape of Ruins: Decay and Emotion in Late Medieval and Early Modern Antiquarian Narratives." In *Gender and Emotions in Medieval and Early Modern Europe: Destroying Order, Structuring Disorder*, edited by Carolyn Broomhill, 109–25. New York: Routledge, 2016.
Marin, Louis. "Théâtralité et pouvoir, magie, machination, machine: *Médée* de Corneille." In *Le pouvoir de la raison d'état*, edited by Christian Lazzeri and Dominique Reynié, 231–59. Paris: Presses Universitaires de France, 1992.
Martin, Henri-Jean, et al. "Typographie et littérature: La mise en text du livre classique." In *La naissance du livre moderne: Mise en page et mise en texte du livre français.* Paris: Ed. du Cercle de la Librairie, 2000.
Maslan, Susan. "Melancholy Racine: Benjamin's 'Trauerspiel' and Literary Jews." *Yale French Studies*, no. 124 (2013): 64–78.
McDermott, Emily. *Euripides' Medea: The Incarnation of Disorder.* University Park: Pennsylvania State University Press, 1989.
McKinley, Kathryn L. *Reading the Ovidian Heroine: "Metamorphoses" Commentaries 1100–1618.* Amsterdam: Brill, 2001.
Melzer, Sara. "'Voluntary Subjection:' France's Theory of Colonization/Culture in the Seventeenth Century." In *Structures of Feeling in*

*Seventeenth-Century Cultural Expression*, edited by S. McClary, 93–116. Toronto: University of Toronto Press, 2013.

Merleau-Ponty, Maurice. *The Visible and the Invisible: Followed by Working Notes*. Edited by Claude Lefort. Translated by Alphonso Lingis. Evanston, Ill.: Northwestern University Press, 1968.

Merlin, Hélène. *Public et littérature en France au XVIIe siècle*. Paris: Les Belles Lettres, 1994.

Miller, Christopher R. *Surprise: The Poetics of the Unexpected from Milton to Austen*. Ithaca, N.Y.: Cornell University Press, 2015.

Mitchell, W. J. T. *Picture Theory: Essays on Verbal and Visual Representation*. Chicago: University of Chicago Press, 1995.

Mohler, Frank. "The Survival of the Mechanized Flat Wing Scene Change: The Court Theatres of Gripsholm, Cesky, Krumlov and Drottningholm." *Theatre Design & Technology* 35, no. 1 (1999): 46–56.

Moreau, Alain. *Le mythe de Jason et Médée: Le va-nu-pied et la sorcière*. Paris: Les Belles Lettres, 2014.

Nagle, Betty. *The Poetics of Exile: Program and Polemic in the "Tristia" and "Epistulae ex Ponto" of Ovid*. Brussels: Latomus, 1980.

Nelson, Robert James. *Immanence and Transcendence: The Theater of Jean Rotrou, 1609–1650*. Columbus: Ohio State University Press, 1969.

Newlands, Carole. "The Metamorphosis of Medea." In *Medea: Essays on Medea in Myth, Literature, Philosophy, and Art*, edited by J. J. Clauss and S. I. Johnson, 178–208. Princeton, N.J.: Princeton University Press, 1997.

Neyrat, Frédéric. *Biopolitique des catastrophes*. Paris: Editions MF, 2008.

Norman, Larry F., *The Shock of the Ancient: Literature and History in Early Modern France*. Chicago: University of Chicago Press, 2011.

———. "Tragic Violence in Performance and Print Illustration: From Monléon's *Thyeste* to Corneille and Racine." *Biblio* 17, no. 161 (2005): 143–56.

Nussbaum, Martha. "Patriotism and Cosmopolitanism." In *For Love of Country: Debating the Limits of Patriotism*. Boston: Beacon Press, 1996.

———. *The Therapy of Desire: Theory and Practice in Hellenistic Ethics*. Princeton, N.J.: Princeton University Press, 2009.

Ost, François. *Antigone voilée*. 2005. Brussels: De Boeck, 2010.

Pasolini, Pier Paolo, dir. *Medea*. Rome, Italy: San Marco S.p.A, 1969.

Pavlock, Barbara. *The Image of the Poet in Ovid's "Metamorphoses."* Madison: University of Wisconsin Press, 2009.

Phelan, Peggy. *Unmarked: The Politics of Performance*. New York: Routledge, 1993.

Phillips, Henry. *Church and Culture in Seventeenth-Century France*. Cambridge: Cambridge University Press, 2002.

———. *The Theatre and Its Critics in Seventeenth-Century France*. Oxford: Oxford University Press, 1980.
Powell, John. *Music and Theatre in France, 1600–1680*. Oxford: Oxford University Press, 2000.
Pyne, Stephen J. "Forged in Fire: History, Land, and Anthropogenic Fire." In *Advances in Historical Ecology*, edited by William L. Balée, 64–99. New York: Columbia University Press, 1998.
———. *World Fire: The Culture of Fire on Earth*. New York: Henry Holt, 1995.
Rancière, Jacques. "The Ethical Turn of Aesthetics and Politics." *Critical Horizons* 7, no. 1 (2006): 1–20.
Richir, Marc. *Fragments phénoménologiques sur le temps et l'espace*. Paris: Jérôme Millon, 2006.
Riffaud, Alain. "Corneille et l'impression de ses livres: de l'indifférence à l'innovation." In *Pratiques de Corneille*, ed. Myriam Dufour-Maître, 55–74. Mont-Saint-Aignan: Presses universitaires de Rouen et du Havre, 2012.
———. "Les succès éditoriaux du théâtre français au XVII siècle." *Revue d'Histoire Littéraire de la France* 117, no. 4 (2017): 797–806.
Rigolot, François. *Les métamorphoses de Montaigne*. Paris: PUF, 1988.
Riley, Kathleen. *The Reception and Performance of Euripides' "Herakles": Reasoning Madness*. Oxford: Oxford University Press, 2008.
Roberts, Jennifer L. "The Power of Patience: Teaching Students the Value of Deceleration and Immersive Attention." *Harvard Magazine*, November/December 2013. http://harvardmagazine.com/2013/11/the-power-of-patience.
Rosensweig, Anna. "Reaching *Antigone:* Relational Rights in Early Modern Drama." Presentation at the University of Rochester, February 2016.
———. "'Toute la cité pleure': Mise en scène du peuple thébain dans *Antigone ou la Pieté* de Robert Garnier." *Cahiers Forell—Formes et Représentations en Linguistique et Littérature: La Foule au théâtre*, April 2015, http://09.edel.univ-poitiers.fr/lescahiersforell/index.php?id=279.
Schérer, Jacques. *La dramaturgie classique en France*. Paris: Librairie Nizet, 1959. Reprinted with preface and notes by Georges Forestier. Paris: Armand Colin, 2014.
Schmidt, Martin. "Psychic Skin: Psychotic Defences, Borderline Process and Delusions." *Journal of Analytical Psychology* 57 (2012): 21–39.
Segal, Naomi. *Consensuality: Didier Anzieu, Gender, and the Sense of Touch*. Amsterdam: Rodopi, 2009.
———. "The Other French Freud: Didier Anzieu—The Story of a Skin." *SAS-Space*, 2006. http://sas-space.sas.ac.uk/id/eprint/62.
Semk, Christopher. *Playing the Martyr: Theater and Theology in Early Modern France*. Lewisburg, Penn.: Bucknell University Press, 2017.

Sharpe, Christina. *In the Wake: On Blackness and Being*. Durham, N.C.: Duke University Press, 2016.
Slimani, Leïla. *Chanson douce*. Paris: Gallimard, 2016.
———. *The Perfect Nanny*. Translated by Sam Taylor. New York: Penguin, 2018.
Smith, Bruce R. *Ancient Scripts and Modern Experience on the English Stage, 1500–1700*. Princeton, N.J.: Princeton University Press, 2014.
Solodow, Joseph B. *The World of Ovid's Metamorphoses*. Chapel Hill: University of North Carolina Press, 1988.
Stanton, Domna. *The Dynamics of Gender in Early Modern France: Women Writ, Women Writing*. Aldershot: Ashgate, 2014.
Starobinsky, Jean. *L'oeil vivant*. Paris: Gallimard, 1970.
Steimatsky, Noa. *Italian Locations: Reinhabiting the Past in Postwar Cinema*. Minneapolis: University of Minnesota Press, 2008.
Stengers, Isabelle. *Cosmopolitics I*. Translated by Robert Bononno. Minneapolis: University of Minnesota Press, 2010.
———. *Souviens-toi que je suis Médée: Medea nunc sum*. Paris: Les Empecheurs de Penser en Rond, 1993.
Stiegler, Bernard. *What Makes Life Worth Living: On Pharmacology*. Cambridge: Polity Press, 2013.
Strauss, Jonathan. *Private Lives, Public Deaths: Antigone and the Invention of Individuality*. New York: Fordham University Press, 2013.
Tarrant, Richard. "Ovid and Ancient Literary History." In *The Cambridge Companion to Ovid*, edited by Philip Hardie, 13–33. Cambridge: Cambridge University Press, 2002.
Torelli, Giacomo. *Giacomo Torelli: L'invenzione scenica nell'Europa barocca*. Fano: Fondazione Cassa di risparmio di Fano, 2005.
Trabant, J. *Der gallische Herkules: Über Sprache und Politik in Frankreich und Deutschland*. Tübingen: A. Francke Verlag, 2002.
van Eck, Caroline. *Classical Rhetoric and the Visual Arts in Early Modern Europe*. Cambridge: Cambridge University Press, 2007.
Vernant, Jean-Pierre. "Prometheus and the Technological Function." 1965. In *Myth and Thought among the Greeks*, 237–47. London: Routledge & Kegan Paul, 1983.
Vernant, Jean-Pierre, and Pierre Vidal-Naquet. *Myth and Tragedy in Ancient Greece*. Cambridge, Mass.: Zone Books, 1988.
Viala, Alain. "Corneille premier auteur moderne." In *Pratiques de Corneille*, edited by Myriam Dufour-Maître, 29–40. Mont-Saint-Aignan: Presses universitaires de Rouen et du Havre, 2012.
Visentin, Hélène. "Le 'Dessein' de la pièce à machines, un cas particulier d'inscription du texte spectaculaire." *Texte* 33/34 (2003): 139–65.
———. "Le théâtre à machines: Succès majeur pour un genre mineur." *Littératures Classiques* 51 (2004): 205–22.

Vuillermoz, Marc. *Le système des objets dans le théâtre français des années 1625–1650: Corneille, Mairet, Rotrou, Scudéry.* Geneva: Droz, 2000.
Ward, Peter. *The Medea Hypothesis: Is Life on Earth Ultimately Self-Destructive?* Princeton, N.J.: Princeton University Press, 2009.
Warner, Marina. *Fantastic Metamorphoses, Other Worlds.* Oxford: Oxford University Press, 2004.
Wetmore, Kevin J., Jr., ed. *Black Medea: Adaptations for Modern Plays.* Amherst, N.Y.: Cambria Press, 2013.
Williams, Gareth. *Banished Voices: Readings in Ovid's Exile Poetry.* Cambridge: Cambridge University Press, 1994.
Wilson, Emily. *Mocked with Death: Tragic Overliving from Sophocles to Milton.* Baltimore: Johns Hopkins University Press, 2004.
Wygant, Amy. *Medea, Magic, and Modernity in France: Stages and Histories, 1553–1797.* Aldershot, Eng.: Ashgate, 2007.
———. "Pierre Corneille's Medea-Machine." *Romanic Review* 85, no. 4 (1994): 535–50.
Yourcenar, Marguerite. "Antigone ou le choix." In *Feux.* Paris: Grasset, 1936.
Zanger, Abby. "On the Threshold of Print and Performance: How Prints Mattered to Bodies of/at Work in Molière's Published Corpus," *Word & Image,* 17, no. 1–2 (2001): 25–41.
———. *Scenes from the Marriage of Louis XIV: Nuptial Fictions and the Making of Absolutist Power.* Stanford, Calif.: Stanford University Press, 1997.

# INDEX

Abbey Theatre, 1, 2, 3
absolutism, 9, 54–55, 174
Aeson (character), 5, 5, 6, 45–46, 66, 114–15
Aète (character), 144, 155–57, 159, 161–62, 166, 170–72
allegory: *La Conquête* temporal dynamics and, 148–50, 151, 154; *Phèdre* as tragedy, 177–78; suspense and, 160; temporal dynamics and, 146–50, 151, 154
Almeida Theater, 1, 2, 3, *3*
Altdorfer, Albrecht, 146–48, 149
*Andromaque* (Racine, J.), 11, 181
*Andromède* (Corneille), 144, 164, 169
Anouilh, Jean, 38
Antigone (character): autonomy and resistance model of, 38–40, 43–44, 51; Creon conflict and duologue with, 21, 37–38, 39, 40, 41, 42, 43; feminist scholarship on, 38, 41; Honig on, 31, 41–42, 213n2; iconography of, 31, 37–39; Medea contrasted with, 31, 37, 44–45, 49, 51; name meaning, 45; sacrifice/self-sacrifice of, 39
*Antigone* (Sophocles): contemporary significance of, 39, 51; democracy and, 42, 43; as melodrama, 42; Polynices burial in, 40; scholarship on, 31, 38–44
Anzieu, Didier, 32, 81–82, 217n24
Apollo (character), 102, 109, 147
Apollonius of Rhodes, 106, 159, 218n27
Appiah, Anthony, 200
archaism/primitivism, 146–47; *Athalie* and, 178; of infanticide, 28–29; with magic and witchcraft, 20, 21, 82; *Medea* film by Pasolini and, 96, 97, 99, 101, 118–19; Medea/Médée, 7, 20–21, 28–32, 37, 44, 47, 82, 96, 99, 118–19, 213n42; of Medean violence, 7, 20, 21, 28–29, 96, 99

*Argonautica* (Apollonius of Rhodes), 159, 218n27
*Argonautica* (Valerius Flaccus), 157, 159, 223n21
Argonauts (characters): in *La Conquête*, 144, 155, 156–59, 162–63, *168*, 168–70; Golden Fleece quest and, 3–4, 46, 50, 54, 61, 66, 68–69, 95, 111, 114, 143–44, 149, 151–53, 155, 157, 159, 161–64, 169–73; in *Medea* film, 95–96; Medea interconnection with, 77, 79; Ovidian, 112, 114; Pollux as, 53–54, 61–64, 69, 71–72, 156
Aristotle/Aristotelian values, 41, 179; catastrophe classical definition and, 185; catharsis and, 141; Medea presence in, 21; Racinian poetics and, 9; on suspense, 160
*Athalie* (Racine, J.), 224n3; about, 34, 175; archaism and, 178; catastrophe in, 176, 178, 180, 186–92, 195, 196; death of Athalie in, meaning of, 188–89; dreams of Athalie in, 181–84, 190–92, 198; King Louis XV and, 176, 178–80, 196; multiplicity of Athalie in, 189–92, 193–94; palimpsestic history and, 192–96; periodization of neoclassical tragedy and, 34, 175, 177–78; *Phèdre* contrasted with, 197–98; prophecy in, 176, 198; Racine, L., memoirs on, 178, 179, 196; religious themes in, 175, 179–82, 192–93; revival in eighteenth century of, 176, 178–79; sacrifice/self-sacrifice in, 188, 192–93, 195; survival thematic in, 179–85, 193–94; temporal disruption and questioning in, 34, 175, 176, 178, 186–87, 189, 192; violence approach and role in, 176, 184–85, 197–98
attente (waiting). *See* suspense

*239*

audience: Corneille on pleasure of, 57–60; in spectacle, role of, 33; violence reaction differences from, 14–15
Auslander, Philip, 124

Bacon, Wallace, 124
Bahti, Timothy, 108
BAM. *See* Brooklyn Academy of Music
Benthien, Claudia, 81
Benveniste, Emile, 45
*bienséance* (decorum), 11–12, 13, 18, 70
Biet, Christian, 210n12, 212n30
blood: in contemporary productions, 1–4, 2; fire relation to, 7; in *Hercule mourant*, 122, 130–31, 132, 139
Briese, Olaf, 186–87, 225n18
Brooklyn Academy of Music (BAM), 1, 2, 3
Burnet, Thomas, 186
Butler, Judith, 31, 38, 41

Callas, Maria, 32, 95–96, *96*
Carlson, Marvin, 52, 126
Carson, Ann, 45
catastrophe: in *Athalie*, 176, 178, 180, 186–92, 195, 196; definition and evolution of, 34, 185–87, 196, 225nn17–19; geological, 186–87, 225n18; religious themes and, 186; survival relation to, 180; temporal dimensions of, 186–87, 225n19
catharsis, 21–22, 141, 212n30
Cavarero, Adriana, 49–51, 205
Cave, Terence, 160
Cavell, Stanley, 129
Chalciope (character), 155–59, 171
Chaney, Michael, 141–42
*Chanson douce* (*Lullaby* or *The Perfect Nanny*) (Slimani), 202–6
Chappuzeau, Samuel, 14–15
Chiron (character), 98–100, *100*
Christian tradition. *See* religious themes
*Le Cid* (Corneille), 9, 22, 54, 58
Clark, T. J., 141
"La Conqueste de la Toison d'or par les argonauts" (engraving) (Lepautre), 168, *168*
*La Conquête de la Toison d'or* (*La Conquête*) (Corneille): about, 33–34, 144; action in, approach and function of, 150–51, 153, 155, 157, 159–62, 164, 170–71; allegory and temporality in, 148–50, 151, 154; Argonauts in, 144, 155, 156–59, 162–63, *168*, 168–70; Chalciope role in past and future interpretations in, 155–59, 171; *Desseins* written for and impact on, 144–45, *145*, 149–50, 166–68; enchantment role in, 153–54, 165–67; flight in, 154, 160, 163–65, 167–73, *168*; future anxiety and interpretations in, 155–60, 171–73; Golden Fleece quest in, 144, 149, 151–53, 155, 157, 159, 161–64, 169–73; historicity regime in, 145–46, 222n4; King Louis XIV marriage and, 144, 145, 147, 148–49, 151–52; as machine play, 144, 150, 159–60, 164–65; magic and witchcraft in, 34; *Médée* (Corneille) contrasted with, 144–45; opera relation to, 144, 145; passion and action relation in, 151, 159–64, 170; prologue for, 144, 151–55, 167; propagandist aspects of, 33, 144, 145, 148–50, 222n2; stage technologies in, 33–34, 144–45, 150, 152–54, 159–60, 164–73; suspense/suspension in, 154, 160–73, *168*; temporal complexity in, 33–34, 144–46, 148–52, 154–59, 164–68, 170–71
Conroy, Derval, 189
Conti, Natale, 149
Coonfield, Gordon, 125
Corneille, Pierre, 7, 9, 200; on audience pleasure, 57–60; on catharsis of violence, 21–22; enchantment themes for, 153–54, 165–67; "Épître"/dedication for *Médée* by, 55–60, *56*, 71, 72; Euripides's *Medea* influence for, 70, 100; "Examen"/prefatory note for *Médée* by, 22, 55, 61, 69–70, 71–72; illustrations for works of, 22–28, *24*, *25*, *27*, 168, *168*, 212n37; on *Medea* (Seneca the Younger), 70, 71; on Medean violence, 59–60, 71–72, 201; *Médée* impact on career of, 54–55; *Médée* printed edition by, 55–57, 93; on *Médée*'s value and role, 22; Ovidian Medea influence for, 68, 100–1, 119, 153; politics of theater for, 55, 57–58; prefatory texts handling by, 216n4; print conventions and versions approach of, 22–23, 55–57, 93, 144, 212n36; printed works, features of, 22–23; Seneca the Younger influence

for, 64, 71, 84–85, 86, 92, 100; suspense approach of, 160–61; on violence in theater, 21–22, 59–60, 71–72, 201; *vraisemblance* approach for, 12, 13, 70, 72
Corneille, Pierre (works): *Andromède*, 144, 164, 169; *Le Cid*, 9, 22, 54, 58; *Imitation de Jesus-Christ*, 212n36; *Rodogune*, 10, 129, 156, 161. See also *La Conquête de la Toison d'or*; *Desseins de la Toison d'or*; *Horace*; *Médée*
cosmopolitanism/cosmopolitics: defining, 200–1; history of, 200; Medean violence and, 201, 205–6
Cracknell, Carrie, 1, 4
Creon/Créon (character): Antigone conflict and duologue with, 21, 37–38, 39, 40, 41, 42, 43; authority and sovereignty of, 21, 41, 65, 73–79, 87–88; death of, 21, 37, 54, 58, 70, 71, 89–90, 97–98, 120; gown test strategy of, 87–88; illustrated depictions of, 23; Médée judgment and banishment by, 72–73, 75–80, 98; tolerance and negotiation of, 75, 78–80
Creusa/Créuse/Glauce (character): death of, 46–47, 88–89, 91, 97–98, *98*, 99, 120, 206; death of, Jason response to, 90–91; ekphrasis of, with Médée gown, 83–86, 218n27; gown of Médée desired by, 71–73, 83–86, 88–89, 218n27; Jason relationship with, 53–54, 62, 63, 83, 84, 90–91; in *Medea* film, 97–98, *98*, 99; sarcophagi depictions of, 46–47, *47*
Cunningham, Valentine, 104
Cusk, Rachel, 1, 3, *3*

d'Aigaliers, Pierre Laudan, 15, *16*
d'Aubignac, François Hédelin, 11–12, 13, 185, 211n20
*De Constantia* (Lipsius), 121
decorum (*bienséance*), 11–12, 13, 18, 70
Déjanire (character), 122, 126, 129–31, 139
Delmas, Christian, 165, 223nn28–29
De Man, Paul, 141
democracy, 42, 43, 50
Derrida, Jacques, 46, 124, 184
Descartes, René, 153–54, 222n17
*Desseins de la Toison d'or* (*Desseins*) (Corneille): about, 144–45, *145*; as ekphrasis, 150; flight described in, 167–68; magic described in, 166; play experience impacted by, 150; source citing in, 149
destruction: blood in symbols of, 7; endurance in, 32, 54; fire symbolism of, 7, 26, 47; literature as art of, 32–33, 35, 82; of Medea and Medean violence, 8, 22, 26, 28, 32–33, 47, 51, 54–55, 92–93, 100; Ovidian description and, 32–33; temporal structures and, 31. See also catastrophe
Diderot, Denis, 176
dreams: *Athalie* use of, 181–84, 190–92, 198; *La Conquête* use of, 157–60, 172–73
Du Ryer, Pierre, 9

Eappen, Matthew, 205
Egginton, Bill, 220n12
ekphrasis: of Créuse with Médée gown, 83–86, 218n27; defining, 103, 104, 108, 110; *Desseins* as, 150; features mobilized by, 110; of Homer, 103–4; Medea and, 101–2, 105, 107–11; Medean violence and, 105; Ovidian Medea and, 101–2, 105, 107–11, 116–17; paintings and visual arts, 104–5, 110, 118, 141; poetry and, 103–4, 105, 107–10; Pygmalion myth and, 109–10
enchantment: in *La Conquête*, role of, 153–54, 165–67; Descartes's admiration/surprise relation to, 153–54, 222n17; stage technologies and theatrical, 151–54, 164–67, 203, 223n18
endurance: in destruction, 32, 54; of Hercule, 33, 123, 125–28, 139–40; tragedy relation to models of, 33, 123, 125–28, 139–40
epiphany, 140–42
Erickson, Jon, 124
*Esther* (Racine, J.), 175, 176, 178, 180
Euripides: feminist perspective on Medea of, 49–52, 214n17; infanticide inclusion by, 50–51, 117; Medea origins and, 106; *Médée* (Corneille) influence from, 70, 100; Ovidian Medean influenced by, 117, 118. See also *Medea*

feminist perspective/theory: on Antigone, 38, 41; on Euripides's Medea, 49–52, 214n17; on maternality, 49, 205; on Medea, 49–52, 212n41, 214n17

Fénelon, François de Salignac de La Mothe, 18
fire and burning: blood relation to, 7; as character in *Hercule mourant*, 129; Creusa death and, 46–47, 88–89, 91, 97–98, *98*, 99, 120, 206; destruction and symbols of, 7, 26, 47; in *Hercule mourant*, 33, 119, 120–23, 129–31, 133–35, 137–40; *Hercule mourant* passion and fury symbolized with, 130–31, 133, 138; *Hercule mourant* performance spectacle of, 33, 134–35, 137–40; Hercule slow death by, 33, 121–23, 128–33, 137–39; for Medea and Medean violence, 4–5, 5, 6, 7, 47–48, 120; in *Médée* unauthorized illustration, 26, 27, 28
Fleetwood, Kate, 1, 3, *3*
Fletcher, Angus, 147
Foley, Helene, 118, 213n2, 214n17
Forestier, Georges, 180, 195–96
Foucault, Michel, 30, 196–97
Fumaroli, Marc, 9–10, 175, 177–78

Garner, Margaret, 28–29, *29*
Garnier, Robert, 9
Glauce. *See* Creusa/Créusej/Glauce
Golden Fleece quest: in *La Conquête*, 144, 149, 151–53, 155, 157, 159, 161–64, 169–73; for Jason and Medea, 3–4, 46, 50, 54, 61, 66, 68–69, 95, 111, 114, 143–44, 149, 151–53, 155, 157, 159, 161–64, 169–73; in *Medea* film by Pasolini, 95–96; in *Médée* (Corneille), 54, 61, 66, 68–69, 143
Gombrich, E. H., 109
Goold, Rupert, 1, 4
Green, Eugène, 137
Greenberg, Mitchell, 216n18
Guillot, Catherine, 212n37
Gumbrecht, Hans Ulrich, 140–41
Gutzwiller, Kathryn, 105
Guyot, Sylvaine, 17, 180

Halpern, Richard, 43, 209n8
Hardy, Alexandre, 9
Hartog, François, 146
Heaney, Seamus, 38
Hercule/Hercules (character): death by burning slowly for, 33, 121–23, 128–33, 137–39; Déjanire love and fury for, 122, 126, 129–31, 139; endurance of, 33, 123, 125–28, 139–40; hero to madman transition, 137–38; immortality of, 126–28; introspection of, 138–39; Iole desired by, 122, 129–30; Medea contrasted with, 120; Medea gown likened to cloak of, 120; in paintings, *136*, 137; Philoctète final portrayal of, 139–40; sacrifice of, 126, 128–29, 131–33, 135; speech and eloquence of, 121–22
*Hercule mourant* (Rotrou): about, 33, 119, 120; beginning of, 129–30; blood in, 122, 130–31, 132, 139; Christ resurrection and sacrifice story and, 126, 131, 133; debut performances of, 120; dedication to Richelieu in, 126–28; endurance model of tragedy in, 33, 123, 125–28, 139–40; fire and burning role in, 33, 119, 120–23, 129–31, 133–35, 137–40; Hercule's slow burning death in, 33, 121–23, 128–33, 137–39; Mahelot's description of spectacle of, 134–35; passion and fury connection with fire in, 130–31, 133, 138; presence in performance of, 123, 125–29, 139, 142; print conventions and versions, 123, 128, 135, 142; Senecan influences for, 121, 134, 219n1; spectacle of fire and burning in performance of, 33, 134–35, 137–40; Stoicism/Neo-Stoicism influence in, 33, 121, 125, 129–34, 138; temporal experience in, 125; transformation narratives in, 127–28, 132–33, 137; violence in, 33, 119
*Hercules furens* (Seneca the Younger), 121
*Hercules Oetaeus* (Seneca the Younger), 121, 134, 219n1
"Hercules on his funeral pyre at Mt. Oeta" (Rousselet), *136*, 137
Herodotus, 106
*Heroides* (Ovid), 106
Hesiod, 106
Hinds, Stephen, 106–7
Hippolyte (character), 17, 18–19, 198
*Hippolyte* (La Pinelière), 121
Homer, 50, 103–4
Honig, Bonnie, 31, 41–42, 213n2
*Horace* (Corneille), 10, 216n4; battle scene approach in, 15, 17, 23; illustrations for, 23, 24, *24*; uncertainty for future in, 156; *vraisemblance* in, 13

# Index

*Horace* (d'Aigalier), 15, *16*
Horace (poet), 11, 12, 211n17
*Horrorism* (Cavarero), 49, 205
Hoxby, Blair, 209n8

Ibbett, Katherine, 161
*Iliad* (Homer), 50, 103–4
illustrations: Corneille works and, 22–28, *24*, *25*, *27*, 168, *168*, 212n37; Hercules portrayal in, *136*, 136–37; of Jason, 23, 25, 26; for *Médée* (Corneille), 23, 25, 26, 27, 28; of Médée flight, 24, *25*, *27*, 28, 168, *168*; violence depictions in, 23, *24*, *25*, 26, 27, 28
*Imitation de Jésus-Christ* (Corneille), 212n36
*Inclinations* (Cavarero), 49
infanticide: *Chanson douce* portrayal of, 202–6; contemporary stagings of, 1, 3–4; Euripides's inclusion of, 50–51, 117; *Médée* (Corneille) approach to, 92; Ovidian Medea approach to, 117–18; primitive nature of, 28–29; real-life narratives of, 28–29, 29, 202; sacrifice and Medean, 29, 50
*in medias res*, 129, 181
Iole (character), 122, 129–30
*Iphigénie* (Racine, J.), 11, 129
Irigaray, Luce, 38

Jameson, Fredric, 175
Jason (character): authority of, 74; Créuse death and, 90–91; Créuse relationship with, 53–54, 62, 63, 83, 84, 90–91; Golden Fleece quest and, 3–4, 46, 50, 54, 61, 66, 68–69, 95, 111, 114, 143–44, 149, 151–53, 155, 157, 159, 161–64, 169–73; illustrated depiction of, 23, 25, 26; justice and negotiations with, 74–75; *Medea* film portrayal of, 96, 98–99; Medea relationship with, 3–4, 34, 44, 45, 54, 60–73, 77, 111, 149, 151–52, 155, 158–60, 162, 172–73; *Médée* debut performance and, 55; as mercenary, 61, 62–63; Pollux relation with, 53–54, 61–64, 69, 71–72, 156
Jézabel (character), 182–84
Jones, Ann Rosalind, 82
Jouhaud, Christian, 209n8
justice, 72–80, 87–88, 92–93, 216n18

Konstan, David, 45
Koselleck, Reinhart, 34, 146–48, 149, 180
Krevens, Nita, 200
Krim, Leo and Lucia, 205

Lacan, Jacques, 38, 217n24
La Harpe, Jean-François de, 186
La Mesnardière, Hippolyte-Jules Pilet de, 11
Langer, Susanne, 19
*Laocoön* (Lessing), 103
La Péruse, Jean de, 8, 29
La Pinelière, Guérin de, 121
Latour, Bruno, 31, 47, 201
Lemak, Marilyn, 28
Lepautre, Jean, 168, *168*
Lessing, G. E., 103, 104–5, 110, 118
*Lettres persanes* (Montesquieu), 225n19
Lipsius, Justus, 121
Longino, Michèle, 61
Loraux, Nicole, 45
Louis XIII (king), 10
Louis XIV (king), 9, 168; *La Conquête* retrofitted for marriage of, 144, 145, 147, 148–49, 151–52; death of, 178; Racine, J., work for wife of, 175, 176; survival of, 179
Louis XV (king), 176, 178–80, 196
*Lullaby* (*Chanson douce*) (Slimani), 202–6
Lully, Jean-Baptiste, 164

machine plays (*pièces à machines*): *La Conquête* as, 144, 150, 159–60, 164–65; defining, 8; flight and technological suspension aspects of, 154, 160, 163–65; function of mythological, 223nn28–29; opera relation to, 144; print conventions and, 15, 221n16
magic and witchcraft: archaic and outsider associations with, 20, 21, 82; in *La Conquête*, 34; *Desseins* description of, 166; empowerment with Medean, 48, 66, 111, 155; healing and medicinal nature of Medean, 45–46, 48, 113, 118; marriage relation to Medean, 154; Medea/Médée, 4–5, 20, 45–48, 66–68, 85, 87, 88, 96, 111–15, 118, 151–53, 155, 164–67, 203; passion relation to, 151; sacrifice and Medean, 46, 67–68; theatrical illusion relation to, 151–54, 164–67, 203; transformation narratives and, 114–15, 152–53

Mahelot, Laurent, 134–35
Maintenon (Racine, J., patron), 175, 176
*Manon Lescaut* (Prévost), 225n19
Marmontel, Jean-François, 176, 225n17
Maslan, Susan, 224n3
maternality: in *Chanson douce*, 203–5; feminist perspective on, 49, 205; sacrifice/self-sacrifice and, 50, 202
Mathieu, Jean, 6
McCrory, Helen, 1
*Medea* (Euripides), 45; Abbey Theatre BAM production, 1, 2, 3; Almeida Theater production, 1, 3, *3*; contemporary productions, 1, 2, *3*, 3–4; Corneille on, 70; Corneille's *Médée* influence from, 70, 100; feminist perspectives on, 49–52, 214n17
*Medea* (film) (Pasolini), 7; archaism aspects in, 96, 97, 99, 101, 118–19; Argonauts portrayal in, 95–96; Callas title role in, 32, 95–96, *96*; Chiron portrayed in, 98–100, *100*; Glauce/Creusa death in, 97–98, *98*, 99; Golden Fleece quest and theft in, 95–96; Jason portrayal in, 96, 98–99; layered approach to, 97–101, *98*, *100*; Medea's alienation in, 96–97; Ovidian Medea in, 32, 94, 97, 100–1, 118–19
*Medea* (Ovid), 106, 117–18
*Medea* (painting) (Timomachus), 104–5, 110, 118
*Medea* (Seneca the Younger): Corneille on, 70, 71; Corneille's echoing of, 64, 71, 84–85, 86, 92, 100; gown described in, 84–85; Ovidian Medea influenced by, 117–18
*The Medea Hypothesis* (Ward), 226n1
Medea/Médée (character): Aeson's rejuvenation and, 5–6, *5–6*, 45–46, 66, 114–15; Antigone contrasted with, 31, 37, 44–45, 49, 51; archaic and premodern nature of, 7, 20–21, 28–32, 37, 44, 47, 82, 96, 99, 118–19, 213n42; Argonauts' interconnection with, 77, 79; backstory, 3–4; cleaving, ethos of, 20, 32, 62, 66, 68, 69–70, 82, 85–86, 88, 91–92; contemporary approaches to, 1–4, *2*, *3*; Corneille on value and role of, 22, 57–59; cosmopolitanism of, 200; destructive power of, 8, 22, 26, 28, 32–33, 47, 51, 54–55, 92–93, 100; ekphrastic, Ovidian, 101–2, 105, 107–10, 116–17; endurance in destruction in, 32, 54; feminist perspective/theory of, 49–52, 212n41, 214n17; fire symbolism and, 4–5, *5*, *6*, *7*, 47–48, 120; flight, illustrations of, 24–28, *25*, *27*, 168, *168*; flight, staging, 164, 167–68, 170–73; flight and suspension in *La Conquête*, 167–73; Golden Fleece quest and, 3–4, 46, 50, 54, 61, 66, 68–69, 95, 111, 114, 143–44, 149, 151–53, 155, 157, 159, 161–64, 169–73; gown, 21, 32, 71–73, 80–92, 120, 218n27; gown, Créuse desire for, 83–86, 218n27; gown, poisoning of and death by, 86–91; gown, selfhood and, 32, 73, 80–82, 86, 90–92; gown, skin relation to, 80–82, 88–92; Hercule contrasted with, 120; horrorism of, 49, 50; identification with, 4; infanticide, contemporary staging of, 1, 3–4; infanticide, Corneille's approach to, 92; infanticide, Euripides's inclusion of, 50–51, 117; infanticide, "modern-day" comparisons to, 28–30, *29*, 202; infanticide, Ovid's approach to, 117–18; Jason's relationship with, 3–4, 34, 44, 45, 54, 60–73, 77, 111, 149, 151–52, 155, 158–60, 162, 172–73; judgment and banishment by Créon, 72–73, 75–80, 98; in literary and political iconography, role of, 20–21, 26; magic and witchcraft, 4–5, 20, 45–48, 66–68, 85, 87, 88, 96, 111–15, 118, 151–53, 155, 164–67, 203; magic empowering for, 48, 86, 111, 155; maternality of, 50; Medusa's relation to, 49, 215n27; multiple and hybrid nature of, 47–48, 99, 111–12, 215n30; in neoclassical tragedy evolution, 9–10; origins in literary history, 106–7; as outsider/foreigner, 3, 4, 20–21, 47–48, 78, 82, 92–93, 96–97, 105, 200, 213n42; Ovidian, 32–34, 68, 94, 97, 100, 101–3, 105–19, 153, 219n24; Pelias's murder by, 45, 46, 50–51, 54, 65–69, 72, 74–75, 77–78, 79, 89–90, 114–15, 117, 172; pharmacological and healer aspects and, 45–48, 51, 113, 118; *Phèdre* reference to, 9–10, 177; political action and anti-politics of, 47–52, 212n41; rehearsive quality of, 4, 30, 31–32, 52, 100; sacrifice/self-sacrifice and, 21, 22, 29, 46, 50, 52, 67–68, 112, 199; sarcophagi interpretations of,

46–47, 47; Timomachus's painting of, 104–5, 110, 118; transformation/anti-transformation narratives and, 33, 102, 111–12, 114–17
Medean violence. *See* violence, Medean
*Médée* (Corneille): about and background, 7, 9, 32, 54–55, 94; career impact for Corneille, 54–55; *La Conquête* relation with, 144–45; debut performances, 55–56; endurance in destruction in, 32, 54; "Épître"/dedication for, 55–60, 56, 71, 72; Euripides influence for, 70, 100; "Examen"/prefatory note for, 22, 55, 61, 69–70, 71–72; Golden Fleece quest and, 54, 61, 66, 68–69, 143; illustrations for, 23, 25, 25–26, 27, 28; infanticide approach in, 92; justice and *justesse* in, themes of, 72–80, 87–88, 92–93, 216n18; opening scene in, 60–61; Ovidian Medea influence in, 68, 100–1, 119; periodization of neoclassical tragedy and, 9–10, 34, 177; print conventions and versions for, 23, 25, 26, 27, 28, 55–57, 93; self-exploration in, 32, 73, 80–82, 86, 90–92; Seneca the Younger influence in, 64, 71, 84–85, 86, 92, 100; singular and plural perspective in, 66–68; stage technology in, 164; unauthorized edition of, 26, 27, 28
*Médée* (La Péruse), 8, 29
Medusa (character), 49, 153, 215n27
Merleau-Ponty, Maurice, 81, 217n21
*Métamorphose Figurée* (Salomon), 5, 5, 7
*Metamorphoses* (Ovid): ekphrastic nature of, 101–2, 105, 107–11, 116–17; Medea as amalgam in, 111–12; *Medea* film influenced by, 32, 94, 97, 100–1, 118–19; Medea in, 32–34, 68, 94, 97, 100, 101–3, 105–19, 153, 219n24; narrative description in, 32–33, 101–5; Pygmalion myth, 109–10, 112; transformation narratives in, 32–33, 102, 108–15; youth and aging in, 112–15, 116–17
Milesien, Denis, 149
Mitchell, W. J. T., 103–4
modernity: "effective history" and, 30–31; Koselleck on temporality and, 146–48; maxims of, 175; Medean violence and, 28–30, 35; neoclassical French tragedy relation to, 174–75
*The Modern Medea* (painting) (Noble), 28–29, 29

Montesquieu, 225n19
*Mythologie* (Conti), 149

neoclassical French tragedy: aesthetic values and purity of, 10, 174–75; antimodernity of, 174–75; French culture relation with, 9–10, 174–75, 209n8; multiplicities of violence in, 210n12; periodization and related works for, 9–10, 34, 175, 177–78; violence in, debates on, 11–28, 57–58; violence in, notable, 10–11. *See also specific works and topics*
Neophron, 106
Neo-Stoics. *See* Stoicism/Neo-Stoicism
Nérine (character), 64–65, 86–87, 88
Newlands, Carole, 111
Noble, Thomas Satterwhite, 28–29, 29
Norman, Larry, 23
Nussbaum, Martha, 200

occult. *See* magic and witchcraft
Oedipus (character), 38, 44
opera, 144, 145
oracles. *See* dreams; prophecy
Ortega, Yoselyn, 205
Ost, François, 38
Ovid, 7, 219n15; Argonauts' portrayal by, 112, 114; Corneille's influence from, 68, 100–1, 119, 153; description and destruction, 32–33; ekphrasis use by, 101–2, 105, 107–11, 116–17; Euripides's Medea influence for, 117, 118; infanticide of Medea approach by, 117–18; *Medea* film influenced by, 32, 94, 97, 100–1, 118–19; Medean violence approach of, 102–3, 117–18; Medea of, 32–34, 68, 94, 97, 100, 101–3, 105–19, 153, 219n24; Medea of, as amalgam, 111–12, 118; Medea versions from, 106; Seneca the Younger, influence for, 117–18; *utile dulci* in poetry of, 12
Ovid (works): *Heroides*, 106; *Medea*, 106, 117–18. See also *Metamorphoses*

paintings: Altdorfer, temporal considerations in, 146–48, 149; dramatic poetry kinship with, 59; ekphrasis of, 104–5, 110, 118, 141; Hercules's portrayal in, 136, 137; of Medea by Timomachus, 104–5, 110, 118; *The Modern Medea*, 28–29, 29
palimpsests, 42, 99, 141, 192–96

Pasolini, Pier Paolo. See *Medea* (film)
passion: in *La Conquête* relation to action, 151, 159–64, 170; French aestheticism and, 174; in *Hercule mourant* symbolized with fire, 130–31, 133, 138; magic and witchcraft relation to, 151; *Phèdre* avoidance of, 177–78
Pelias/Pélie (character): Medea portrayal in relation to, 45, 51, 66–68, 114–15; murder of, 45, 46, 50–51, 54, 65–69, 72, 74–75, 77–78, 79, 89–90, 114–15, 117, 172
*The Perfect Nanny* (*Chanson douce*) (Slimani), 202–6
performance studies, 33, 123–25, 140–42
*Phèdre* (Racine, J.): *Athalie* contrasted with, 197–98; death soliloquy of Phèdre in, 9–10, 177; falls of Phèdre in, 17–18, 135; Medea referenced in, 9–10, 177; neoclassical tragedy periodization and, 9, 34, 175, 177–78; passion avoidance in, 177–78; religious themes in, 177; self-poisoning death of Phèdre in, 9–10, 18, 129, 135, 177, 198; Théramène soliloquy, critics on, 18–19; as tragedy allegory, 177–78; violence approach and role in, 17–19, 177–78, 197–98
Phelan, Peggy, 124
Philoctète (character), 139–40
Phineus (character), 112, 113
Phryxus (character), 156–57, 161–62, 223n21
Picart, Bernard, 6
*pieces à machines*. See machine plays
Pindar, 106
plausibility (*vraisemblance*), 11–12, 13–14, 18, 70, 72
*Poetics* (Scaliger), 185
poetry, dramatic: Aristotelian values and, 9; ekphrasis and, 103–4, 105, 107–10; Horace on function of, 11, 12; Medean influence in, 22–28; painting and visual arts kinship with, 59; spectacle of performance tension with, 135
Pollux (character), 53–54, 61–64, 69, 71–72, 156
Polynices (character), 40
*Pratique du théâtre* (d'Aubignac), 13
presence (theatrical): epiphany relation to, 140–42; in *Hercule mourant*, 123, 125–29, 139, 142; performance studies on, 33, 123–25, 140–42; temporal dimensions and dynamics and, 124–25
Prévost, 225n19
primitivism. See archaism/primitivism
print conventions and versions: *Le Cid*, 22; *La Conquête*, 144–45, 145, 149–50, 166–68; Corneille use of and approach to, 22–23, 55–57, 93, 144, 149, 212n36; *Hercule mourant*, 123, 128, 135, 142; machine plays and, 15, 221n16; *Médée* (Corneille), 23, 25, 26, 27, 28, 55–57, 93; theatrical performance contrasted with, 221n16; theatrical performance impacted by, 15, 17, 123, 128; theatrical violence and, 15, 16, 17. See also illustrations
propaganda, 33, 144, 145, 148–50, 222n2
prophecy: in *Athalie*, 176, 198; *La Conquête* use of, 157–60, 172–73
Pygmalion myth, 109–10, 112

Racine, Jean, 7, 9–10, 200; legacy, 176; Louis XIV's wife as patron for, 175, 176; playwrighting break and return for, 175; religious themes in, 175, 177, 180–82
Racine, Jean (works): *Andromaque*, 11, 181; *Esther*, 175, 176, 178, 180; *Iphigénie*, 11, 129. See also *Athalie*; *Phèdre*
Racine, Louis, 178, 179, 196
"Rajeunissement d'Eson" (illustration) (Picart), 6, 6
Rancière, Jacques, 41, 44
Rapin, René, 12
"Rejeunisement d'Eson" (illustration) (Mathieu), 6
religious themes: in *Athalie*, 175, 179–82, 192–93; catastrophe and, 186; *Hercule mourant* resurrection and, 126, 131, 133; *Phèdre*, 177; temporal dynamics in works with, 146–47, 148, 180–81; in theater of 1600s, 121
Reni, Guido, 136, 136–37
Richelieu (cardinal), 10, 126–28, 216n8
Richir, Marc, 217n21
Roberts, Jennifer, 141
*Rodogune* (Corneille), 10, 129, 156, 161
Rose, Heidi, 125
Rosensweig, Anna, 43
Rotrou, Jean, 33, 119, 200; *Hercule mourant* dedication to Richelieu,

126–28; print conventions use by, 123, 128, 135, 142; religious themes revival and, 121; Senecan influences for, 121, 134, 219n1. See also *Hercule mourant*
Rousselet, Gilles, *136*, 137

sacrifice/self-sacrifice: Antigone, 39; in *Athalie*, 188, 192–93, 195; in *Hercule mourant*, 126, 128–29, 131–33, 135; in *Iphigénie*, 11; maternality and, 50, 202; Medea infanticide without, 29, 50; Medean, 21, 22, 29, 46, 50, 52, 67–68, 112, 199; Medean magic and, 46, 67–68
Saint-Évremond, Charles de, 12
Salomon, Bernard, *5, 5*, 7
sarcophagi, 46–47, *47*
Scaliger, Julius César, 185
Schérer, Jacques, 225n17
Schmidt, Martin, 216n19
Segal, Naomi, 32, 81–82, 217n24
self: Médée's gown relation to, 32, 73, 80–82, 86, 90–92; Merleau-Ponty on division of, 81, 217n21; skin-ego theory of, 32, 81–82, 217n24
Seneca the Elder, 117
Seneca the Younger, 8–9, 15, 70; Corneille's echoing Medea of, 64, 71, 84–85, 86, 92, 100; *Hercule mourant* influenced by, 121, 134, 219n1; Ovidian Medea influenced by, 117–18
Seneca the Younger (works): *Hercules furens*, 121; *Hercules Oetaeus*, 121, 134, 219n1. See also *Medea*
Shakespeare, William, 153
Shaw, Fiona, 1, 2, 3
*The Sight of Death* (Clark), 141
skin: gown of Medea, relation to, 80–82, 88–92; psychoanalytic and phenomenological exploration of, 81, 216n19; skin-ego and, 32, 81–82, 217n24; transformation narratives and, 81–82, 102
Slimani, Leïla, 202–6
Solodow, Joseph B., 219n15
Sommaville, Antoine de, 56
Sophocles, 38–39. See also *Antigone*
spectacle: audience role in, 33; of fire and burning in *Hercule mourant*, 33, 134–35, 137–40; performance studies and, 123–24; of theatrical illusion and magic, 151–54, 164–67, 203
stage technologies: in *Andromède*, 144, 164, 169; in *La Conquête*, 33–34, 144–45, 150, 152–54, 159–60, 164–73; flight and suspension, 154, 160, 163–65, 167–73, *168*; inventors of, notable, 154, 223n18; *Médée* (Corneille), 164; propagandist use of, 144, 148, 222n2; theatrical illusion and enchantment with, 151–54, 164–67, 203, 223n18; in transformation narratives of *La Conquête*, 152–54, 166–67. See also machine plays
Stallybrass, Peter, 82
Starobinski, Jean, 86
Steimatsky, Noa, 99
Stengers, Isabelle, 29, 34, 201
Stiegler, Bernard, 48, 51
Stoicism/Neo-Stoicism, 33, 121, 125, 129–34, 138, 181
Strauss, Jonathan, 39–40, 213n2
surprise, 153–54, 222n17
survival thematic, 179–85, 193–94
suspense, dramatic: in *La Conquête* relation to technological suspension, 160–73; Corneille's approach to, 160–61; in rhetoric, 160; scholarship on, 160

Targa, François, 56
Tarrant, Richard, 106
*The Tempest* (Shakespeare), 153
temporal dimensions and dynamics, 221n1; allegory and theatrical, 146–50, 151, 154; *Athalie* disruption and questioning of, 34, 175, 176, 178, 186–87, 189, 192; of catastrophe, 186–87, 225n19; *La Conquête* approach to, 33–34, 144–46, 148–52, 154–59, 164–68, 170–71; disruption, importance of, 31, 34–35; flight technology and, 164–68, 170–71; *Hercule mourant*, 125; *in medias res* and theatrical, 129, 181; Koselleck on premodern, 34, 146–48, 149, 180; of Medean violence, 94–95, 143–44, 226n1; in painting by Altdorfer, 146–48, 149; performance presence and, 124–25; religious thematic and, 146–47, 148, 180–81; with theatrical illusion and enchantment, 151–54, 164–67, 203; violence role in disrupting, 7–8, 11, 35, 94–95, 143–44, 226n1
theater: aesthetics and purity of French neoclassical, 10, 174–75; allegory and temporality in, 146–50, 151, 154;

theater (cont.)
    antimodernity of French neoclassical, 174–75; catastrophe meaning in, 34, 185–86, 187, 225n17; democracy and, 43; diverse history of, 31; epiphany relation to presence in, 140–42; historical truth and, 12, 13; *in medias res* and temporality in, 129, 181; *Medea* (Euripides) productions in contemporary, 1–4, *2*, *3*; mimesis of, 14; politics for Corneille, 55, 57–58; presence in, 33, 123–29, 139–42; print conventions and versions impacting performance, 15, 17, 123, 128; print version contrasted with performance, 221n16; religious themes in 1600s, 121; sense of time in, 124–25; "thisness" in, 125, 220n12; *utile dulci* value of, 11–12; violence and print technology in, 15, *16*, 17; violence in, audience response to, 14–15; violence in, debates on, 11–28, 57–58, 210n12, 211n21; *vraisemblance* and, 11–12, 13–14, 18, 70, 72. *See also* neoclassical French tragedy; tragedy; *specific works and topics*
Théramène (character), 17–19
*Thésée* (Lully), 164
Timomachus, 104–5, 110, 118
Torelli, Giacomo, 154, 223n18
tragedy: as cadential form, 19; contemporary significance of, 39, 206; death relation to, scholarship on, 213n2; endurance model of, 33, 123, 125–28, 139–40; Medean, nature of, 34–35; Medean influence in premodern, 8–11; Medean tragedy role in history of, 8–9, 34; narrative description role in, 18–19, 101–2; periodization and related works for neoclassical, 9–10, 34, 175, 177–78; rehearsal of violence role in, 4, 8, 19, 30, 31–32, 37, 39–40, 52, 100, 176, 205; scholarship on nature of, 209n8; survival role in, 180–85. *See also* neoclassical French tragedy; *specific works and topics*
transformation narratives: Aeson's rejuvenation and, 5–6, *5–6*, 45–46, 66, 114–15; *La Conquête* stage technology role in, 152–54, 166–67; in *Hercule mourant*, 127–28, 132–33, 137; magic and witchcraft and, 114–15, 152–53;

Medean violence tension with, 33, 112, 117; *Metamorphoses*, 32–33, 102, 108–15; skin and, 81–82, 102; youth and aging in, 112–15, 116–17

Valerius Flaccus, 157, 159, 223n21
*Le Véritable Saint Genest* (Rotrou), 121
Vigarani, Gaspare, 154
violence: in *Athalie*, approach and role of, 176, 184–85, 197–98; audience reaction to, differences, 14–15; catastrophe relation to theatrical, 185–86; catharsis of, 21–22, 141, 212n30; Corneille on theatrical, 21–22, 59–60, 71–72, 201; epistemological structure of, 199; French aestheticism and, 10; function of, critics on, 19, 57–58; in *Hercule mourant*, role of, 33, 119; Horace on theatrical, 211n17; illustrated depictions of, 23–28, *24*, *25*, *27*; multiplicities of neoclassical theatrical, 210n12; notable neoclassical tragedy, 10–11; in *Phèdre*, approach and role of, 17–19, 177–78, 197–98; as pleasant and instructional, 11–12; print technology and theatrical, 15, *16*, 17; rehearsal of, 4, 8, 19, 30, 31–32, 37, 39–40, 52, 100, 176, 205; temporal disruptions with, 7–8, 11, 35, 94–95, 143–44, 226n1; theatrical, debates on, 11–28, 57–58, 210n12, 211n21
violence, Medean: anti-transformative nature of, 33, 112, 117; *Chanson douce* depictions of, 202–6; cleaving in, logic of, 20, 32, 62, 66, 68, 69–70, 82, 85–86, 88, 91–92; contemporary significance of, 51–52, 93, 201, 226n1; Corneille on, 59–60, 71–72, 201; cosmopolitical dimension to, 201, 205–6; destructive force of, 8, 22, 26, 28, 32–33, 47, 51, 54–55, 92–93, 100; ekphrasis and, 105; as exceptional, 20–21; features of, 19–22, 199–200; fire and burning in, 4–5, *5*, *6*, *7*, 47–48, 120; gown significance in, 80; in *Hercule mourant*, 119; illustrated versions depicting, 23, *25*, *26*, *27*, 28; "in wake of," meaning, 30–31; modernity and, 28–30, 35; as nonredemptive, 21–22, 29; Ovid's approach to, 102–3, 117–18; primitive nature of, 7, 20, 21, 28–29, 96, 99; purpose and approach of, 7–8; real-life

narratives of, 28–30, 29, 202; rehearsive nature of, 4, 30, 31–32, 52, 100; as relational and networked, 20, 203; temporality and temporal disruption of, 94–95, 143–44, 226n1; as unassimilable, 20; as untimely, 21, 29–30
Visentin, Hélène, 221n16
Voltaire, 176, 186
*vraisemblance* (plausibility), 11–12, 13–14, 18, 70, 72
Vuillermoz, Marc, 221n16

waiting. *See* suspense
Ward, Peter, 226n1
Warner, Deborah, 1, 4
Warner, Marina, 109
Wilson, Emily, 19, 180–81
Woodward, Louise, 205
Wygant, Amy, 64, 87, 154, 215n30

Yourcenar, Marguerite, 38

Zanger, 168–69, 170, 212n36

JULIETTE CHERBULIEZ is Professor of French and Italian at the University of Minnesota–Twin Cities, and Director of its Consortium for the Study of the Premodern World. She is the author of *The Place of Exile: Leisure Literature and the Limits of Absolutism* (Bucknell, 2005).

www.ingramcontent.com/pod-product-compliance
Lightning Source LLC
Chambersburg PA
CBHW030438300426
44112CB00009B/1053